Gin Before Breakfast

W. Dale Nelson

Gin Before Breakfast

The Dilemma of the Poet in the Newsroom

 SYRACUSE UNIVERSITY PRESS

Syracuse University Press
Syracuse, New York 13244-5160

First Edition 2007

07 08 09 10 11 12   6 5 4 3 2 1

The paper used in this publication meets the minimum requirements
of American National Standard for Information Sciences—Permanence
of Paper for Printed Library Materials, ANSI Z39.48–1984.∞™

For a listing of books published and distributed by Syracuse University Press,
visit our Web site at SyracuseUniversityPress.syr.edu

ISBN-13: 978-0-8156-0888-2
ISBN-10: 0-8156-0888-8

Library of Congress Cataloging-in-Publication Data

Nelson, W. Dale.
    Gin before breakfast : the dilemma of the poet in the newsroom / W. Dale Nelson.—1st ed.
        p. cm.
    Includes bibliographical references and index.
    ISBN-13: 978-0-8156-0888-2 (cloth : alk. paper)
    ISBN-10: 0-8156-0888-8 (cloth : alk. paper)
    1. Poets, English—Biography.   2. Journalists—Great Britain—Biography.   3. Poets, American—
Biography.   4. Journalists—United States—Biography.   I. Title.

PR502.N39 2007
821.009—dc22
[B]   2007006247

Manufactured in the United States of America

For Eric and Aspen

Our old songs are lost,
Our sons are newspapermen
At the singers' cost.

—Edwin Muir

W. DALE NELSON spent forty years as a reporter with the Associated Press. During twenty years in Washington, he won the Aldo Beckman Award for excellence in reporting about the presidency. His poetry has appeared in general and literary magazines in the United States, Canada, England, and Australia. Nelson is the author of *The President Is at Camp David* and *Who Speaks for the President?*, both published by Syracuse University Press. He received a creative writing fellowship in poetry for 2004 from the Wyoming Arts Council and has received awards from *Poetry Northwest, Plainsongs,* and *Visions.* He and his wife, Joyce Miller Nelson, a painter and writer, live in Laramie, Wyoming.

Contents

Illustrations

Acknowledgments

The lines of Edwin Muir quoted as the epigraph are from "Complaint of the Dying Peasantry," from *Collected Poems* by Edwin Muir, copyright © 1960 by Willa Muir. Used by permission of Oxford University Press, Inc.

Portions of the introduction and chapter 1 appeared in somewhat different form in the March 2000 issue of *Daybreak* under the title "The Poet in the Newsroom."

The author wishes to thank Dale Eckhardt for locating one of the countless columns written by her late husband, Charles Levendosky, for the *Casper (Wyo.) Star-Tribune* and for permission to quote from the column and to reprint Levendosky's poem, "All the Blue Rooms," published in his *Circle of Light* (Glendo, Wyo.: High Plains Press, 1995).

Thanks are also due to Mary Selden Evans, executive editor of Syracuse University Press, for her help and encouragement. I also wish to thank three outside readers who critiqued the manuscript for Syracuse. While I did not always agree with them, their overall suggestions contributed to whatever merit this book has.

Introduction

Young poets, Archibald MacLeish once wrote, are generally advised by their elders "to avoid the practice of journalism as they would wet socks and gin before breakfast."[1]

Leonard Woolf wrote that "generally habitual or professional journalism destroys any ability to write literature."[2]

Felix Frankfurter feared that MacLeish had "sold himself down newspaper row" with his writing for *Fortune* and other journals.[3]

On the other hand, the editor of London's *Morning Post* thought having to write under deadline pressure improved Coleridge's prose.[4]

And Rudyard Kipling, who covered Hindu-Moslem riots for newspapers in India before making his reputation as a poet, wrote:

Ah! What avails the classic bent
   And what the cultured word
Against the undoctored incident
   That actually occurred?[5]

The undoctored incident. The journalist has to get it right. That is what he works at. That is his trade. Not so, or not necessarily so, the poet.

Henry James, speaking of facts, tells us, "Nine-tenths of the artist's interest in them is that of what he shall add to them and how he shall turn them." Thus John Keats could get away with saying that it was "stout Cortez," not Balboa, who gazed upon the Pacific with eagle eyes from a mountaintop in Panama.[6]

The journalist could not get away with it. For him, accuracy is paramount. But words are his trade, too, as they are the poet's.

"The poet's material is words that for all we may say and feel against them are more manageable than men," said Robert Frost. "Get a few words alone in a study and with plenty of time on your hands you can make them say anything you please."[7]

So, says Frost, the poet is engaged in word management. Likewise the journalist. They manage the words in ways that are vastly, but not entirely, different.

Charles G. Ross, a professor of journalism when he was not being a reporter and editor for the *St. Louis Post-Dispatch* or Harry Truman's White House press secretary, wrote: "If your story is pathetic, it is not necessary to tell the reader so. Let him find it out from the simple, human facts. In describing a pretty girl, don't stop with saying she is pretty; tell how she is pretty—tell the color of her hair and eyes. Strive always to be specific."[8]

Not bad advice for poets. Despite their distance from the clamor of Kipling's newsroom, they, too, must keep in mind what actually occurs. Ezra Pound, in his *Imagiste* days in Paris in 1913, advised them to "go in fear of abstractions" and practice "Direct treatment of the 'thing,' whether subjective or objective."[9]

As a journalist for more than fifty years and a publishing poet during most of that time, I have long been intrigued by the phenomenon of the poet-journalist.

When he was twenty-two years old, Ernest Hemingway complained that newspaper writing was "gradually ruining" his ability as a creative artist. Shortly before his death, though, he told an interviewer, "Newspaper work will not harm a young writer and may help him if he gets out of it in time." It "may help him." It probably helped Hemingway, who wrote both journalism and fiction throughout his life and whose work sometimes straddled the borderline between the two. His spare prose often bears the earmarks of good journalism.[10]

So what is the dilemma of the poet, or the fiction writer, in the newsroom? The most obvious answer is the simplest one. Journalism is hard, demanding work, and it takes up too much of a writer's time. Ernest Hemingway thought he could be European correspondent for the *Toronto Star* and write fiction on the side. Hemingway was a conscientious workman, and he worked conscientiously for his employer. The work did not leave him enough spare time for fiction, so he gave up his newspaper job. The poet and critic Yvor Winters, who grew wine grapes on his California acreage, felt the same way about farming as Hemingway felt about journalism. "A farmer," Winters said, "has no time to be a scholar or a poet, regardless of how big a place he runs."[11]

There have been notable poets, of course, who practiced other professions while writing poetry. Wallace Stevens was vice president and general counsel of the Hartford Accident and Indemnity Company. William Carlos Williams was a physician in general practice in Rutherford, New Jersey. Unlike the poet-journalists, however, neither of them had a day job that dealt primarily with words. The journalist writes on the job, and if he or she wants to write poetry or fiction, goes home and writes some more.

Despite this burden, many poets, including MacLeish himself, have wandered into the newsroom. Most of them have wandered out again.

Woolf may have put it best: "What you write for a paper, you write for a moment of time. You write it for consumption with the kipper or eggs and bacon at the breakfast table. Literature is written not with the eggs and bacon but in the mold of eternity."[12]

Perhaps a glimpse at some of my own experience could help illustrate the relationship.

As a reporter in the Washington, D.C., bureau of the Associated Press in 1980, I covered a congressional committee hearing on the aftermath of the eruption of Mount St. Helens in the other Washington, my home state. The story I wrote gave the names, states, and party affiliations of the committee members and the names and occupations of the witnesses. None of this information made it into the poem I wrote as a result of the experience. The exchanges between lawmaker and witness were used, but transformed. The poem began simply enough:

There will be damage: fruit will fall
At a finger's touch, crops rot
Under the hard ash, machines fail
In the field, and the first slight

> Particles of silica enter
> The logger's lung.

As the son of a logger, the last touch may have struck home to me the most. There was a jibe at the bureaucracy in which "The managers of desolation, measuring / Deer by the acre, gauge the loss." Then the poem took a dogleg and explored Vesuvius. It ended by saying that we know more about Mount St. Helens than Pliny the Elder did about Vesuvius, but "We do not know more about the moment's / Change" and that "Mountains, we say in our metaphors / Are the place for transfigurations."[13]

In 1964, when I was working for the AP in Seattle, I was sent to Alaska as part of a team covering an earthquake that devastated parts of the state. After arriving in Anchorage, I flew to the badly damaged port city of Valdez. I no longer have a copy of my story about Valdez, but I believe I mentioned that the name of the city is, oddly, pronounced with a long *e*. The news coverage made careful distinctions between what happened in different parts of the state, but a poem I wrote years later mingled armed nighttime patrols in Anchorage with the tsunami, then known as a tidal wave, that wiped out Valdez.

> The port we flew to over glaciers
> was a wreck. We found few answers
> to our questions. Tidal, the wave
> washed brutal things ashore.
> . . . .
> . . . The people pronounced
> their town's name strangely, and nobody
> we found could say why. When flights out
> resumed, we still did not know
> enough about those odd, shaken slopes.[14]

Shortly after my retirement in 1992, I wrote a sort of summing-up poem about my "Forty Years as a Reporter for the Associated Press." I had been covering the Justice Department off and on and had noticed tourist buses lined up outside the building for such destinations as Arlington National Cemetery. I wrote:

> At the Department of Justice
> (There is no department of mercy),
> Monuments waited for buses.
> One run, they rode to graves.

The poem then asked questions:

> Did you get it right? Did the hours
> Add up to anything? How should you get
> The answers to your questions?

It did not answer them except to say unhelpfully, "Look under Truth in the yellow pages." It then dodged to my reporting experiences after an airliner crashed into a bridge over the Potomac River, asked more questions, and concluded: "The sunlight embassies / Walking on Massachusetts, / Mean things we do not understand."[15]

Glancing over these poems, I am struck by something I did not realize at the times, separated by intervals of several years, at which they were written. They are about mystery, about things we do not know. We understand the fragility of life no better than Pliny did. We ask questions, but find few answers. Leaving Valdez, we have still not satisfied our curiosity about its "odd, shaken slopes." Driving down Massachusetts Avenue on a sunny afternoon, we find ourselves puzzled by the embassy buildings and what secrets of international diplomacy they may hide. Newspaper stories tell us about names and titles, distances and populations, fatality totals and investigations. Poems tell us about ourselves.

Not far from where the buses loaded outside the Justice Department, I saw another bus. In the space for its destination, it said, "Not in Service. Express." An oddity on Pennsylvania Avenue. A vehicle to take us where we are going, and get there in a hurry.

Well, enough of me. These pages tell the stories of other journalists who have assayed, with varying success, to write in the mold of eternity.

Gin Before Breakfast

1 "I Will Write for the Permanent"

As Prime Minister William Pitt spoke on and on, the reporter in the dimly lit press gallery of the House of Commons dropped off to sleep. When he woke he went to his office and wrote an account based on what he had heard.

It is a scenario familiar enough to journalists covering legislative debates, whether in Westminster or West Virginia.

But the sleepy scribe for the London *Post,* a nine-year-old newspaper subtitled the *Cheap Morning Advertiser,* was no ordinary journeyman reporter. His name was Samuel Taylor Coleridge, and at the age of twenty-eight he had already written "The Rime of the Ancient Mariner" and "Kubla Khan."[1]

Coleridge's fatigue as the younger Pitt, second of a father-and-son dynasty of prime ministers, delivered his February 17, 1800, speech on Britain's aims in its war against France was not surprising. It was three in the morning, and the writer had been in the "hideously crowded" gallery since 7:15 A.M. the day before.[2]

Throughout most of his life, Coleridge was both intrigued and repelled by journalistic work. He professed to despise it, yet he often sought it. He worked as a reporter, an editorialist, and a feature writer—disciplines different in themselves and in their relation to his poetry.

Growing up as the youngest member of a Devonshire clergyman's large family, Coleridge acquired early in life the journalist's eye for an anecdote, his ear for a memorable phrase—talents that would echo in the "dancing rocks" flung up by Kubla Kahn's fountain like "chaffy grain beneath the thresher's flail." As a student at Cambridge, he was an

1

avid reader of political articles in the London press, a pastime that might not have served the lyric poet so well but is reflected in the moral and civic anguish of the ancient mariner.

"To be wholly successful," wrote Coleridge's nineteenth-century biographer H. D. Traill,

> the journalist—at least the English journalist—must not be too eloquent, or too witty, or too humorous, or too profound. Yet the English reader likes, or thinks he likes, eloquence; he has a keen sense of humor, and a fair appreciation of wit; and he would be much hurt if he were told that ingenuity and profundity were in themselves distasteful to him. How then to give him enough of these qualities to please and not enough to offend him? . . . This is a problem that is fortunately satisfied for most journalists by the fact of their possessing these qualities in no more than, if so much as, the minimum required. But Coleridge, it must be remembered, possessed most of them in embarrassing superfluity.[3]

This superfluity may have been both his strength and his weakness as a newspaperman. Coleridge was a wit and a great talker, although his platform delivery was described as monotonous. He was a man intensely interested in public affairs. He was also a man little concerned with dress or demeanor, whose wife "thought him a clown in appearance." A writer who attended one of Coleridge's lectures called him slovenly and said that he "would do well to appear with cleaner stockings . . . and if his hair was combed out every time he appeared in public it would not depreciate him in the esteem of his friends."[4]

Certainly he brought assets, beside his wit and eloquence, to the newsroom. He was a stout advocate for an independent press who realized, as all reporters need to remind themselves, that "after all, (government) Ministers do not *love* newspapers in their hearts, not even those that support them." Tempering principle with realism, he declared, "I will never write what, or for what, I do not think right. All that prudence can justify is *not* to write what at certain times one may yet think." He deplored scandal-mongering, asking, "In the name of God, what

Samuel Taylor Coleridge, author of "The Rime of the
Ancient Mariner," also wrote editorials and personality
profiles for London newspapers. Artist Robert Hancock
may have flattered him a little in this portrait; the poet's
wife thought him "a clown in appearance." Courtesy of
the National Portrait Gallery, London.

have we to do with Lord Nelson's mistresses, or domestic quarrels?"
His daughter, Sara, said of him, "His policy with regard to reporting
news was to state the facts simply and nakedly, without epithets or com-
ments," a policy not common in his time.[5]

But Coleridge had other qualities that were less at home on Fleet
Street. Much as he loved pontificating, he loved also to be at home with
his old folios, to devote himself to the literary, religious, and philosophical musings that he considered of ultimate importance.[6]

"I think there are two ways of good writing—one for immediate and wide impression, though transitory—the other for permanence," he said. "Newspapers are the first. The best one can do is the second."[7]

Both were good ways of writing. But newspaper work, Coleridge rightly felt, was not the best he could do.

His first professional publication, a poem "To Fortune," about buying a ticket to the Irish Lottery, appeared on November 7, 1793, in London's *Morning Chronicle*. It earned him a guinea, a British coin of the time that was worth a little more than a pound.[8]

At Cambridge, in 1791, Coleridge began taking laudanum, a tincture of opium, at first for the relief of neuralgia brought on by the damp climate. It was the beginning of a dependence that would dog him throughout his life. He left Cambridge in December 1794, probably because he was in debt. In London, he and fellow poet Robert Southey tried unsuccessfully to secure jobs as reporters on the *Telegraph*.[9]

In January, Coleridge and Southey made their way to the West Country seaport of Bristol. Coleridge at first intended to return to London, possibly to work on the *Telegraph* or *Citizen*. But, he decided, "I love Bristol, and I do not love London." The two discussed starting a monthly to be called *The Provincial Magazine* but dropped the idea after a quarrel.[10]

Still Coleridge did not give up. He wrote in his autobiography that he was "persuaded by sundry Philanthropists . . . to set on foot a periodical work entitled, *The Watchman*." It is likely that he, not the philanthropists, took the initiative. After an evening meeting in Bristol's Summer Tavern in December 1795, he announced that the first issue would appear on February 5, 1796. It actually appeared on March 1, with a prospectus promising to give people outside of London "the opportunity of hearing calumnies exposed and false statements detected." With the financial backing of prosperous Bristol tradesman Josiah Wade, Coleridge embarked January 8 on a five-week advertising tour of industrial towns in the Midlands and northern England. He found Worcester too dominated by aristocrats and clerics to be a likely market for a periodical embodying his then-liberal politics. In Birmingham, however, he thought he had lined up a hundred or so subscribers in his "first stroke in the new business I had undertaken." One he didn't sign up was a black-haired candlemaker who listened to his half-hour spiel while melting wax, agreed with his political views, and then asked for the price. Only fourpence for thirty-two pages, Coleridge told him.

"Thirty and two pages?," asked the chandler. "Bless me! Why except what I do in a family way on the Sabbath, that's more than I ever reads, Sir! all the year round. I am as great a one as any man in Brummagem, Sir! for liberty and truth and all them sorts of things, but as to this (no offence, I hope, Sir!) I must beg to be excused."[11]

Things went no better in Manchester. Armed with a letter of introduction, he bearded a "stately and opulent wholesale dealer in Cottons" who took his measurements, from head to toe, twice, and then asked if he had a bill or invoice. Coleridge offered what he described as a "flaming prospectus" for *The Watchman*. "Overstocked with these articles," grumbled the tradesman. "People always setting up some new thing or other." Crushing the prospectus in his palm, he stuffed it into his pocket. Coleridge retired from the canvassing business.[12]

His friends filled the vacuum. His backer Wade, visiting London, lined up an agent. Booksellers in Bristol gathered nearly four hundred orders. One of Coleridge's representatives in Nottingham ran into a patrician who read the motto on the prospectus, "That all may know the Truth; and that the Truth may make us Free!!" and sniffed that it must have been written by some "seditious dog." Actually, the words paraphrase those of Jesus, preaching in the Temple in Jerusalem in the eighth chapter of the Gospel according to John.

The poet was not asleep during the newspaper promoter's tour. On his way from Nottingham to Sheffield on February 1, Coleridge spotted an early primrose unfolding in "This dark, frieze-coated, hoarse, teeth-chattering month."[13]

With the help of his supporters, the would-be editor amassed a subscription list bearing nearly a thousand names. In a canny dodge to avoid the stamp tax levied on weekly newspapers, *The Watchman* was published every eighth day. The first issue contained essays by Coleridge on such subjects as the slave trade and the government's call for a public fast. The editor at first left the domestic and foreign news summaries to an acquaintance, George Burnett, who rewrote them from the London papers. Coleridge found Burnett's contributions so bad that he threw them in the fire. After this aggressive form of editing, he did the work over, adding capital letters, italics, exclamation points and other adornments.[14]

Subscribers, unfortunately, found the paper dull. One called the editor a "Newspaper paragraph thief." Many were offended by the second issue, in which Coleridge continued his discussion of fast days under an epigraph from Isaiah: "Wherefore my Bowels shall sound like an Harp." Coleridge admitted his choice of a biblical text was "most censurable" and said he was ashamed of the flip essay but had not time to revise it. It lost him, he said, five hundred of his more pious subscribers and brought him many abusive letters.[15]

By mid-April, sales were hardly keeping the paper afloat, and back issues were selling for a penny. On May 5, Coleridge told Thomas Poole, a well-to-do tanner he had met while on a walk in the Quantock Hills near Bristol, that issue number twelve would be the last.

As it turned out, he gave up in the tenth issue, just eight days later. "Henceforward, I shall cease to cry the state of the political atmosphere," he told his readers. "The reason is short and satisfactory—the work does not pay its expenses. Part of my subscribers have relinquished it because it did not contain sufficient original composition, and a still larger because it contained too much." As he had in announcing the paper's beginning, he turned to the Bible to proclaim its end, paraphrasing the words of Ezekiel: "Watchman, thou hast watched in vain."[16]

A sympathetic printer had given Coleridge forty pounds worth of paper when he started *The Watchman*. Nevertheless, the poet told Poole, the publication was now five pounds in the red, with no receipts in prospect. "It is not pleasant, Thomas Poole! to have worked 14 weeks for nothing—for nothing—nay—to have given the public in addition to that toil five & 40 pounds," he said.[17]

Reader dissatisfaction with the awkward eight-day schedule of publication, described by one commentator as an "arrangement . . . ingeniously calculated to irritate and alienate its public," undoubtedly contributed to the paper's demise. The poet-editor seems also not to have identified the specific audience he was writing for.[18]

Coleridge abandoned his Bristol quarters and retired to a cottage at Nether Stowey in the Quantocks. Even there he could not escape reminders of his paper's failure. Arising early one morning, he admonished a servant for using too much paper to start a fire in the fireplace. It didn't matter, she said: "Why, it is only Watchmen." Hardly comforting words to a troubled publisher.[19]

Most reviews of Coleridge's first book of poems, published in April 1796 by Bristol bookseller Joseph Cottle, were from favorable to enthusiastic. They did not put food on the table, however. Coleridge, with a wife at home and a child expected, concluded that "there are two giants leagued together, whose most imperious commands I must obey, however reluctant,—their names are BREAD and CHEESE."[20]

On July 1, James Perry, editor of the *Morning Chronicle,* wrote from London offering a position as coeditor. A Bristol friend and confidant, the radical physician Dr. Thomas Beddoes, urged the poet to accept the offer, saying it could lead to a promotion. Coleridge was skeptical. "I rather think," he wrote Poole, "that Perry means to employ me as a mere Hireling, without any proportionate Share of the Profits." Coleridge apparently went to London to see Perry, but he did not go to work for the *Chronicle.* Perhaps the editor was not impressed with the applicant's notoriously untidy dress and appearance.[21]

Coleridge returned to Stowey and made odd bits of money by sending verses to the *Morning Post.* He turned down a position as tutor to the child of a wealthy widow, telling a friend, "I could not love the man who advised me to keep a school, or write for a newspaper. He must have a hard heart."[22]

But something had to be done. Coleridge's first child, Hartley, had been born, and his friends despaired of his plan to get by through subsistence farming on his acre and a half of land at Stowey. William Wordsworth moved into a cottage forty miles from Coleridge's, and together they wrote the volume of *Lyrical Ballads,* but Coleridge's contribution, "The Rime of the Ancient Mariner," was ridiculed by critics.[23]

A chance encounter in December 1797 at the country estate of the Wedgwood family, wealthy and philanthropic Staffordshire potters, led Coleridge into a fourteen-year association with Scotsman Daniel Stuart, who had recently become editor of the liberal, antigovernment *Morning Post*. Among the Wedgwoods' other guests was philosopher and historian James Mackintosh, Stuart's brother-in-law. On Mackintosh's recommendation, the editor invited Coleridge to contribute "verses or political essays" at a retainer of a guinea a week. Mackintosh told Coleridge that Stuart was "ashamed of offering you so small a pittance," and the editor assured him it might be increased later.

He needed the money. A guinea a week would cover about half of his expenses, which he calculated at one hundred pounds a year or a little more. He was getting a forty-pounds-a-year annuity, inaugurated by his friends two years earlier, so the additional funds would just barely get him by. Skilled craftsmen at the time earned about ninety pounds a year; a comfortable living in London for a gentleman with a small household and one servant came to two hundred pounds.[24]

The first of Coleridge's contributions to the *Post,* a political satire on Pitt's war policies entitled "Fire, Famine and Slaughter," appeared on January 8, 1798. In April, two months after the French invasion of Switzerland, his "France: An Ode" was published along with a laudatory editorial by Stuart. "It is very satisfactory," wrote the editor, "to find so zealous and steady an advocate of France as Mr. Coleridge concur with us in condemning the conduct of France toward the Swiss Cantons."[25]

Newspapers of the time often published poems dealing with vital issues of the day. Writing from his Lake District home in the fall of 1801, Coleridge told Stuart that in submitting poetry he would "certainly labor to make the poems in general suited to a daily morning paper" and that "some kinds ought to recur more frequently than others; and these, of course, temporary and political." His friends Wordsworth and Southey were also submitting poems to the *Post,* and Wordsworth wrote articles in 1809 on such issues as the Spanish struggle against French domination. Whether Wordsworth was paid is uncertain. Stuart had loaned him money, and he once wrote asking whether the editor would accept an article as payment. Four decades later, Wordsworth, by then a distinguished literary figure who probably thought journalism a grubby occupation, denied that he had ever written for a newspaper for money.[26]

Coleridge's off-again, on-again association with the paper had been interrupted in 1798. The poet's second child, Berkeley, was born in June of that year, but his marriage to the former Sara Fricker was already showing strains. In September, he left for Germany with Wordsworth and Wordsworth's sister, Dorothy, planning to study chemistry and anatomy and collect the works of German philosophers. He promised Stuart occasional travel pieces but, desultory as he often was, failed to deliver. Sara remained at home with Berkeley. In February 1799 the child, not yet a year old, died of pneumonia. Coleridge returned to Stowey that July, determined to pursue his goals in poetry, philosophy, and criticism.[27]

First, he must try to make some kind of living. Although he submitted nothing to Stuart while abroad, he apparently stopped in to see him on his way home.[28]

By the middle of October, Coleridge's luggage had arrived from Germany, and he traveled from Stowey to London to retrieve it. Stopping en route in Bristol, he heard false reports that Wordsworth was seriously ill, and he headed north. He found his fellow poet in good health at Sockburn farm, near the home of Thomas Hutchinson, whose daughter Mary would later be Wordsworth's wife. Coleridge's stay with the Hutchinson family was marked by two events of signal importance in his life. He met Sara Hutchinson, the second of the farmer's three daughters, and he caught his first sight of the shores and mountains of the Lake District. "It was to me a vision of a fair country," he exclaimed. London was soon beckoning, though. A letter from Stuart offered a position on the staff of the *Morning Post*.[29]

As Coleridge put it, he was "solicited to undertake the literary and political department" of the newspaper. He said he "acceded to the proposal on the condition that the paper should thenceforward be conducted on certain fixed and announced principles, and that I should neither be obliged nor requested to deviate from them in favor of any party or any event."[30]

He wrote to Southey that the position would enable him and his wife to live in London for four or five months. The demands of newspaper work, however, added to other difficulties in the Coleridge marriage. On March 2, 1800, Sara left their lodging at 21 Buckingham Street,

Strand, near the *Post* offices, took Hartley with her, and went to stay with friends. Coleridge moved in with the essayist Charles Lamb. He wrote to Southey that Sara, while a good mother, did not appreciate his "studies, temperament, and—alas—infirmities."[31]

Before he left the Lake District, Coleridge went hiking with Wordsworth, parting from him on November 18, 1799, and returning to Sockburn. There he renewed acquaintance with the Hutchinsons, particularly Sara. Soon he had fallen in love with her. After only a week, however, he had to catch an all-night coach to London to take up his work on the *Post*. Within a year he was asking Stuart to please send a quarter's issues to "one very dear friend, to whom the pleasure of seeing a Paper during the time I wrote in it, would be greater than you can easily imagine." The friend was Sara Hutchinson.[32]

Coleridge's duties were not quite as he had described them. Stuart was in charge, and the poet was a writer of leaders, or editorials. In the next five months, he wrote seventy-six of them, beginning on December 7 with an analysis of the new French constitution proclaimed by Bonaparte.[33]

As an editorialist, he was the voice of moderation. His paragraphs warned against the rigidities of government policy and at the same time the excesses of the radical Jacobin political society in France. "It is the fate and nature of revolutions," he wrote, that "the people at first are more than angels in their notions of rights and liberties; and less than men in their enjoyment and practice of them." He condemned Napoleon's seizure of power, but also criticized Pitt's refusal to accept an offer of peace negotiations. "Good men should now close ranks," he said. "Too much of extravagant hope, too much of rash intolerance, have disgraced all parties."[34]

When asked to write on farm issues, he would sometimes ask Poole, who knew more about the subject, to help him out. Like many journalists, he complained about his job. By February, he had twice put in long hours attending and reporting debates in the Commons, and found the work "of a very unpleasant kind." "We newspaper scribes are true Galley-Slaves," he wrote to Josiah Wedgwood.[35]

Galley slave or no, he found some things attractive about the work, writing to Wedgwood that "it is not unflattering to a man's vanity to reflect that what he writes at 12 at night will before 12 hours is over have perhaps 5 or 6000 readers." He also had the pleasure of seeing some of his work reprinted in provincial papers and in journals as far away as America. He asked a friend to send Poole some of the issues with his leaders in them and said, "They are important in themselves, & excellent Vehicles for general Truths. I am not ashamed of what I have written."[36]

He need not have been. He was, said biographer Traill, "a workman of the very first order of excellence in this curious craft." So much so that Stuart offered him a half share in both the *Morning Post* and its companion evening paper, *The Courier*. He estimated he could make two thousand pounds a year if he accepted, but it would mean giving up poetry. So he told Stuart "that I would not give up the Country, & the lazy reading of Old Folios for two thousand times two thousand Pound." In later years, to the annoyance of his benefactor, he wrote that he had "wasted the prime and manhood of my intellect" in Stuart's service.[37]

On Christmas eve, 1799, he wrote to Southey that he had been working from nine in the morning until midnight as "a pure scribbler." But he still managed time occasionally to drink too much at a party and have to apologize to his host. On one occasion, he blamed a fit of bad temper partly on a "glass of punch of most deceitful strength" mixed by Lamb's sister, Mary. The opium was also taking its toll. By January 1800, two years after his prose contributions first appeared in the paper, he was writing Stuart that he was "very unwell." If the editor needed a leader for the paper that day, the poet could write it, but the editor would have to come and get it. "I cannot come out," said Coleridge, "and if it will do as well tomorrow, so much the better." Later in the day he felt well enough to promise "three or four paragraphs of seven or eight lines each," delivered that evening by Lamb.

In a letter to Stuart a month later, he was questioning "whether we continue connected or no." Still, although preoccupied with the translation of three Schiller plays from the German, he told his editor that in a few days "I shall be able to give you some assistance, probably as much as you may want."[38]

How much effect Coleridge's contributions had on the circulation
of the *Post* was debatable. Stuart said the paper had daily sales of 350
copies in August 1795 and had risen to slightly more than 2,000 in April
1802, making its circulation the highest of any London paper. Coleridge
called this "a pledge that genuine impartiality, with a respectable portion
of literary talent, will secure the success of a newspaper." He also took
credit for increasing the circulation in a conversation in which he mis-
takenly said it had soared to 7,000. Stuart took exception to this, and
the poet's daughter, editing her father's essays after his death, conceded
that "while my Father may have done much to raise the reputation, and
enhance the importance, of the *Morning Post*," its general sale depended
on other factors.[39]

Looking back years later, Stuart gave the poet high marks as an editorial writer: "To write the leading paragraph of a newspaper, I would
prefer him to . . . any other man I ever heard of. His observations not
only were confirmed by good sense, but displayed extensive knowledge,
deep thought and well-grounded foresight; they were so brilliantly or-
namented, so classically delightful. They were the writings of a Scholar,
a Gentleman and Statesman, without personal sarcasm or illiberality of
any kind. But when Coleridge wrote in his study without being pressed,
he wandered and lost himself." The editor might well have added that
Coleridge's day-to-day newspaper writings were the work of a poet,
reflecting the same ornament and classicism of such poems as his "De-
jection: An Ode." Stuart's criticism of the prose Coleridge wrote at
his leisure was also apt. Much of his critical work has been fittingly
described as labored and tortuous. Traill wrote that the poet's editorial
pieces "hit the nail on the head in nearly every case, and . . . take the
plainest and most direct route to their point."[40]

Coleridge's approach to journalistic writing is perhaps best shown
in a three-thousand-word profile of Pitt that appeared in March 1800.
He likened the prime minister to "a plant sown and reared in a hot
house . . . who had had the sun without the breeze; whom no storm had
shaken, on whom no rain had pattered; on whom the dews of heaven
had not fallen." Two years before the editorialist wrote these lines, the
poet had written:

The silly buckets on the deck
That had so long remained,
I dreamt that they were filled with dew
And when I awoke it rained.

Rain did not patter on the prime minister but did on the ancient mariner. Clearly Coleridge possessed what one critic has called "extra-journalistic skill in the portrayal of experience or character."[41]

Stuart said the Pitt profile "made a sensation which any writings unconnected with the events of the day rarely did" and that "the Paper was in demand for days and weeks afterward."[42]

Coleridge also complained of Pitt's arid prose, which may have helped put him to sleep on the morning when he reported only half of the prime minister's speech. He wrote that "not a sentence of Mr. Pitt's has ever been quoted, or formed the favorite phrase of the day." This, he declared, could not be said of any man of equal reputation. It could not be said of Coleridge either. His language was so vivid that Stuart sometimes toned it down. His description of Napoleon Bonaparte as "an upstart Corsican" became a byword during the turmoil that followed Napoleon's seizure of power in France.[43]

Coleridge's reports of Pitt's speeches were often more colorful than the originals. A visitor to the *Post* remarked that one of them "did more credit to his head than to his memory." Hearing his own arguments against Pitt's policies toward France used by opposition speakers, Coleridge told Wedgwood of the pleasure of hearing his "own particular phrases in the House of Commons" and chuckling over the plagiarism.[44]

The "upstart Corsican" phrase would haunt Coleridge. In a note accompanying his "Character of Mr. Pitt," he promised that a similar portrait of Bonaparte would follow. It did not, and he began to be asked why. A little over a month after the Pitt piece appeared, a French diplomat asked Stuart when the Napoleon profile would be published. When Stuart failed to give a satisfactory response, a friend of the diplomat appeared at the newspaper office and said it was the French emperor himself who wanted the answer. He had been much taken with the article on Pitt and was looking forward to reading the one about himself.

Stuart was delighted and rushed to Coleridge with the news. Coleridge, according to his own recollection three years later, was not delighted. "Stuart," he said, "that man will prove a Tyrant, & the deadliest enemy of the Liberty of the Press." He said it saddened him to see "the Dictator of a vast Empire, to be so childishly solicitous for the panegyric of a Newspaper Scribbler."[45]

Nevertheless, Coleridge seemed proud of his scribbling. "Anything not bad in the paper, that is not yours, is mine," he told Southey. When some politicians tried to get London newspapers to moderate their attacks on Bonaparte, the poet was among the most vociferous protesters. Always he argued that freedom of expression was needed to keep the government from becoming a despotism.[46]

In the summer of 1800, Coleridge left London for a new home in the Lake District, telling Poole that Stuart was "importunate against" his leaving the *Post*. He continued to write for the paper, sending his contributions by mail from Greta Hall, the house he had leased in Keswick, a few miles north of Wordsworth's home in Grasmere. On November 13, he boarded a coach from Grasmere, bound once more for London. Stuart found him a set of rooms over a tailor's shop in King Street, Covent Garden, presided over by a middle-aged housewife "who I knew would nurse Coleridge as kindly as if he were her son." The editor would pay mid-morning calls on him to talk over the news and discuss a leader for the next morning's paper, much in the manner of editorial conferences today. Coleridge, however, was increasingly in the grip of his addiction. Before long, Stuart found that although the poet "could talk over everything so well, . . . he could not write on the daily occurrences of the day." Eventually, his editor became convinced that at that time Coleridge "never could write a thing that was immediately required of him. The thought of compulsion disarmed him."[47]

In 1801, Stuart became seriously ill with a fever, perhaps brought on by the unsanitary condition of a London street he walked through. He sold the *Post* and moved to the suburbs. Coleridge returned to the Lake District.[48]

A story came along that summer that was too good for the sometime newspaperman to pass up. John Hadfield, an ex-convict and con man, checked in at the Queen's Head in Keswick in July under the name of Colonel the Honorable Alex Augustus Hope, member of Parliament for Linlithgowshire. Hadfield had already seduced and abandoned two women and was ingratiating himself with a wealthy tourist's young ward at the Queen's Head. That did not stop him from spending time at the Fish Inn in nearby Buttermere to court Mary Robinson, the landlord's pretty daughter. Business at the Fish Inn had picked up over the past decade, since writer Joseph Budworth celebrated the then fourteen-year-old Mary as "The Beauty of Buttermere." Hadfield was still married to a woman named Michelli Nation, who had got him released from prison by paying his debts. Like Miss Nation, Mary was taken in by the smooth-talking visitor with thick black brows and fair hair, and they were married on October 1 at Loweswater Church. On their honeymoon in the Scottish Borders, word reached Hadfield of rumors that he was an imposter, and he rushed back to Keswick with his bride. Unfortunately for him, a barrister named George Hardinge had arrived at the Queen's Head. Hardinge happened to know the real Colonel Hope. Hadfield fled by boat after persuading a gullible constable to allow him one last fishing trip on Derwent Water. During a nationwide search, Hadfield was spotted at a theater in Chester in November, but he escaped.

Patching the story together from interviews, rumors and local clippings, Coleridge wrote a five-part series that appeared in the *Morning Post* between October 11 and December 31, 1802. The first installments, datelined Keswick, were headed "The Romantic Marriage" and the later ones "The Keswick Imposter." A typical passage by the editorialist turned feature writer told readers, "From this time our adventurer played a double game. It seems to have been a maxim with him to leave as few interspaces as possible in the crowded map of his villainy."

The story continued to fascinate the poet. After Hadfield was finally arrested at an inn near Swansea, in South Wales, Coleridge attended his trial in the north England county town of Carlisle. Impersonating a member of Parliament was a capital offense at the time, and Hadfield was sentenced to hang. In August 1803, Coleridge secured the crime reporter's plum: an interview with the condemned man. He wrote about it only in his notebook. He briefly considered turning Hadfield's story into fiction but concluded that "it is not by mere Thought, I can understand this man." Mary Robinson, incidentally, married farmer Richard Harrison in 1807, had seven children, and lived out her life among the lakes.[49]

In 1804, Coleridge left England for a stint as secretary to the civil commissioner of Malta. By this time Stuart was back in fair health and had bought a half share in the *Courier*, an evening newspaper. Active management of the paper was left to his partner, T. J. Street.

When Coleridge returned to London on August 17, 1806, he was determined finally that he and his wife must separate. He moved in again with Lamb, but left in mid-September for a room at the *Courier*, where he became an assistant to Stuart and Street. He was to find neither his quarters nor his employment much to his liking. The building was too noisy to sleep comfortably in, and his combined bed and sitting room, up two flights of stairs, was tended by an "unlovable old woman" named Mistress Bainbridge. Again he was busy writing short paragraphs on domestic and foreign affairs, but Street was not as impressed with his work as was Stuart. Added to this was Coleridge's growing disenchantment with the *Courier*. He chafed, like many another journalist, when publication of his pieces was deferred, and believed that the paper had lost its independence and become an organ of the government.[50]

By the end of 1807, Coleridge was spending much of his time at the *Courier* working on a series of lectures culminating in his celebrated work on Shakespeare. He spent the next two years shuttling between the lakes and London, both writing for the *Courier* and lecturing. He hoped that he and Wordsworth might start something like the eighteenth-century essay journal the *Spectator*.

Wordsworth, however, did not join in this venture, declaring that "I am sorry for it—as I have not the least hope that it can proceed." His opium-dependent friend, said the poet, could not in his opinion "execute anything of important benefit either to himself, his family or mankind."[51]

The first number of the journal appeared on June 1, 1809, with a title page reading, "THE FRIEND: A Literary, Moral, and Political Weekly

Paper, excluding Person and Party Politics and Events of the Day." As this description suggests, it was an odd newspaper. "The mode of publication is not the proper one for matters so abstract as are frequently treated of," wrote Dorothy Wordsworth. An anonymous writer in the *Eclectic Review* complained that "though coming with some of the exterior marks of a newspaper" it was more like "a commentary on Aristotle or Plato." Interestingly, Coleridge considered this a "flattering review." To Stuart he wrote that "as to anything, ordinarily understood by Politics, I have as little to do with it, as with News." Nevertheless, he said, *The Friend* "was and I trust is to be a newspaper."[52]

Coleridge was discovering some of the disadvantages of living in his beloved Lake District. Mail was delivered three times a week, on Wednesday, on Friday, and at 10:00 P.M. on Sunday. He had to walk three miles from his house to Rydale to pick it up. If it was Sunday, a reply could not leave the district until Tuesday because the mail was held up at Hawkshead all day Monday. "It is not once in ten times that we can answer by the same post that brings the letter," he told Stuart. Wordsworth said that he sometimes had to leave his home in Grasmere as late as two o'clock in the morning to meet the carrier with his newspaper from Keswick.[53]

Coleridge also struggled with getting the journal printed. An elderly printer in the Lake District town of Kendal decided against taking the work on. Having it printed in London was a possibility, but would cut down the profits. Would it be practical, he asked Stuart, who was providing the paper, to set up a press at Grasmere and hire a printer from Liverpool? Stuart did not encourage the idea, and Coleridge lined up a young printer in Penrith, John Brown, who might take on the work. Penrith was closer than Kendal, but still required a strenuous hike over a 1,929-foot pass in the Cumbrian Mountains. While leaping an icy stream, the poet badly sprained his knee.[54]

In addition to hiking, he had to deal with the government Stamp Office, procure subscribers, and arrange for payment for issues. Was the paper to be weekly or monthly? Was it to be delivered in the mail or sold at bookstores? Many people, argued Coleridge, "like to have the *newspaper feeling* of receiving a Paper at their own doors." How large should the editions be? In the end, it was weekly, with 644 copies, all but a dozen of them delivered by mail at the price of a shilling—one twentieth of a pound. "Me, unused to business," groaned the poet. "I find the writing of the Essays quite delightful, by comparison with the business of setting up a shop." To make matters worse, his "fatal habit" still troubled him. He had been "extremely unwell for eight days . . . so as to be incapable of sitting upright for half an hour together."[55]

Sara Hutchinson was with him at Grasmere, and was taking down his dictation both for *The Friend* and for the *Courier.* Despite his disagreement with Street's pro-government stance, he offered to provide the evening paper with two columns a week, as it "needs a little BRIGHTENING UP."

Stuart complained that the first issues of *The Friend* were written in "too hard and laborious a style," but Coleridge assured him in September that "every number after those will become more and more entertaining." Entertaining or not, the paper ceased publication on March 15, 1810, after twenty-eight issues. Coleridge's hopes that his unconsummated love for Sara Hutchinson would be reciprocated were soon dashed. Sara left Grasmere to join her brother at his new farm in Wales.[56]

At the end of 1810, Coleridge was back in London, offering his services to the *Courier* for a six-month period and saying he could be in the office every morning at 9:30, read the morning papers and point out to Street "whatever seemed valuable." He might, he hoped, write occasional leaders when the editor was otherwise occupied. He promised that he would have "no pretense to any control or intermeddlement; but merely during a certain space of time to be in part his assistant, and in part a political writer in the service of the paper." He reported for work May 6 at 8:30, an hour earlier than he had said.

The editor was, by Coleridge's account, "very pleased" with the arrangement, but before long the poet found cause for discontent. Five days after he went to work, a visitor to his lodgings reported that he "expressed liberal opinions on politics, and I doubt not the *Courier* would assume a different air if he were allowed to give it his complexion." But he was not. A friend said Coleridge considered Street, who was believed

by some to be in the pay of the Treasury, "altogether a corrupt man."
Coleridge was unhappy when the paper killed an article he wrote in June
criticizing the reappointment of the Duke of York as commander in chief
of the army by his brother, the Prince of Wales. The prince had by then
become Prince Regent because of the mental incapacity of King George
III. It later appeared that the article, printed in the first two thousand
copies of the paper, was withdrawn because of pressure from the government. Stuart refused the government's offer to pay for the large number
of copies that had to be destroyed, saying later that he feared influential
readers would believe the article was "designedly sent by ministers to the
paper for a crooked purpose."[57]

Coleridge also thought some writings in the *Courier* were longer
than they merited, and others were not timely. "Freshness of effect," he
said, was "the point which belongs to a newspaper and distinguishes it
from a library book." He said one story in the paper ran to more than
two columns when it could have been covered in a third of a column.
An account of a "stupid" parliamentary debate, he said, could have been
cut by half. Street was picking up copy from the morning papers, and
Coleridge hoped the editor would let him spend his first half hour at
work condensing them. This, he said, would make room for more interesting material and "give somewhat of an original cast to the paper."
Street seems to have paid little attention, and to have left work early, as
Coleridge found him gone one day when he tried to call on him a little
after two o'clock. The last of Coleridge's forty-five articles was published September 27. He appeared to have lost heart for his job. Traill
said his writings for the *Courier* in 1811 and 1812 had "much more of
the character of newspaper hack work than his earlier contributions."
The poet wrote his patron, George Beaumont, "I will write for the PER-
MANENT or not at all."[58]

On October 5, Coleridge wrote to Street that he had finished three
political profiles, but they did not appear and may not have been written. He tried unsuccessfully to get a position with the *London Times*.

In 1812 the poet was spending most of his time lecturing. Members of his aristocratic audience paid a guinea for admission to Willis's
Room, the Surrey Institute, and other fashionable venues. By August, he

no longer wished "to write for any given time for the Courier," although he was still trying to sell the paper a series of twenty articles on subjects ranging from the War of 1812 in America to his long-promised "Character of Buonaparte." Nothing came of them.[59]

In a bitter letter to Stuart in September 1814, after reading a harsh review of his work, Coleridge "for the very first time in my whole life, opened out my whole feelings and thoughts concerning my past fates and fortunes." His newspaper writing, he told his old friend, "would read to you now, AS HISTORY. And what have I got for all this? . . . to think and toil, with a patent for all the abuse, and a transfer to others of all the honors." Two months later, he was nonetheless submitting copy to the *Courier*, as he continued to do through 1816. By May of that year, he was writing to Stuart that "had the paper maintained and asserted not only its independence but its appearance of it, it is true that Mr. Street might not have . . . received as many nods or shakes of the hand from Lord this, or that, but equally true, that the Ministry would have been far more effectually served" by a more independent newspaper. Stuart replied that he had withdrawn from the paper altogether after it "slid into a mere ministerial journal, or instrument of the Treasury, Street making it acquire the reputation even of being official."[60]

In 1816, Coleridge collapsed from an opium overdose while in London to work on his play, *Zapolya*, for production at Covent Garden. The play was rejected, and a doctor persuaded the author to cut back on the opium. The physician, Dr. Joseph Adams, put Coleridge under the care of Dr. James Gillman in the London suburb of Highgate. The poet would live with the Gillmans until his death in 1834. Despite Gillman's efforts, Coleridge made covert arrangements with a local chemist to assure a continued supply of opium.[61]

Coleridge was now trying to concentrate his weakened energy on philosophy and lamenting that "it is a hard thing to be compelled to turn away from such subjects to scribble essays for the newspapers."

His journalistic days were soon over, and the best of his poetry was behind him. He would spend the rest of his life on such works as a justification of Trinitarian Christianity and treatises on logic and the constitution of church and state. In July 1826, he listed the types of visitor he had recently had: a merchant, a manufacturer, a physician, a member of Parliament, clergymen, painters, political economists. As ever, he fascinated his visitors with eloquent talk on an enormous range of subjects. He talked of Bonaparte, of popular representation, of love and friendship, of poetry, of the Papacy and Reformation.[62]

No talk of his newspaper days is recorded.

2 "A Wonderful and Ponderous Book"

When a mob led by working-class agitator Mike Walsh stoned the Manhattan home of Bishop John Hughes in 1842 to protest the bishop's support of public funds for parochial schools, a twenty-two-year-old editor who signed his name Walter Whitman wrote, "Had it been the reverend hypocrite's head, instead of his windows, we could hardly find it in our soul to be sorrowful." As if this were not enough, he went on to describe the bishop as "a false villain, who uses his pontifical robes to cover the blackest, most traitorous heart in the broad limits of the American republic."[1]

The editorialist Coleridge may have cautioned against intemperate zeal and rash intolerance and warned that passion makes men blind, but the editorialist Walt Whitman was cut from other cloth.

Although professing to have "no antipathy or bigotted [sic] ill will to *foreigners*," Whitman railed against "coarse, filthy, unshaven Irish rabble" and backed the so-called nativists, who fought bitterly against immigrants, many of them Irish Catholics.[2]

The great poet was at the time the youthful "leading editor" of the *New York Aurora*, but the billingsgate was fairly representative of his editorial style on other papers as well.[3]

At the *Aurora*, he denounced an earlier employer, New York publisher and poet Park Benjamin, as "one of the most vain pragmatical nincompoops in creation," a "witless ape," and a man regarded by his associates as they would regard "a pert, ungainly fellow, half boor and half fop—who has, by some mistake, gained admittance in the society of decent and fashionable people." After becoming editor of the *Evening Tattler,* he described his former employers at the much larger *Aurora,*

22

Anson Herrick and John F. Ropes, as journalists incapable "of constructing two lines of grammar or meaning," two "ill bred vagabonds" who displayed "more low deceits . . . more gross blasphemy and prurient conversation" than he had ever heard.[4]

As an editor in Brooklyn, he called New York, then a separate city, "one of the most crime-haunted and dangerous cities in all Christendom" and "The Gomorrah across the river."[5]

"Some day," he declared, "decent folk will take the matter into their own hands and put down, with a strong will, this rum-swilling, rampant set of rowdies and roughs."[6]

Along with the rash intolerance, though, there was plenty of intemperate zeal. The poet who would "hear America singing," the apostle of the country's "manifest destiny," began as a civic booster.

As editor of the *Brooklyn Daily Eagle,* he proposed that Long Island be made into the new state of Paumanok, with Brooklyn as its capital.[7]

At the *Aurora,* not yet seeing New York with the eyes of a Brooklyn editor, he described the city as "a great place—a mighty world in itself."[8]

Already, his theme was America, and he was a booster for it. "We glory in being *true Americans,*" he wrote. "And we profess to impress *Aurora* with the same spirit. We have taken high American ground."[9]

As a poet, Whitman took the same ground. *Leaves of Grass* is a curious mixture of great poetry and rampant editorializing for a nineteenth-century view of America's manifest destiny. There is, for instance, more egalitarian editorializing than poetry in "America," which appeared in the first annex of his magnum opus:

> Centre of equal daughters, equal sons,
> All, all alike endear'd, grown, upgrown, young or old,
> Strong, ample, fair, enduring, capable, rich,
> Perennial with the Earth, with Freedom, Law and Love,
> A grand, sane, towering, seated Mother,
> Chair'd in the adamant of Time.

By the age of twenty-eight, Whitman had edited or helped to edit eight newspapers. His journalistic work was by no means over even

This daguerreotype of Walt Whitman was made early in
the 1840s, when the author of *Leaves of Grass* was editor
of the *New York Aurora*. A young printer at the paper
described the poet as "tall and graceful in appearance,
neat in attire." Courtesy of the Walt Whitman Archive.
Ed. Ed Folsom and Kenneth M. Price. March 30, 2005.
http://www.whitmanarchive.org.

then. "I have had to do, one time or another, during my life, with a long
list of papers, at diverse places, sometimes under queer circumstances,"
he would say in 1882, when he was in his early sixties.[10]

His newspaper career began in 1831, when he was apprenticed at the age of twelve to Samuel E. Clements, editor of a four-page weekly called the *Long Island Patriot*. Young Walter was no stranger to the *Patriot*. His father, a carpenter with political interests, subscribed to it. The boy contributed minor items to the paper, but the early appearance in print that meant most to him was a now-unidentified "piece or two" in the *New York Mirror*.[11]

Five decades later, Whitman remembered "with what half-suppressed excitement I used to watch for the big, fat, red-faced, slow-moving, very old English carrier who distributed the *Mirror* in Brooklyn; and when I got one, opening and cutting the leaves with trembling fingers. How it made my heart double-beat to see my place on the pretty white paper, in nice type."[12]

At the *Patriot*, Whitman got his first instruction in typesetting, an important skill when the editor of a paper—not usually called an editor but more often a proprietor or publisher—repaired the press as needed, composed type on the forms and ran the business office as well as seeing to the editorial and news content.[13]

Whitman was soon to put his lessons to use. Clements, a "hawk-nosed Quaker and Southerner" recalled by associates as eccentric and indiscreet, was fired in November 1831, six months after his young apprentice came to work. This left the boy adrift, but he soon found work in the *Brooklyn Evening Star* printing department. In his midteens he qualified as a journeyman printer and worked for a while as a compositor in New York.[14]

He then took a leave from journalism, teaching instead for two or three years in country schools in Queens and Suffolk counties. However, as he recalled in 1882, he "liked printing . . . and was encouraged to start a paper in the region where I was born." The result was the *Huntington Long Islander*, launched in the spring of 1838 with Walter Whitman as editor and publisher. Whitman took the ferry to New York and bought a press and some type, probably with money loaned him by friends. He also bought a "good horse" named Nina "and every week went all around the country serving my papers, devoting one day and night to it." He may not have made this thirty-mile circuit every week as he said, because by other accounts the paper, which had a circulation of about two hundred, was issued spasmodically, sometimes once a week, sometimes once in two or three weeks. Although Whitman recalled that he had "hired some little help" on his shopping trip to New York, the paper appears to have been mainly a one-man operation, published on the upper floor of a small frame house with Main Street in front and wooded fields in the back. In 1839, Whitman sold the *Long Islander* to E. C. Crowell, who told readers he planned to "continue it regularly." Whitman said he might have stayed at the paper indefinitely if had not been for "my own restlessness."[15]

In August 1839, three months after the sale of the *Long Islander,* Whitman went to work for the *Hempstead Inquirer,* soon to be renamed the *Long Island Democrat.* He set type and wrote sentimental poems and essays under the heading, "Sun-Down Papers from the Desk of a Schoolmaster." In one of these, the young journalist "considered with pain that the golden hours of youth were swiftly gliding; and that my cherished hopes of pleasure had never yet been attained." Later, he expressed a wistful hope that he might someday produce "a wonderful and ponderous book . . . And who knows but that I might do something very respectable?" The *Leaves of Grass* were beginning to sprout, perhaps in hours spent lying under a blooming apple tree when he was supposed to be at the office. Already, the *Democrat*'s editor, James Brenton, found him "of great value to the 'literary' end of the newspaper work."[16]

Walter Whitman's restlessness soon took him to the metropolis across the East River. He contributed some writings to the *Democratic Review* and worked in the large printing office of the publisher and poet Park Benjamin. That he was already taking his poetry seriously is shown by revisions he made to his "Fame's Vanity," first published in the *Democrat* on October 23, 1839, when it was republished under the title "Ambition" in Benjamin's *Brother Jonathan* on January 29, 1842. "Fame's Vanity" began:

O, many a panting, noble heart
   Cherishes in its deep recess

The hope to win renown o'er earth
    From Glory's prized caress.

And some will reach that envied goal,
    And have their fame known far and wide;
And some will sink unnoted down
    In dark Oblivion's tide.

In the revision, the poem opens with ten lines of blank verse introducing the rhymed quatrains, which are spoken to "an obscure youth, a wanderer" by "a shape / Like one as of a cloud," and the second quatrain reads:

And some will win that envied goal,
    And have their deeds known far and wide;
And some—by far the most—will sink
    Down in oblivion's tide.

Two prose contributions to the same publication throw some light on Whitman's development as a poet. Commenting on "The Angel of Tears," in which "the angel Alza" is one of "a million million invisible eyes which keep constant watch over the earth," Whitman biographer Bliss Perry remarked on "how very neatly the young journalist could play, if need be, upon the flute of Edgar Allan Poe." But the Poe influence did not last long. The prose piece, "The Last of the Sacred Army," reflected a penchant for lengthy catalogs that would become a hallmark of Whitman's poetry. A twentieth-century historian would say that the "quick, slick" approach favored by nineteenth-century newspapers would "rust out a writer's style," but it does not seem to have had that effect on Whitman's. Witness "The blab of the pave, tires of carts, sluff of boot-soles, talk of the promenaders" and on through seven lines to "The excited crowd, the policeman with his star quickly working his passage to the center of the crowd." A reporter's city editor would have loved it.[17]

In February 1842, Whitman joined the daily *New York Aurora* as "a sort of free lance." A new opportunity arose when the editor, New

Englander Thomas Low Nichols, got in trouble over a libelous editorial charging graft on a pipe-laying project and left the paper on February 22. On March 28, the publishers announced that they had "secured the services of Mr. Walter Whitman, favorably known as a bold, energetic and original writer, as their leading editor." In his first editorial, Whitman told readers the paper would be "a picture of American life and character—a mirror of society," much like what he would view his poetry as being. He said the paper would be, to a great extent, local but added, "No important movement, in city or country, will escape it."[18]

From the quiet life of a country editor and schoolteacher, Whitman had plunged into one of the nation's hottest newspaper wars. Since the birth of the American republic, newspapers had been partisan organs, owing their existence to political parties. The entry of James Gordon Bennett's *New York Herald* into the field in 1835 signaled the transformation of journalism into a fiercely competitive business. The change prompted attacks on Bennett and the *Herald* by the *Wall-Street Press,* smaller New York papers, and Whig party organs in Albany, Boston, Philadelphia, and Baltimore. Whitman joined the fray, calling the *Herald* "a scandal to the republic."[19]

The new atmosphere also triggered stunning growth in the number of New York newspapers. Nine were launched in 1839, two in 1841, another nine in 1842, and twenty in 1845—forty new newspapers in six years.

The *Aurora* entered this competitive field carrying local and out-of-town news on its 21 x 15¾-inch front page, editorials on the second page, and mostly advertising on its remaining two pages. The staff was small, with one reporter covering police and courts and the rest of the copy written by the editor or freelance writers known as penny-a-liners. The formula apparently worked. During the three months of Nichols's tenure, circulation reached five thousand, a respectable figure, although only about half of the *Herald*'s circulation and less than that of several other competitors.

After a week as editor, Whitman said the *Aurora* was meeting with almost unprecedented success, telling his readers, "Our regular edition has been completely exhausted by eight or nine o'clock every morning;

and we have made arrangements to increase it next week to a thousand beyond what it has hitherto been."

"Editing a daily paper, to be sure, is an arduous employment," he wrote. "The consciousness that several thousand people will look for their Aurora as regularly as for their breakfasts . . . implies no small responsibility upon a man. Yet it is delightful."

From across the river, the *Brooklyn Eagle* chimed in on March 30 with a mixed verdict: "A marked change for the better has come over this spirited little daily since the accession of Mr. Whitman to the 'vacant chair.' There is, nevertheless, a dash of egotism occasionally."[20]

Whitman dressed the part—frock coat, high hat, cane, and boutonniere. The future "good grey poet" seems to have adopted different costumes for different roles. To Charles Roe, one of his students in his schoolmaster days, he "dressed neatly—very plain in everything—no attempt at what would be called fashion. . . . He dressed mainly as other people dressed"—frock coat, vest, black pants, and a white shirt. Another former student, Sandford Brown, when shown in his old age the portrait of Whitman in *Leaves of Grass,* told a pair of English visitors that it reminded him of his first teacher's "Negligent style of the dress, the open collar and the 'way of wearin' the hat.'" Ovetta Hall Brenton, the daughter-in-law of his employer at the *Democrat,* complained that he "cared nothing at all about clothes" and would sit in his shirt sleeves at the Brenton home.[21]

Whitman's egotism may have contributed to his departure from the *Aurora.* At first, his employers were satisfied that "whatever change has occurred in its editorial management, the united opinion of all best qualified to judge, is that the change is far more to advantage than evil."

His midday strolls down Broadway to the Battery and back were ending in sometimes heated discussion with Herrick over "the toning of the leaders," as editorials were still called in America as well as England. Associates described Herrick advising his editor against being "occasionally so trenchant with his pen", and Whitman responding, "if you want such stuff in the *Aurora* write it yourself." The meetings sometimes ended with Whitman picking up his hat and cane and stamping out of the office, then cooling down and returning. There came a time, though, when he did not return. On May 16, the newspaper announced: "Mr. Walter

Whitman desires us to state that he has been for three or four weeks past, and now is, entirely disconnected with the editorial department of the *Aurora*." There were differing versions of his departure—one that he was fired for being lazy and obstreperous and the other that he was tired of "editing a party organ."[22]

He moved on to the *Tattler* and the *Sun*, writing crime stories for both. At the *Sun* he began a practice he would follow often of writing anonymous and favorable reviews of his own work—in this case a novel, *Franklin Evans,* about a country boy from Virginia who falls into evil ways in the city. The patrician poet James Russell Lowell spotted Whitman in 1842 at his editorial desk in the appropriately titled *Plebeian* and later recalled, "He used to do stories then, *a la* Hawthorne." In 1842 and 1843, Whitman was editing the *New York Sunday Times.* For two or three months in 1843, he was an editor at the New York semi-weekly the *Statesman.* His journalistic chores kept him so busy that he was writing less poetry. He was still polishing it, although not quite enough to suit one editor. When "My Departure," first published in 1839 in the *Long Island Democrat,* was reprinted with extensive revisions as "The Death of the Nature Lover" in Park Benjamin's *Brother Jonathan,* the editor commented, "The following wants but a half-hour's polish to make of it an effusion of very uncommon beauty." One of the most striking revisions was that Whitman changed from first to third person. "Would I, when the last hour has come" became "Wisht he, when the dark hour approached." It was a change of stance not to be pursued by the poet who would proclaim, "One's self I sing, a simple, separate person."[23]

In September 1845, Whitman crossed the river again and went to work for the *Brooklyn Evening Star.* In six months there, he wrote on subjects ranging from music to the coercion of juries. The journalistic opportunity for which he is best remembered came in March 1846, when he assumed the helm of the *Brooklyn Daily Eagle* after the death of editor William B. Marsh. The *Eagle,* a Democratic organ in its fifth year of publication, was the *Star*'s rival to be the leading newspaper in the state's second largest city. Whitman was probably eased into the job by Henry C. Murphy, who was both a local Democratic leader and an owner of the paper. The poet had known Murphy at the *Patriot* fifteen years before.[24]

Whitman was to recall the post as "one of the pleasantest sits of my life—a good owner, good pay, and easy work and hours." In his upstairs office at the *Eagle*'s quarters, he wrote editorials denouncing the slave trade as the "most abominable of all man's schemes for making money," assailing capital punishment, expressing his interest in phrenology, celebrating spring flowers, and thanking the Democrats for their "warm kindness" toward the paper. "We really feel inclined to talk on many subjects, to *all* the people of Brooklyn," he wrote. Introducing himself to his readers, he said that an editor "should have a fluent style," but "elaborate finish we do not think requisite in daily writing," apparently an acknowledgment of his own occasionally shaky syntax. When he praised the "grateful Brooklyn air," the *New York Morning News* asked what the air was grateful for, and the *Eagle* replied that the air was thankful for "not being confined, like its sister air, in the odious precincts of New York."[25]

A persistent editorial theme was the Revolutionary War Battle of Brooklyn, in which Washington's heavily outnumbered forces were beaten back and forced to retreat and the British gained control of Long Island. One of Whitman's great-uncles died in the battle, which he saw as an emblem of national unity, with Northerners and Southerners fighting side by side. It was a telling argument as mounting tensions led toward civil war. In his "Drum-Taps," Whitman tells a "Centenarian's Story" of the rout of inexperienced young soldiers facing the disciplined and well-equipped British, and how

> We fought the fight in detachments,
> Sallying forth we fought at several points, but in each the luck
>   was against us,
> Our foe advancing, steadily getting the best of it, push'd us
>   back to the works on this hill,
> Till we turn'd menacing here, and then he left us.
>
> That was the going out of the brigade of the youngest men,
>   two thousand strong,
> Few return'd, nearly all remain in Brooklyn.

Whitman's efforts contributed to construction of a 148-foot Doric column as a monument to American soldiers who died in prison ships that the British moored in Brooklyn's Wallabout Bay after the battle. In a poem, he called them editorially "The stepping stones to thee today and here, America."[26]

Whitman's arrival at the *Eagle* saw the inauguration of a literary department of one to three columns on the front page, which before had been entirely devoted to advertising. The new editor announced the aim of publishing works "on American subjects, particularly those relating to Long Island, and the neighboring section of the United States." He published eight of fellow newspaper editor William Cullen Bryant's poems and pronounced Bryant "among the first in the world" as a poet. Henry Wadsworth Longfellow appeared in twenty-four issues of the *Eagle*—more than any other poet—and was saluted by Whitman as "an honor and glory to the American name." Reviewing a now-forgotten work of fiction, he praised "the patriotism and truth running through it,"—a foretaste of goals he would set in his own literary work. For the most part, Whitman the journalist favored the sentimental and moralistic fare that readers were accustomed to in their newspapers. He printed two of his own poems, "The Playground," which was signed "W," and an ode to be sung at a Fourth of July celebration, to the tune of "The Star-Spangled Banner." The ode returned to the theme of "The battle, the prison ship, martyrs, and hill," and urged that they be remembered "For how priceless the worth of the sanctified earth."[27]

One of Whitman's successors as editor of the *Eagle*, Arthur M. Howe, reviewed the poet's editorials and commentary and said they conveyed "the impression of one who regarded his occupation in journalism as something to which he was compelled by circumstances rather than as a vocation for which he had any positive affection." Whitman scholar Thomas L. Brasher found him "fairly representative" of the journalists of his day. Whitman himself, on his sixty-ninth birthday, told a friend that he was "no use in any situation which calls for instant decision" and that his opinions were "so hazy—so slow to come" that he lacked the makings of a good journalist.[28]

Nevertheless, the *Eagle* prospered under Whitman's hand. The paper acquired a new typeface and moved to new quarters as "increasing business . . . made a necessity for more room." Its hand press was replaced by a steam-driven cylinder press of the kind that had been introduced in the newspaper business eleven years earlier. Whitman may have been the entire editorial staff, although by some reports he eventually acquired the aid of one reporter. The poet obviously did some of the reporting, as he interviewed P. T. Barnum, himself a former newspaper proprietor and editor, in the spring of 1846 after the great showman's return from a tour of Europe. As Whitman reported the interview, Barnum gave his impressions of the continent in words that fortified the poet's own chauvinistic views: "There everything is frozen—kings and *things*—formal, but absolutely *frozen:* here it is *life*. Here it is freedom, and here are *men*." "A whole book might be written on that little speech of Barnum's," Whitman wrote.[29]

The poet-editor did find one good thing to say about Europe. Grousing about his earnings as journalists so often do, he wrote, "In London, or Paris, the payment for a single 'leader' is frequently more than the month's salary of the best remunerated American editor." The passage of time had apparently softened his outlook when he mused thirty-six years later on what "good pay" he got. Well paid or not, he seemed to enjoy the work, or at least parts of it. Elaborating on his desire to "talk on many subjects to *all* the people of Brooklyn," he wrote, "Daily communion creates a sort of brotherhood and sisterhood between the two parties. As for us, we like this. We like it better than the more 'dignified' part of editorial labors, the grave political disquisitions, the contests of faction, and so on."[30]

The "contests of faction" played a role in Whitman's departure from the *Eagle* two years after joining it. "The troubles in the Democratic party broke forth about those times (1848–'49) and I split off with the radicals, which led to rows with the boss and 'the party,' and I lost my place," he said. The troubles in the party revolved around the Wilmot Proviso, a proposal in Congress that would outlaw slavery in disputed lands that the United States was thinking of buying from Mexico. Whitman was for it and spelled out his view in a December 21, 1846, editorial: "If there

are to be states to be formed out of territory lately annexed, or to be annexed, by any means to the United States, let the Democratic members of
Congress, (and Whigs, too, if they like,) plant themselves quietly, without
bluster, but fixedly and without compromise, on the requirement that
Slavery be prohibited in them forever."

The regular Democrats in Brooklyn were against the proviso, but
a dissident group of "Free Soil" Democrats bolted the party, and came
to be known as the Barnburners. Isaac Van Anden, treasurer of the party's General Committee in Kings County, was a kingpin of the regular
Democratic faction, known as the Old Hunkers. The trouble for Whitman was that Van Anden was also publisher of the *Eagle*. Whitman
continued to write Barnburner editorials, and on January 18, 1848, the
Brooklyn Advertiser reported a "great disturbance" at the *Eagle* office.
What this disturbance was is unclear. One report was that Whitman had
kicked a prominent politician down the stairs. Another report, in Brooklyn and New York papers, was that Whitman had been fired and that the
Eagle would now support the Old Hunkers. The paper did realign itself
with the Old Hunker faction, but of Whitman's departure Van Anden at
first said only that "business arrangements" had made it "necessary to
dispense with one of its editors." After rumors about the nature of the
"great disturbance" continued into 1849, he changed his story, saying
he had reluctantly dismissed Whitman because he was "slow, insolent,
heavy, discourteous" and "has no political principles, nor, for that matter, principles of any sort." During the interim, Whitman apparently
continued on good terms with Van Anden, who published several pieces
that he wrote. Still, he was out of a job.[31]

Reports circulated that the Barnburners planned to start their own
paper, with Whitman in charge, but for one reason or another nothing
came of this plan. Another opportunity—and one that Whitman, weary
of factionalism as he had said he was, may have found more appealing—came along that summer. Whitman, a lover of plays, fell in with
a stranger while walking through the lobby of the Broadway Theater
during intermission. The stranger was J. E. McClure, who was starting
a daily in New Orleans, to be called the *Crescent*. McClure needed an
editor and, after a fifteen-minute visit with Whitman at the theater's bar,

he had one. He gave Whitman two hundred dollars to bind the agreement, and the poet was on his way to New Orleans two days later. He took his fourteen-year-old brother, Jeff, already a compositor, with him. He also took his time. After all, the first issue of the Crescent wasn't due to appear for three weeks.[32]

The trip was an eye-opener for Whitman, who had never before ventured more than a few miles from Brooklyn, and prompted literary touches that prefigured some of his later poetry. In Cumberland, Maryland, he marveled at "the immense Pennsylvania wagons, and the drovers from hundreds of miles west." In an account of the trip that he wrote for the Crescent, he described stagecoach stops "with the mountains on all sides, the precipitous and turning road, the large bare-armed trees looming up around us, the room half filled with men curiously enwrapped in garments of a fashion till then never seen." In Louisiana, he saw a live oak standing alone and it became a metaphor:

> . . . a curious token, it makes me think of manly love;
> For all that, and though the live-oak glistens there in Louisiana,
>   solitary in a wide flat space,
> Uttering joyous leaves all its life without a friend a lover near,
> I know very well I could not.[33]

In New Orleans Whitman had a staff of twelve or more that included an editorial writer, a city news reporter, and a translator of items from the foreign press. In one of his own contributions, he defended a traveling show called "Dr. Collyer's Model Artists," depicting such scenes as Adam's first sight of Eve. Although pretty tame by twenty-first-century standards, the displays of flesh had been condemned by northern papers. Whitman in turn condemned "the sickly prudishness that bars all appreciation of the divine beauty evidenced in Nature's cunningest work—the human frame, form and face." In "Starting from Paumanok," the poet would exclaim, "Whoever you are, how superb and how divine is your body, or any part of it!"[34]

The editor's "Free Soil" views soon got him into as much trouble in the South as they had in the North even though, recognizing that he was in slave territory, he avoided the subject in his editorials. He and Jeff detected "a singular sort of coldness" from McClure and his partner, and the older brother responded "with equal haughtiness." On May 24, Whitman and McClure quarreled over a cash advance. Three days later the Whitmans left New Orleans and returned to Brooklyn by way of the Mississippi River and the Great Lakes.[35]

In September 1848 Whitman published the first issue of the *Brooklyn Freeman*, a campaign sheet on behalf of the Democratic presidential ticket headed by Martin Van Buren. A fire destroyed the building where the paper was printed, and he was not able to resume publication until after the election, which Van Buren lost. Further political maneuvering lost Whitman the party's support, and the last issue of the *Freeman* was published in September 1849. In 1850, he contributed sixteen freelance "Sketches of Brooklynites" to the *Advertiser*, saluting in one of them the "bold masculine discourses" of the abolitionist clergyman Henry Ward Beecher.[36]

The poet of *Leaves of Grass* was continuing to take shape. A poem published in the *New York Tribune* on June 14, 1850, shows striking changes in his style. There was something of his name-calling editorial voice in it, but the poetry was now cast in loose free-verse cadences.

THE HOUSE OF FRIENDS

"And one shall say unto him, What are these wounds in thy
hands? Then he shall answer, Those with which I was wounded
in the house of my friends."
                                        —Zechariah, xiii. 6

If thou art balked, O Freedom,
The victory is not to thy manlier foes;
From the house of friends comes the death stab.

Vaunters of the Free,
Why do you strain your lungs off southward?
Why be going to Alabama?
Sweep first before your own door;
Stop this squalling and this scorn

Over the mote there in the distance;
Look well to your own eye, Massachusetts—
Yours, New-York and Pennsylvania;
—I would say yours too, Michigan,
But all the salve, all the surgery
Of the great wide world were powerless there.

Virginia, mother of greatness,
Blush not for being also the mother of slaves.
You might have born deeper slaves—
Doughfaces, Crawlers, Lice of Humanity—
Terrific screamers of Freedom,
Who roar and brawl, and get hot i' the face,
But, were they not incapable of august crime,
Would quelch the hopes of ages for a drink—
Muck worms, creeping flat to the ground,
A dollar dearer to them than Christ's blessing;
All loves, all hopes, less than the thought of gain,
In life walking in that as in a shroud:
Men whom the throes of heroes,
Great deeds at which the gods might stand appalled
The shriek of a drowned world, the appeal of women,
The exulting laugh of untied empires,
Would touch them never in the heart,
But only in the pocket.

Hot-headed Carolina,
Well may you curl your lip;
With all your bondsmen, bless the destiny
Which brings you no such breed as this.

Arise, young North!
Our elder blood flows in the veins of cowards—
The gray-haired sneak, the blanched poltroon,
The feigned or real shiverers at tongues

That nursing babes need hardly cry the less for—
Are they to be our tokens always?

    Fight on, band braver than warriors,
Faithful and few as Spartans;
But fear not most the angriest, loudest, malice—
Fear most the still and forked fang.
That starts always from the grass at your feet.[37]

While working as an editor, Whitman had begun keeping notebooks in his off hours, at home. They were not tidy. Sometimes, when he got to the end of one, he would turn it over and write on the other sides of the leaves, proceeding from the back to the front. Sometimes, he would skip pages and then return and use them later. The notebooks included records of payment to masons for work in the basement of his Brooklyn home and of his final pay from Van Anden. But there was less prosaic material also. Immediately after the Van Anden entry, dated 1847, he wrote, "I am the poet of Equality/ And a mouse is enough to stagger trillions of infidels." In "Song of Myself," the poet of equality made this, "And a mouse is miracle enough to stagger sextillions of infidels." A prose passage in the earliest known notebook, written in 1847 or possibly earlier observed that no two people "have exactly the same language, and the great translator and power of the whole is the poet. He has the divine grammar of all tongues, and says indifferently and alike, How are you friend? To the President in the midst of his cabinet, and Good day my brother, to Sambo, among the hoers of the sugar field, and both understand him and know that his speech is right." When the first edition of *Leaves of Grass* appeared in 1855, the prose had been turned into characteristic long-lined poetry in "Song of the Answerer":

He says indifferently and alike *How are you, friend?* to the
    President at his levee.
And he says *Good day, my brother,* to Cudge that hoes in the
    sugar-field
And both understand him and know that his speech is right.

Whitman scholar Edward F. Grier, who made a painstaking study of the poet's notebooks and the twelve passages in them that would find their way into *Leaves of Grass,* concluded that "Whitman found his mature style early in 1847," when he was editing the *Eagle.*[38]

With the first publication of *Leaves of Grass* in 1855, Walter Whitman the journalist became Walt Whitman the poet, but he still was not through with the craft he learned as a youth. Two years after the book came out, pinched for money and complaining that his publishers "retard my book very much," he accepted a position with the politically independent *Brooklyn Daily Times.* As a sports writer, he covered a New York–Brooklyn baseball game and reported that three Brooklyn players were injured; as an editorial writer, he campaigned for a new city water works and touched on such delicate subjects as sexual repression and the treatment of prostitutes. The editorials prefigured his 1860 poem, "To a Common Prostitute."

> Be composed—be at ease with me—I am Walt Whitman, liberal and lusty as Nature,
> Not till the sun excludes you do I exclude you,
> Not till the waters refuse to glisten for you and the leaves to rustle for you, do my words refuse to glisten and rustle for you.
>
> My girl I appoint with you an appointment, and I charge you that you make preparations to be worthy to meet me,
> And I charge you that you be patient and perfect till I come.
>
> Till then I salute you with a significant look that you do not forget me.

There evidently were differences over editorial policy with the owner of the *Daily Times,* George C. Bennett, and Whitman was unemployed by mid-1859.[39]

The outbreak of the Civil War in 1861 brought Whitman to Washington, where he freelanced for the *New York Times* and other publications.

He also contributed to the *Armory Square Gazette,* published by Washington hospitals caring for the wounded. The boy who most likely read issues of the *Patriot* in his Brooklyn home remained an avid newspaper reader. After the Union defeat in the first battle of Bull Run, he eagerly perused the "magnificent editorials," full of "unfaltering defiance," in all of the New York papers he could lay his hands on. "The *Herald* commenced them—I remember the articles well," he recalled years later. "The *Tribune* was equally cogent and inspiriting—and the *Times, Evening Post,* and other principal papers were not a whit behind."

Whitman's view of journalists may have changed when they started writing about him. "According to the papers I am crazy, dead, paralyzed, scrofulous, gone to pot in piece and whole: I am a wreck from stem to stern," he declared in 1888. A year later, he added: "It seems to be a penalty a man has to pay, even for very little notoriety—the privilege of being lied about. Yet I rest the case finally on the good sense of my friends—their knowledge that, of printed matter anyhow, fully half, three-quarters perhaps—even a greater proportion, is lie—is admitted to be such."[40]

Meanwhile Whitman had been doing some anonymous newspaper writing about himself. A *United States and Democratic Review* piece from his pen in 1855 welcomed the author of *Leaves of Grass* as "An American bard at last!" In the *Brooklyn Daily Times* the same year, he proclaimed that the author of the then new book was a poet "for the south the same as the north." The review began, "To give judgment on real poems, one needs an account of the poet himself. Very devilish to some, and very divine to some, will appear the poet of these new poems." Whitman biographer Gay Wilson Allen writes that "A defense of *Leaves of Grass* in the *Brooklyn City News* on October 10 [1860] was almost certainly written by him." The self-reviewing dodge did not escape criticism, even though the practice was fairly common at the time. An unsigned and unfavorable review in the *New York Daily Times* in 1856 said, "It is a lie to write a review of one's own book, then . . . send it out to the world as an impartial editorial utterance. It is an act that the most degraded helot of literature might blush to commit." This did not stop Whitman. In 1876, in a piece submitted to *West Jersey Press* and widely reprinted, the poet declared: "Whitman's poems in their public reception have fallen stillborn in this country. They have been met, and are met today, with the determined denial, disgust and scorn of orthodox American authors, publishers and editors, and, in a pecuniary and worldly sense, have certainly wrecked the life of their author. . . . Whitman has grown gray in battle. Little or no impression, (at least ostensibly), seems to have been made. Still he stands alone."[41]

Before the decade of the 1870s was over, Whitman had achieved the recognition he sought. In the autumn of 1879, he traveled to Kansas to speak at the territory's twenty-fifth anniversary celebration, and continued on to Colorado, where he recalled "casually" contributing a piece of writing to a newspaper. When newspapers failed to interview him along the route, he wrote out imagined interviews and submitted them for publication. The following year, he was in Quebec, where he "went into the queerest little old French printing-office near Tadousac [sic]," and found it "far more primitive and ancient than my Camden friend William Kurtz's place up on Federal Street." In the printing of his own work, he was "sensitive to technical slips, errors. . . . Having been a printer myself, I have what may be called an anticipatory eye—know pretty well as I write how a thing will turn up in the type." He cautioned printing offices not to "put on a slouchy printer" to work on his books.

The aging poet had not forgotten the twelve-year-old apprentice compositor who was thrilled by the "nice type" in which the *Mirror* printed his work.[42]

He may also have remembered some advice he gave, under the title, "How to Write for Newspapers," on April 24, 1846, a month after he became editor of the *Eagle:* "1. Have something to write about. 2. Write plain; dot your i's; cross your t's; point sentences; begin with capitals. 3. Write short; to the point; stop when you have done. 4. Write only on one side of the leaf. 5. Read it over, abridge and correct it, until you get it into the shortest space possible. 6. Pay the postage."[43]

3 "Something More Than Ordinary Journalistic Prose"

When Rudyard Kipling was a boy in school in 1890, a teacher predicted he would end his days as a "scurrilous journalist." The forecast by W. F. Haslam, an English and classics master at the United Services College near Bideford on the north coast of Devon, could hardly have been more wrong.[1]

When Kipling died in 1936, his poems, short stories, and novels were known throughout the world, and he had won the Nobel Prize for Literature nearly three decades before.

He also achieved another distinction, shared with only a few writers such as Robert Frost and Ernest Hemingway: reporters asked his opinions on subjects he knew little or nothing about. Sometimes, he even answered.

As a celebrity, he was offended by the prying of journalists, but still remembered with affection the life of the "mysterious and ghostly" presses that he had first tasted in his teens in India.[2]

The first child of John Lockwood Kipling and the former Alice Mc-Donald was born on December 30, 1865, in Bombay, an Indian city whose European streets and brick buildings concealed the squalid dwellings of the cotton-mill workers on whom its prosperity depended. They named their son Joseph Rudyard, the second name drawn from the lake in Staffordshire on whose shores they had courted in 1863. Like his father, who taught architectural sculpture in a Bombay art school, the future writer would be known by the middle name he preferred.[3]

Kipling came into a world in which the line between journalism and literature was not as strict as it was later to be. Indian newspapers that employed him as a reporter and editor would also welcome his stories and poems. The literary world was not always as welcoming. In 1904, when his books were at the height of their popularity, a writer in the *Atlantic Monthly* described him as "the most conspicuous modern instance of the reporting journalist turned story-writer," and added that, perhaps because of this, "Mr. Kipling will eventually rank with a class of writers separated by a whole limbo from the greatest creative spirits." The judgment was qualified, a bit condescendingly, with the concession that "one need not in the least grudge them their immediate effectiveness."[4]

Before any of this, the boy must be educated. To English civil servants abroad, that meant sending him to the home country. When he was five years old—an age at which, one of his father's Indian friends would recall, the boy never forgot a face or a name—he was boarded out to a retired sea captain, Pryse Agar Holloway, and his wife in Southsea, near Portsmouth on England's south coast. In memoirs and fiction, Kipling gave grim descriptions of the "bitter waters of Hate, Suspicion and Despair" that he endured with the Holloways and in the day school he was sent to. These tales probably should be taken with healthy skepticism. The bright, difficult child had lived a pampered existence in India, catered to by servants and unused to discipline. The home of a pensioner and his wife, so anxious for extra income that they advertised to take in boys as boarders, must have been a let-down. Whatever the truth, Kipling's accounts show he learned lessons that would be useful in his life as a journalist and creative writer. His six years at Southsea, he said, "demanded constant wariness, the habit of observation, and dependence on moods and tempers"; and also, perhaps most important, "the noting of discrepancies between speech and action."[5]

When Rudyard was twelve, his parents took him away from Southsea and entered him in the United Services College, founded four years earlier "to provide for the sons of the officers of the Army and Navy an inexpensive education of the highest class and of a general nature." Lockwood Kipling was not an army or navy officer, but the "inexpensive" part of the school's advertisement in the *Illustrated London News* no doubt appealed to him. The Kiplings did not come from wealthy families, and a teacher's salary in Bombay probably required economies.[6]

Besides, Cormell Price, the thirty-three-year-old headmaster of the school, was a personal friend. Price had been a schoolmate of Alice Kipling's brother, Henry, at King Edward's School in Birmingham. He was already known to young Rudyard as his lean, bearded "Uncle Crom," one of the "deputy uncles" (another was the poet and artist William Morris) who frequented the London home of his aunt Georgy. Georgiana, Rudyard's mother's sister, was married to the painter Sir Edward Burne-Jones, and the young Kipling stayed with them on welcome vacations from his Southsea school.[7]

At United Services College, Rudyard sparred with his hot-tempered housemaster and literature teacher William Crofts, under whom, he said, "I came to feel that words could be used as weapons, for he did the honor to talk at me plentifully." Once, Crofts assigned students to write an essay about what they did on their vacation, and asked the feared Haslam to grade it. Kipling recalled in his memoirs that his essay was "of variegated but constant vileness. . . . Even I had never done anything worse." Haslam thought so, too. Taking over the floor from Crofts, the English and classics master "told me off before my delighted companions in his best style, which was acid and contumelious" and "wound up by a few general remarks about dying as a 'scurrilous journalist.'" Crofts, Kipling recalled, "added a word or two" after Haslam left.[8]

Not long after this incident, Price revived the *United Services College Chronicle,* a school magazine that had been abandoned after its first three issues, and made Kipling the editor. Apparently, said Rudyard, his "Uncle Crom" saw that he was "irretrievably committed to the ink pot." He did the job for his last two years at the school, writing most of the magazine himself and getting his introduction to the composing room by overseeing the journal's printing at a shop in Bidesford. On the side, he contributed occasional news items to a local newspaper.[9]

As part of the journalistic assignment, Price gave his students unlimited access to his "brown-bound, tobacco-scented" library. Kipling recalled the glories of it in his semiautobiographical *Stalky & Co.:*

There were scores and scores of ancient dramatists, there were Hakluyt, his voyages; French translations of Muscovite authors called Pushkin and Lermentoff; little tales of a heady and bewildering nature, interspersed with unusual songs—Peacock was that writer's name; there were Borrow's *Lavengro;* an odd theme, purporting to be a translation of something called a "Rubaiyat," which the Head said was a poem not yet come into its own; there were hundreds of volumes of verse—Crashaw; Dryden; Alexander Smith; F. E. L.; Lydia Sigourney; Fletcher and a Purple Island; Donne; Marlowe's *Faust;* Ossian; *The Earthly Paradise; Atalanta in Calydon;* and Rosetti—to name only a few.

To a boy already embarked on writing verse, it was heady stuff.

Occasionally, he said, "the Head, drifting in under pretense of playing censor to the paper, would read here a verse and here another of these poets, opening up avenues."[10]

Another avenue would open.

In India, Lockwood Kipling had been pulling strings. In December 1881, he wrote to a friend that he planned to "bring Rudyard out to India next year, and get him some newspaper work. Oxford we can't afford. Ruddy thirsts for a man's life, a man's work." Newspaper work seemed a good choice, as Rudyard's poor eyesight would disqualify him for the Civil Service. Lockwood by now had moved from Bombay to Lahore as principal of the new Mayo School of Industrial Art and curator of the Lahore Museum. Both he and Alice wrote occasionally for the local paper, the *Civil and Military Gazette.* It was obviously not a coincidence that in the spring of 1882, Stephen Wheeler, editor of the *Gazette,* called on the young Kipling while on a visit to England. An associate of Wheeler's, George Allen, was said to have visited England about the same time, seen Rudyard, and wired back, "KIPLING WILL DO."[11]

That summer, Price told his student that two weeks after the end of summer term he would leave for India to work on the Lahore newspaper. Kipling described himself as joyous at the prospect, but his first biographer, Lord Birkenhead, said the youth would have preferred to make his own way in London as a writer. He had, after all, sold an article to a London newspaper and received a guinea for it.[12]

At any rate, on the drizzly day of September 20, Kipling sailed from Tilbury, Essex, on the steamer *Brindisi.* The Lahore at which he arrived, after a four-day train trip from the port of Bombay, was the capital of the Punjab. The slightly more than 110,000 people in the city and its suburbs were predominantly Muslim. Many of its 1,723 English belonged to an infantry battalion and battery of artillery stationed at the military cantonment of Mian Mir.[13]

The evening *Civil and Military Gazette* had been founded ten years earlier by the Lahore barrister William Walker and James Rattigan, an Anglo-Indian businessman. It was largely supported by a printing contract with the provincial administration, which led to charges that it was in the pocket of the Punjabi government. Kipling went to work in its offices—two sheds behind a grove of acacia trees—with the title of assistant editor. He was, as he described it, "fifty per cent of the 'editorial staff.'" His salary of 150 rupees a month (about 13½ British pounds at the time) was fifty more than Price had told him he would be paid. The neophyte journalist, not yet seventeen years old, found the workload heavy and said he loathed Wheeler for the first three years he worked for him.[14]

"He had to break me in, and I knew nothing," he wrote. "What he suffered on my account I cannot tell; but the little that I ever acquired of accuracy, the habit of at least trying to verify references, and some knack of sticking to desk work, I owed wholly to Stephen Wheeler." Like many journalists he remembered being given the sage advice to take nothing for granted if he could check it. In a letter to a former teacher, he wrote, "One of the first things a sub editor has to learn is to altogether give up original writing. I have not written three words of original matter beyond reports and reviews since I have joined the staff."[15]

E. Kay Robinson, who succeeded Wheeler as editor of the *Gazette,* said his predecessor "had done his best to make a sound second-rate journalist out of the youngster by keeping his nose at the grindstone of proof-reading, scissors-and-paste work, and the boiling down of government Blue Books into summaries for publication." Robinson conceded that after he became editor he could not help "burdening Kipling with a good deal of daily drudgery," but added that "if you want to find a man who will cheerfully do the office work of three men, you should catch a young genius." Working in a room with green paper covering the windows as a shield from the glare outside, the young subeditor sat at a desk littered with papers that were weighted down to keep the fans from blowing them about. He must have cut a striking figure in the newsroom. Short and hairy, with a bulky moustache and thick glasses, he was, like his father, given to sudden, jerky movements. Unlike his father, he was also bumptious, aggressive, and notably foul-mouthed. As he dipped his pen frequently and deeply into the ink pot, the white cotton trousers and vest he wore in the summer were often, said Robinson, "spotted all over like a Dalmatian dog."[16]

A work day of ten to fifteen hours in the sweltering heat of Lahore— 116 degrees in the shade, he said—apparently told on Kipling's health. Once, he and Wheeler "made a compact to work the paper at the lowest possible pressure throughout the hot weather." Nevertheless, he wrote, "I discovered that a man can work with a temperature of 104, even though next day he has to ask the office who wrote the article." A poem Kipling wrote years later, called "The Galley Slave," may well have referred to his newspaper days as he put himself in the person of a slave recalling "the welts the whips have left me" and "the scars that never heal." By 1884, he had been freed to do some of his own work, and the first of the poems that would form his *Departmental Ditties* began to appear in the paper. He wrote to Robinson two years later that such "rhymed rubbish" was writ- ten for his own amusement and on his own time. In addition to his own verse, he contributed, to mark the 1885 New Year celebration, a parody beginning, "From the pines of the Alleghanies I, Walt Whitman—colossal, pyramidal, immense—send salutation. / I project myself into your person- ality—I become an integral part of you" and climaxing with "Oh! Civil- ian, Superior Being, Loafer, Subaltern, Grass-Widow and Grass-Mother of many conflicting domesticities, I salute you / . . . Happy New Year."[17]

Lockwood Kipling wrote to a friend that his son had mastered the work quickly although Wheeler was "very tetchy and irritable, and by dint of his exertions in patience and forbearance, the boy is training for heaven as well as for the editorship."[18]

The son of the Rattigan who was one of the paper's founders re- ported that "in the day-to-day business of journalism Kipling did not by any means shine. He had little taste for mere routine duties; he was apt to neglect the rather tedious assignments that inevitably fell to the lot of the junior members of a very small staff."[19]

These tedious assignments included agricultural fairs, village festivals, and race meets. Later, Kipling was sent to cover openings of bridges and spent "nights in the wet with wretched heads of repair gangs" while covering a railway flood that washed out tracks of the North Western Railway line to Rawalpindi during the first week in August 1887. He rode to the scene, about fifty miles north of Lahore, in the inspection car of an overnight North Western train, by invitation of a government inspector. In his second-person account of the trip, in which he described himself as a Perfectly Disinterested Observer, he wrote, "The observer, . . . comforted with a big arm chair and a broad and stately bunk, feels so good, so impartial, so calm—so secretariatish and administrative, in fact" that he "can watch 'another man's break' with satisfaction." The passage bears marks of the jocose style that caused Kipling to say apologetically in the prelude to *Departmental Ditties:*

> I have written the tale of your life
>   For a sheltered people's mirth,
> In jesting guise—but ye are wise,
>   And ye know what the jest is worth.[20]

When they arrived at the scene of the flooding, Kipling's growing talent for descriptions of action took over:

> After the train had cleared the Shadera Bridge, the Ravee [river] growling angrily among the piers in the watery moonlight, it seemed suddenly and without warning to shoot forth into the deep still sea. Never was transformation more complete. Lahore . . . had been suffering sadly from want of rain: but here was the explanation. All the heavy clouds that for weeks past had come up from the South, circled over our heads and departed, must have spent themselves from Muridki [hill] onward, for the country-side was swamped. [The first telegraphic report had been right] for the railway was "washed as far as the eye could reach." The leaden

levels of water were broken only by the line of embankment and, in the uncertain distance, by island-like clumps of trees.

Here the warm rain began to fall and the rest of the journey till dawn was as a journey in a dream. On both sides lay nothing but water—flush it seemed with the culverts and the top of the wire-fencing; when the train stopped, was heard nothing but the noise of a hundred waters—the murmur of the rain on the carriage roof—the lap, lap, lap of water by the side of the line, the gurgle of tiny streams running down to the borrow-pits—and the sullen splashing from the eaves of the carriage. . . . Then the train would stand out to sea, and in a moment, all trace of dry earth would vanish.

After the repair work had been done, passengers were transferred to another train. "Yet another Departmental Head was superintending this," Kipling wrote, "and, since a lady, even with both hands free, cannot walk comfortably in inch-deep slime, . . . [the department head] took, as it were the most natural thing in the world, a certain small and very much astonished baby from her arms, and bore it for half a mile, issuing orders meantime."[21]

In his poem "The Floods," Kipling used the same material in ways that are strikingly different and yet strangely similar.

> The rain it rains without a stay
>   In the hills above us, in the hills;
> And presently the floods break way
>   Whose strength is in the hills
> The trees they suck from every cloud,
> The valley brooks they roar aloud—
> Bank high for the lowlands, lowlands,
>   Lowlands under the hills!
>
> The first wood down is sere and small,
>   From the hills—the brishings off the hills;
> And then come by the bats and all

We cut last year in the hills;
And then the roots we tried to cleave
But found too tough and had to leave—
Polting down through the lowlands, lowlands,
        Lowlands under the hills!

The eye shall look, the ear shall hark
        To the hills, the doings in the hills!
And rivers mating in the dark
        With tokens from the hills.
Now what is weak will surely go,
And what is strong must prove it so—
Stand fast in the lowlands, lowlands,
        Lowlands under the hills!

The floods they shall not be afraid—
        Nor the hills above 'em, nor the hills—
Of any fence which man has made
        Betwixt him and the hills.
The waters shall not reckon twice
For any work of man's device,
But bid it down to the lowlands, lowlands,
        Lowlands under the hills!

The floods shall sweep corruption clean—
        By the hills, the blessing of the hills—
That more the meadows may be green
        New-mended from the hills.
The crops and cattle shall increase,
Nor little children shall not cease.
Go—plough the lowlands, lowlands,
        Lowlands under the hills![22]

Both journalist and poet recognized the simple fact that the flooding came from the hills and both noted the endurance, at the end, of

children. But the poet is alone in calling the hills blessed and noting their benign effect on the arid lands below.

Kipling the reporter also saw troops waiting in timber yards off side alleys "till the order came to go in and hit the crowds on the feet with gun butts" to break up Hindu-Muslim rioting. "The science of defense lay solely in keeping the mob on the move," he wrote. "If they had a breathing space they would halt and fire a house, and then the work of restoring order would be more difficult, to say the least of it. Flames have the same effect on a crowd as blood on a wild beast." He heard British soldiers ordering the rioters to move on, followed by "the ringing of rifle-butts and shrieks of pain."

On a walk in the Khyber Pass, Kipling was shot at by an opponent of an Afghan potentate whose courtship by the Indian government he was on assignment to cover. In the course of investigative reporting on the percentage of lepers among butchers who supplied beef and mutton to Europeans in Lahore, he "first learned that crude statements of crude facts are not well seen by responsible official authorities."[23]

Kipling called Lahore a "wonderful, mysterious, dirty ant hill" and told a friend, "I'm in love with the Country and would sooner write about her than anything else." Of British society in Lahore, he spoke scornfully. In an article in the *Gazette,* disguised as a tourist's letter, he wrote, "There are no books, no pictures, no conversation worth listening to. . . . They have a high opinion of themselves, and I think they have a right to, so far as work goes. But they don't seem to realize the beauties of life."

In 1885, at age nineteen, Kipling received an offer of a bribe—the first of several—on a visit as a roving correspondent to one of the Indian Native States, the provinces not under direct British rule. When he opened the basket of fruit laid at the flap of his tent each morning, he found a five-hundred-rupee note and a cashmere shawl. Kipling was seasoned enough in the subcontinent's politics by that time to conclude that the local administration wanted to have more guns added to the salute the province's ruler would receive when he visited British India. He rejected the gift by sending it to the high-caste ruler in the hands of a camp-sweeper.

When Kipling returned to Lahore, Wheeler was ill, and he found himself in charge. Among correspondence addressed to the editor came a letter from the offended Native State ruler complaining of "your reporter, a person called Kipling." He replied that he would investigate, "but they must expect me to be biased because I was the person complained of." That, it seems, was the end of the matter.[24]

Some years later, on a visit to Rajputana in what is now Pakistan, Kipling wrote:

> With the exception of such journals as, occupying a central position in British territory, levy blackmail from the neighboring states, there are no independent newspapers in Rajputana. A King may start a weekly, to encourage a taste for Sanskrit and high Hindi, or a Prince may create a Court Chronicle; but that is all. A "free press" is not allowed, and this the native journalist knows. With good management he can, keeping under the shadow of our flag, raise two hundred rupees from a big man here, and five hundred from a rich man there, but he does not establish himself across the Border. To one who has reason to hold a stubborn belief in even the most elementary morality of the native press, this bashfulness and lack of enterprise is amusing.

Kipling's observations were biased by his devotion to the British ideal of empire-building, just as his Indian writings were politically motivated to serve the cause of the empire.[25]

After Robinson moved into Wheeler's slot, Kipling seems to have had an easier time at the *Gazette*. His new superior, not much older than he, consulted him on policy questions and gave him "a greater insight into the higher workings of a paper than ever before." Robinson had come to India from a Fleet Street job with the evening *London Globe* to be assistant editor of the *Pioneer* in Allahabad. He met the Kipling family while on a visit to Lahore and discovered in Lockwood "a rare, genial soul, with happy artistic instincts, a polished literary style and a generous cynical sense of humor." Not long afterward he moved to the Lahore paper as editor and found Rudyard "bubbling over with poetry which his hard day's office work gave him no time to write."[26]

The work consisted partly of editing contributions from readers. Once he severely trimmed a literary discourse on Milton, only to discover "that the writer was a relative of one of our proprietors, who thought our paper existed to air his theories." He skimmed Far Eastern and Middle Eastern newspapers every morning, and English papers once a week, for usable items. He checked the contributions of local correspondents for possible libel and sometimes translated from French-language journals.[27]

Making his customary visit to the all-white Punjab Club after work one day, he was hissed because his paper had come out for an unpopular government bill that would permit native judges to try white women. When a sympathetic captain intervened and said, "The boy's only doing what he's paid to do," Kipling said he saw a great light. "I was a hireling, paid to do what I was paid to do—and I did not relish the idea."[28]

Robinson encouraged Kipling to contribute fiction and poetry to the paper. The first of the thirty-nine *Plain Tales from the Hills* to be published by the *Gazette* appeared in 1885 and additional *Departmental Ditties* —"digressions from office work," he called them—the following year.[29]

One, published later in book form, while not great poetry, told a revealing story.

THE MAN WHO COULD WRITE

Boanerges Blitzen, servant of the Queen,
Is a dismal failure—is a might-have-been.
In a luckless moment he discovered men
Rise to high position through a ready pen.

Boanerges Blitzen reckoned therefore: "I
With the selfsame weapon can attain as high."
Only he did not possess, when he made the trial,
Wicked wit of C-l-v-n, irony of L——l.

(Men who spar with government need, to back their blows,
Something more than ordinary journalistic prose.)

Never young Civilian's prospects were so bright,
Till an Indian paper found that he could write:
Never young Civilian's prospects were so dark,
When the wretched Blitzen wrote to make his mark.

Certainly he scored it, bold and black and firm,
In that Indian paper—made his seniors squirm,
Quoted office scandals, wrote the tactless truth—
Was there ever known a more misguided youth?

When the rag he wrote for praised his plucky game,
Boanerges Blitzen felt that this was Fame:
When the men he wrote of shook their heads and swore,
Boanerges Blitzen only wrote the more.

Posed as young Ithuriel, resolute and grim,
Till he found promotion didn't come to him;
Till he found that reprimands weekly were his lot,
And his many Districts curiously hot.

Till he found his furlough strangely hard to win,
Boanerges Blitzen didn't care a pin:
Then it seemed to dawn on him something wasn't right—
Boanerges Blitzen put it down to "spite."

Languished in a District desolate and dry;
Watched the Local Government yearly pass him by;
Wondered where the hitch was; called it most unfair.

      •   •   •   •   •

That was seven years ago—and he still is there.[30]

It was not poetry but "ordinary journalistic prose" that Kipling had
to deal with most of the time. He found his critics at the Punjab Club
"not concerned with my dreams. They wanted accuracy and interest,
but first of all accuracy." It took him, he said, "an impatient while to

learn" that newspaper spaces "limited my canvasses and, for the reader's sake, prescribed that within these limits must be some sort of beginning, middle, and end."[31]

He admitted later that he got a magnified idea of his importance. "The difference, then, between me and the vulgar herd who 'write for the papers' was, as I saw it, the gulf that divides the beneficed clergymen from ladies and gentlemen who contribute pumpkins and dahlias to Harvest Festival decorations."[32]

In 1886, Kipling collected some of his newspaper poems and a few others and paid to have them printed on the *Gazette* press as *Departmental Ditties and Other Verses*. It was the first book of verse that he alone had written, although three collections privately printed by the family contained work by Rudyard and his sister, Trix, and their parents. The first printing of *Departmental Ditties* was bound in light brown paper with red tape around it, much like a government envelope, and addressed facetiously to "All Heads of Departments and all Anglo-Indians" from "Rudyard Kipling, Assistant, Department of Public Journalism, Lahore District."[33]

While the newspaper verses were for the most part quickly written light verse, the "Other Verses" were more ambitious. As a reporter covering Indian railways, Kipling had been told, "Yes, a driver of the mail *is* somebody." In "The Overland Mail," he wrote that not only the drivers but the runners who delivered on foot to outposts in the hills were indeed somebody. He also displayed a growing deftness of poetic technique.

Is the torrent in spate? He must ford it or swim.
Has the rain wrecked the road? He must climb by the cliff.
Does the tempest cry "Halt"? What are tempests to him?
The Service admits not a "but" nor an "if."
While the breath's in his mouth, he must bear without fail,
In the Name of the Empress, the Overland Mail.[34]

In November 1887, the twenty-two-year-old Kipling left the Lahore District for Allahabad to edit *The Week's News,* a new magazine supplement to the *Pioneer.* Here, he was "a new boy at a big school" and living for the first time in Hindu, rather than Muslim, India. He was also a bit uncomfortable at being under the eye of the paper's proprietor, Sir George Allen, instead of at a distant outpost in Lahore.

Still, *The Week's News* ran fiction as well as news, and Kipling jumped to take advantage by publishing his own work. He conceded that "my editing of the *Weekly* may have been a shade casual—it was but a re-hash of news and views after all. My head was full of, to me, infinitely more important material."[35]

The "more important material" was increasingly to dominate Kipling's output. He was making the transition from being one of those who "write for the papers" to recognition as a creative writer. It was slow going.

His reputation flourished in India, where publication of *Departmental Ditties* and *Plain Tales from the Hills* by a Calcutta publishing house brought him the heady experience of strangers turning to look at him and "asking to be introduced when I dance or dine in strange places beyond my district." His work, however, failed at first to catch fire on the English literary scene. When a friend tried to market an early Kipling story, *The Mark of the Beast,* to London magazines, one editor called it "poisonous stuff which has left an extremely disagreeable impression on my mind." Another urged Kipling's friend to "burn this detestable piece of work."[36]

Nevertheless, *Plain Tales from the Hills* drew a flattering notice from London's *Saturday Review. The Review's* critic, Edmund Gosse, while favorably impressed, found fault with "the noisy newspaper bustle of the little peremptory sentences."[37]

The encouragement prompted Kipling to give up both journalism and India and to once again set his sights on London. Before leaving, he paid one more visit to Lahore, and found it "packed with ghosts." After a reunion with his family, he visited the office where he had worked at the *Gazette* and found it empty. The paper had moved. At the new location in a grove of orange trees, he listened to the clunk of the Columbia press and smelled the familiar odors of printing. "No man can put in seven years on an Indian journal when he is half the staff, and the sheet is part of his being, without loving her dearly," he wrote in a piece called

"Home," which the *Gazette* published. Privately, he expressed a less sentimental view, writing to a correspondent, "I have just come off a fifteen hour spell with my loathing for the occupation tenfold increased."[38]

On March 3, 1889, Kipling embarked from Calcutta for a leisurely trip by way of Rangoon; Singapore; Hong Kong; Japan; San Francisco; Portland; the states of Washington, Montana and Utah; Washington, D.C.; Boston; Pennsylvania; and Liverpool. By now, he was well enough known to be interviewed by journalists, instead of interviewing others. Both the papers he had worked for commissioned him to write about his trip, and the articles were later used as the basis for a travel book. In the "queer mad town" of Tacoma, Washington, he reported, "men were babbling of money, town lots and again money" on "the rude, crude streets, where the unshaded electric light was fighting with the gentle northern twilight." The town on Puget Sound, he said, was "literally staggering under a boom of the boomiest." He may have foreseen that he was in for a boom of his own when a copy of the *Spectator* made its way to his Tacoma hotel, containing an encouraging review of his *Soldiers Three*. When Kipling arrived in London in October, he was twenty-four years old.[39]

Two months later, his "Ballad of East and West" was published in *Macmillan's* magazine to critical acclaim. Kipling was on his way. The poem was excellent at its best, and very bad at its worst, and shows that the poet's newspaper experience may have both helped and hindered him. The ballad tells the story of an outlaw on the Indian-Afghani border who steals a British colonel's favorite mare. The colonel's son sets out to recapture the horse, but instead is cornered by the outlaw. In the end the boldness of the soldier converts the outlaw to the British cause, and the two ride back together. The theme fitted Kipling's imperialist convictions perfectly, but the strength of the poem is in the telling, in such passages as: "There was rock to the left and rock to the right, and low lean thorn between, / And thrice he heard a breech-bolt snick tho' never a man was seen."

Kipling the newspaperman had learned that "every word should tell, carry, weigh, taste and, if need were, smell." The lesson served the poet well. The reader is in the Khyber Pass, riding through thorny brush between rocks that have plagued so many warriors. He does not hear the breech bolt once or twice, or a few times; he hears it thrice. The writer also knows the value of the right verb. The bolt does not open, or close, or snap. It snicks, and the reader hears it. But the best known lines in the poem are those at the end.

> Oh, East is East, and West is West, and never the twain shall meet,
> Till Earth and Sky stand presently at God's great Judgment Seat,
> But there is neither East nor West, Border, nor Breed, nor Birth,
> When two strong men stand face to face, though they come from
>   the ends of the earth![40]

The poem would have been better without them. As a reporter, the poet made his point, but Kipling the editorialist all but wrecked a good poem. It was a fault that would do more damage to his reputation than he deserved. W. H. Auden said that time pardoned Kipling's views because he wrote well, but not everyone joined in the pardon.[41]

March 1891 saw the first publication of Kipling's novel *The Light That Failed*. While not his best work, it is interesting for its portrayal of correspondents covering General Charles George Gordon's doomed 1885 campaign in Sudan.

> With the soldiers sweated and toiled the correspondents of the newspapers, and they were almost as ignorant as their companions. But it was above all things necessary that England at breakfast should be amused and thrilled and interested, whether Gordon lived or died, or half the British army went to pieces in the sands. The Soudan campaign was a picturesque one and lent itself to vivid word-painting. Now and again a "Special" managed to get slain,—which was not altogether a disadvantage of the paper that employed him,—and more often the hand-to-hand nature of the fighting allowed of miraculous escapes which were worth telegraphing home at eighteen-pence the word. There were many correspondents with many corps and columns,—from the veterans who had followed on the heels of cavalry that occupied

Cairo in '82, what time Arabi Pasha called himself king . . . to youngsters jerked into the business at the end of a telegraph-wire to take the places of their betters killed or invalided.

Writing of the Central Southern Syndicate, which employed his fictional black-browed correspondent Gilbert Belling Torpenow, Kipling continued: "The syndicate did not concern itself greatly with criticism of attacks and the like. It supplied the masses, and all it demanded was picturesqueness and abundance of detail; for there is more joy in England over a soldier who insubordinately steps out of a square to rescue a comrade than over twenty generals slaving even to baldness at the gross details of transport and commissariat."

Eventually Kipling's artist hero, Dick Heldar, is "made free of the New and Honorable fraternity of war correspondents, who all possess the inalienable right of doing as little work as they can and getting as much for it as Providence and their owners shall please." One night, he gets a telegraph clerk drunk and, while the clerk sleeps, copies out some "laboriously acquired exclusive information, forwarded by a confident correspondent of an opposition syndicate." After Torpenhow assures him that "all was fair in love or war correspondence," he constructs "an excellent descriptive article from his rival's riotous waste of words."

Another time, after a colleague with a taste for military tactics tells Torpenhow that a dispatch he has written is worthless, the correspondent replies, "It's off my hands at any rate. . . . Thirty-seven, thirty-eight, thirty-nine slips altogether, aren't there? That should make between eleven and twelve pages of valuable misinformation."

Despite his cynical depiction of a correspondent's work, Kipling the novelist conceded, "It was not an easy life in any way."[42]

With his growing success, Kipling was becoming more and more antipathetic to the "vulgar herd who write for papers." On a visit to Australia in 1891, one of the leading newspapers offered him an assignment to cover the Melbourne Cup horse race, but he recalled his race meeting jobs in India and "knew it was not in my line."[43]

In January 1892 Kipling was married to Caroline Balestier, the sharp-tongued daughter of the American literary agent Wolcott Balestier. The

Kiplings emigrated to America and settled in Vermont. In 1896, bad feeling between Kipling and his brother-in-law, Beatty Balestier, burst into the open. Kipling believed Balestier was drinking too heavily and neglecting a responsibility he had undertaken to supervise work on the Kiplings' home, Naulakha. When reporters sought to interview Kipling about the dispute, they were repulsed. "I decline to be interviewed," Kipling said. "American interviewing is brutal and immoral. It is an outrage to be insulted on the public highways and asked to give the details of one's private life. . . . When I have anything to say, I write it down and sell it. My brains are my own."[44]

Once Kipling, harried by visitors he believed were reporters, took refuge in neighbor John Bliss's barn. When Bliss asked him, "Why don't you tell them to go to hell?," he replied, probably rightly, "Can't do that, they would write it all up in their papers."[45]

The dispute with Caroline's brother became even more public when a team of horses Beatty was driving almost ran Kipling down as he was bicycling on a steep, wooded trail near his home. The Kiplings sent a sheriff to arrest Beatty for assault, resulting in a hearing attended by so many reporters from Boston, New York, Philadelphia, and Washington that it had to be moved from the courthouse to the large hall in which town meetings were held.[46]

Kipling was upset by the publicity, but it may have been something on a larger scale that precipitated his departure from America. When British Guiana and Venezuela became embroiled in a border dispute in 1896, Kipling was angered by anti-British statements by President Grover Cleveland. He believed war between Britain and the United States was a real possibility and envisioned returning to England and possibly serving as a war correspondent, as he wrote to a friend. "You see," he wrote, "it is obviously absurd for me to sit still and go on singing from a safe place while the men I know are on the crown of it; and it may be that when I am closer to the scene of the action I may be able to help with a little song or two in the intervals of special correspondence."[47]

War did not break out, but in September 1896 Kipling rented a house in Devon and took his family to England.[48]

On their only return to America, in February 1899, Kipling was met by reporters who got nothing from him but a vapid statement in favor of truth and sincerity, and left, according to one newspaper's fanciful account, singing:

We've met with many men from overseas,
An' some of 'em was shy and some was not.
The Frenchmen and the Germans and Chinese.
But Kipling was the hardest of the lot.
Some of 'em talked English an' the rest
Would talk from early winter to the fall,
But the Mowgli-man we found the greatest pest,
For the bloomin' sod 'e wouldn't talk at all.[49]

In 1900, the Boer War brought Kipling himself into another fling at journalism. The author, ardent as always in his country's cause, had gone to South Africa to see for himself. The press-conscious commanding general, Lord Roberts, apparently discussed with him early in February at the Mount Nelson Hotel in Cape Town the possibility of editing a paper for the troops. Kipling said Roberts merely instructed him to go to Bloemfontein, a Boer stronghold that had fallen to the British, and do as he was told. He was met at the station by correspondents H. A. Gwynne of Reuters and Perceval Landon of the *Times* of London. They led him to the office of a small local newspaper, the *Friend*, which they were taking over. Kipling found on the floor a "really rude" editorial about himself.

Soon he seemed to relish his return to the smells and sounds of his *Civil and Military Gazette* days. "Oh, how good to be a worker in a newspaper office again," he exclaimed, even though he did it for only two weeks before returning to England. In South Africa, as in India, he was seldom seen without a pen in his hand.[50]

One night, impatient to get a new poem he had written into print, he walked over to the composing room, broke in through a window, and set up the last lines himself. The poem saluted the Boer General Joubert, whose death he had just learned of, as one who "gave his life / To a lost cause, and knew the gift was vain."[51]

During the Boer War in 1900, Rudyard Kipling was recruited to edit a paper for British troops. The British army took over a small local newspaper, the *Friend*. Here, Kipling is seated on the table at far right. H. A. Gwynne, later editor of the London *Morning Post* is at the left end of the table. Courtesy of the Kipling Society.

Although their provincial capital had fallen, roving bands of Boers continued to harass the countryside. The entire staff of the *Friend*, with a military escort, turned out to cover the Battle of Kari Siding in "a vacant world full of sunshine and distances, where now and again a single bullet sang to himself." Except for one shot in the Khyber Pass years before, it was Kipling's first experience of "being under aimed fire—being, as it were, required as a head." His party had apparently been mistaken for a British cavalry regiment. He later described the experience as "a cross between poker and Sunday School."[52]

The award of the Nobel Prize in 1907 brought Kipling new acclaim, although one commentator lamented that such "goldsmiths" as Meredith, Hardy, and Swinburne had been passed over and the award given to a "literary blacksmith."[53]

In the following years, Kipling's predictions that a war was coming fell largely on deaf ears and earned him the reputation of a militaristic Cassandra. The English writer Jerome K. Jerome, visiting the continent, said, "Kipling was known, but was discussed rather as a politician than a poet."[54]

The war he had foreseen brought sorrow, and perhaps guilt, to Rudyard Kipling. Through his old benefactor Lord Roberts, he arranged to get his son, John, into the army at age seventeen, despite his bad eyesight. Visiting the front, he wrote to the boy that it was "a grand life . . . and does not give you a dull minute." John went to France on August 15, 1915, and was killed while leading a platoon into combat six weeks later. Kipling's grief was so great that he could not accept a friend's offer of a bulldog as a gift. John had owned a bulldog when he was little.[55]

In the same month that he lost his son, Kipling was asked by the Admiralty to write a series of articles about the work of the Royal Navy. On November 17, 1915, the *Daily Telegraph* announced that the Nobel laureate would describe "the adventurous work of the armed trawlers, patrol boats, mine sweepers and submarines, which ceaselessly maintain our naval grip of the enemy in the North Sea and the home waters." Variations on traditional sea songs, written in much the style of *Departmental Ditties,* accompanied the articles.

Perceval Landon, whom Kipling had met as a fellow member of the *Friend*'s staff in Bloemfontein, had become a close friend with whom he could trade newspaper gossip. Landon still traveled on assignment to such places as Tibet or Turkey, but his home base was a cottage Kipling built for him on the grounds of Bateman's, the rural home he and Caroline had chosen in Sussex.[56]

To Bateman's in September 1922 came a visitor who brought Kipling's dislike of most reporters to the fore. Clare Sheridan, a sculptor who had known the Kiplings as a child, apparently did not tell them she was on a commissioned tour for the anti-British *New York Evening World.* When her story appeared, Kipling heatedly denied making the anti-American remarks she attributed to him in reconstructing their conversation.[57]

In a curious observation on the relationship of journalism and poetry, Kipling said he always wrote his stories and poems with a pen. "With a lead pencil I ceased to express—probably because I had to use a pencil in reporting."[58]

A few years before his death, he wrote to H. A. Gwynne, another companion from the *Friend* who had become editor of the London *Morning Post.* The letter was mostly about the need of good headlines in a newspaper. It was shop talk between "the likes of you and me, who were bred among the presses."[59]

The ghosts Rudyard Kipling had found when he visited Lahore so many years before had not faded away.

4 "Anything but Matter-of-Fact Life"

On September 19, 1835, T. W. White, proprietor of the *Southern Literary Messenger* in Richmond, wrote to his troublesome contributor and assistant Edgar Allan Poe, "No man is safe who drinks before breakfast! No man can do so, and attend to business properly."

The words, to be echoed wryly by Archibald MacLeish 104 years later, expressed White's regret for having had to dismiss Poe and left the door open for him to return from his home in Baltimore. However, the proprietor added, "If you would come to Richmond again, and again should be an assistant in my office, it must be expressly understood by us that all engagements on my part would be dissolved, the moment you got drunk."[1]

The theme would haunt Poe's brief career as a journalist.

Poe's parents were actors. His father, David Poe Jr., was the son of an Irish immigrant who served as a major in George Washington's Revolutionary War army. His mother, Elizabeth, was born in England to parents who foresaw a theatrical career for her in America. She began as a child actor and played Ophelia in *Hamlet* at age fourteen. After her marriage to David in 1806, they appeared together, once in a production of *King Lear* in which she played the sympathetic role of Cordelia and he was cast as the villainous Edmund. Regardless of roles, Elizabeth consistently got the better reviews. Like his more celebrated son, David Poe had a drinking habit that grew steadily worse. Shortly after Edgar's birth, David deserted his family. Elizabeth died on December 8, 1811. Edgar was raised by his godfather, Baltimore merchant John Allan, with whom his relations were hostile.[2]

This watercolor miniature of Edgar Allan Poe at about age 37 was painted by John A. McDougall. Courtesy of SuperStock, Inc., for the Henry E. Huntington Library and Art Gallery.

Poe began writing verse as a schoolboy, and by 1831, when he was twenty-two, he had written "To Helen" and "The City in the Sea," later to become anthology favorites. Always in financial difficulty, he wrote that same year to William Gwynne, editor of the *Federal Gazette and Baltimore Daily Advertiser,* seeking employment, possibly in Gwynne's office, adding that salary would not be a first point considered. He said he no longer regarded Richmond as his home and wanted to move to Baltimore.[3]

He apparently did not get the job; Gwynn showed a friend a copy of Poe's poem "Al Aaraaf" and described it as "indicative of a tendency to anything but the business of matter-of-fact life." At any rate, Poe was living in Baltimore by October 12, 1833, when he won a fifty dollar prize in a short story contest sponsored by the *Baltimore Saturday Visiter* [*sic*]. The three judges sat around a table at the home of John P. H. Latrobe, one of their number, deliberating over wine and cigars and tossing discarded stories into a basket, until they came to a group of sixteen tales entered by Poe. After that, the only question was whether to choose "MS. Found in a Bottle," as they eventually did, or "The Descent into the Maelstrom." Poe also entered the poetry competition, entering his notable ballad "Ulalume" among other works. The twenty-five dollar prize, however, went to John H. Hewitt, the editor of the *Saturday Visiter,* for a poem called "The Song of the Winds."[4]

On October 21, nine days after the announcement of the prizes, Poe paid a thank-you call on Latrobe, wearing all-black clothes that "had very evidently seen their best days." He had already made a similar call on John Pendleton Kennedy, a Baltimore lawyer and writer who was one of the other judges. He had found a valuable friend. Writing in his journal a few days after Poe's death in 1849, Kennedy recalled finding the poet "in a state of starvation" and providing him with "clothing, free access to my table and the use of a horse for exercise." Early in 1835, Kennedy wrote to White recommending that he consider Poe as a contributor and possibly a permanent employee. "He wants experience and direction, but I have no doubt he can be made very useful to you."[5]

White was impressed, and tried. He began publishing Poe stories in March, paying five to twenty dollars by mail to Baltimore. By August, Poe was in White's office in Richmond and promised to "aid me all that lies in his power," but was expected to stay only one month. White found him "unfortunately rather dissipated" but hoped he would be able to help with proofreading. Poe did more. In the next issue, he wrote all of the critical and literary notices and was earning about forty dollars a month. By September 21, however, he "flew the track" as "his habits were not good." He had been despondent, complaining of "a depression of spirits which will ruin me should it be long continued." White feared that Poe might commit suicide.[6]

The neophyte magazine publisher didn't seem to be in much better spirits himself. "Stick by me, or I may perish," he wrote to his friend the journalist Lucian Minor, who had previously declined an offer to be editor of the *Messenger.* By October 20, White had relented, and Poe was with him again, reading copy and writing reviews. White was editing the paper himself and cautioned Minor, should he mention Poe, "not to say as editor." In January 1836, Poe gave his annual salary as $520, but said he earned enough for extra work to make the total $800, with a promise of $1,000 for the next year. In February, he was finding "no difficulty in keeping pace with the demands of the magazine," although White had "got so far behind in regard to time" that they had to skip an issue. By the end of the year, White felt he had been patient long enough. "Highly as I really think of Mr. Poe's talents, I shall be forced to give him notice," he said. Poe had forfeited the conditions on which he had been allowed to return.[7]

White also worried that Poe's sometimes trenchant criticism might get him into trouble with libel laws. When he asked James E. Heath, a former editor of the *Messenger,* to go over one article, Heath suggested striking out references to James Fenimore Cooper and Washington Irving. The editor may have been responding to barbs some southern newspapers had launched. The *Newbern Spectator* of New Bern, North Carolina, wrote, "Every man of proper feelings, every lover of literature, who peruses the work, is disgusted with the superficial criticism and uneducated flippancy . . . and with the low, egotistical means resorted to." Poe said he thought the writer of the editorial was "the identical gentleman who once sent us from Newbern an unfortunate copy of verses," and added, "If the Editor of this little paper does not behave himself we will positively publish his verses." Another North Carolina newspaper, the *Oxford Examiner,* found Poe's strictures "unnecessarily, perhaps, strictly severe in some instances." Not all editors agreed. The *Charlottesville Advocate* acclaimed Poe's criticism as "acute, just, and pungent." James Russell Lowell, writing later, found him the country's "most discriminating, philosophical, and fearless critic."[8]

The January issue of the *Messenger* announced, "Mr. Poe's attention being called in another direction, he will decline, with the present number, the Editorial duties" of the magazine. White said Poe had "retired" from the publication on January 3 but would "continue to furnish its columns from time to time with effusions of his vigorous pen." His last review, of Columbia College Professor Charles Anthon's edition of Cicero's orations, was mild enough. Anthon, he wrote, "has given the world evidence of comprehensive as well as of an acute and original understanding" of the Roman statesman and orator. "What follows," said the editorial announcement, "is from another hand." Poe, the statement said, "is now desirous of bidding all parties a peaceable farewell." He now headed for New York.[9]

"Before quitting the *Messenger,*" Poe would later write, "I saw, or fancied I saw, through a long and dim vista, the brilliant field for ambition which a magazine of bold and noble aims presented to him who would successfully establish it in America." Such a magazine, he said, should lean to "the curt, the terse, the well-timed, and the readily diffused, in preference to the old forms of the verbose and ponderous and the inaccessible." He envisioned a circulation of twenty thousand copies selling at five dollars each and netting seventy thousand dollars after expenses. He boasted that he had increased the *Messenger*'s circulation from seven hundred copies to fifty-five hundred in fifteen months and that it was netting ten thousand dollars a year when he left. This differs from the account of White, who wrote in January 1837, while Poe was still at the magazine, that he was "so overwhelmed in debt that I scarcely dare think of such an editor as I know I ought to have."[10]

As early as 1834, Poe had nourished a plan to publish "a monthly magazine of a superior intellectual character." "As soon as Fate allows I will have a magazine of my own—and will endeavor to kick up a dust," he wrote to a friend in September 1839. Four months later, he heard that "Some one of capital in Baltimore" was interested in starting a magazine. Poe asked a Baltimore acquaintance to tell him all about it "*by return of mail.*" By January 1841, he was making arrangements for the magazine, which he had named the *Penn Monthly.* J. R. Pollock, a periodical agent and publisher on Chestnut Street in Philadelphia agreed to handle the magazine's business affairs and printed a supply of prospectuses promising the first issue would come out on March 1. On January 17, Poe declared his prospects "*glorious,*" began soliciting manuscripts, and said he had "cut the bridges behind me." He even ordered stationery. A financial crisis intervened, however, and the *Penn* was postponed.[11]

In the midst of this crisis, the comic actor William Burton, who had doubled as publisher of *The Gentleman's Magazine* for four years, needed money for a new theater and put his magazine on the market for thirty-five hundred dollars, or one dollar a subscriber. George R. Graham, publisher of the *Casket,* which had only fifteen hundred subscribers, jumped at the chance, and combined the two periodicals as *Graham's Magazine.* It was a lucky break for Poe, who had been hired as associate editor of *Gentleman's Magazine* in July 1839. Burton had offered him ten dollars a week to work about two hours a day, with an understanding for the future. The future turned out to be a disaster. Burton objected to many of Poe's articles because they were too long or for other reasons. Poe "grew discouraged and could feel no interest in the journal." To a friend he wrote, "Do not think of subscribing." Nevertheless, his salary was increased to twenty dollars, apparently at the beginning of 1840. By June 1, however, Burton was balking at paying him fifty dollars a month. In 1841, he may still have been on the payroll, as Burton asked Graham to "take care of my young editor." In February 1841, Poe was hired to conduct the book review department of *Graham's Magazine* at a salary of eight hundred dollars a year. By the 1850 census, the magazine's circulation had grown to thirty thousand a year.[12]

At *Graham's,* Poe often printed revised versions of previously published poems of his own, including "To Helen," "The Raven," and "The Bells." In April 1941, *Graham's* published Poe's tale "The Murders in the Rue Morgue." In June 1842, Poe offered the sequel, "The Mystery of Marie Roget" to a Boston publication called *Mammoth Notion* for fifty dollars, although he said he would have received one hundred dollars for it from *Graham's.* He said he was anxious to have it published in Boston "for reasons . . . which I need not specify." Actually, he had left *Graham's* and been succeeded by Rufus Griswold. Griswold said Poe was fired, but Graham told a visitor that Griswold was hired as a temporary replacement when Poe "was, from illness or other causes, absent for a short time from his post." According to this account, Poe came back unexpectedly, saw Griswold in his chair, and "turned on his heel without a word, and left the office, nor could he be persuaded to enter it again."[13]

On leaving *Graham's,* Poe again turned his attention to the projected *Penn* magazine. He told an acquaintance that Graham had agreed to join him in the project, provided he would edit Graham's, but had kept putting him off and then backed out. *Penn* came to nothing, despite

Poe's giving it a more appealing name, *The Stylus,* trying tirelessly to line up backers, and even signing a contract with artist Felix Darley to be its illustrator. Soon, Poe joined the ranks of New York's poet-journalists. In October 1844, he took a job as "mechanical paragraphist" for the *Evening Mirror,* working as a subeditor responsible for short articles and reviews. In March 1845, his name appeared on the masthead of the *Broadway Journal* as one of its three editors. One of the trio, Charles F. Briggs, had played a key role in establishing the paper two months earlier with the aid of John Bisco, a former school teacher from Massachusetts, who became publisher. Briggs said Poe was "only an assistant to me and will in no way interfere with my own way of doing things." The poet was announced as editor, he said, "as his name is of some authority."[14]

Poe later conceded that at this time he was only a contributor to the paper, with no editorial control. Briggs and Poe split the editorial share of the profits with the third editor, former *New York World* music critic Henry C. Watson. The profits were meager. By May, Poe said he was working fourteen to eighteen hours a day and yet was "as poor now as ever I was in my life." Briggs said Poe had "lately gotten into his old habits." The editorial *troika* did not last long. After an outbreak of feuding between Briggs and Bisco, with the former agitating for a new publisher, the issue for the first two weeks in July failed to appear. When the paper resumed on July 12, the names of Poe and Watson were alone on the masthead and a notice said that the editorial content of the paper was "under the sole charge of Edgar A. Poe," while Watson would continue to run the music department. In October, a discouraged Bisco sold the paper to Poe for fifty dollars, in the form of a note from Horace Greeley that was never redeemed. Poe was now editor and publisher. "By a series of manoeuvres almost incomprehensible to myself I have succeeded in getting rid, one by one, of all my associates," he wrote to his old benefactor Kennedy.[15]

Neither the paper nor its new captain fared any better. James Russell Lowell, who had recommended Poe to Briggs on the basis of his writings, met him for the first time when he called at the office one day and found him drunk. Walt Whitman also came by to talk about a piece of his that the *Journal* had published. Although more favorably impressed than Lowell, Whitman thought Poe "subdued, perhaps a little jaded." With no one left to help him put one December issue together, the beleaguered editor went off on a binge and left a column and a half empty. When the *Journal*'s last issue came out on January 3, 1846, Poe wrote, "Unexpected engagements demanding my whole attention, and the objects being fulfilled, so far as regards myself personally, for which the *Broadway Journal* was established, I now, as its Editor, bid farewell—as cordially to foes as to friends."[16]

In May of the same year, the editor of the Philadelphia magazine *Godey's Lady's Book* wrote, "We have received several letters from New York, anonymous and from personal friends, requesting us to be careful what we allow Mr. Poe to say of the New York authors." Poe had contributed a series on "The New York Literati" in which he took on some of the city's biggest literary reputations and created what journalistic historian Frank Luther Mott called "*Godey*'s greatest sensation." The editor replied that "we have nothing to do but publish Mr. Poe's opinions, *not our own*. Whether we agree with Mr. Poe or not is another matter." Publisher Louis A. Godey was no doubt pleased by the controversy. Magazine agents in New York ran out of copies of the May issue and took newspaper ads to assure their customers that they were ordering more.[17]

Poe's most severe criticism was saved for Briggs, his former rival for editorial power at the *Journal*. "Mr. Briggs has never composed in his life three consecutive sentences of grammatical English," he wrote. He conceded that an article by Briggs was "quite easy and clever in its way, but the way is necessarily a small one." A critical article on Thomas Babington Macaulay, Poe said, might have been "the silliest thing of this kind ever penned." Aside from his treatment of Briggs, it is difficult to see what the fuss was about. Poe described the theological arguments of the minister and Columbia University professor George Bush as "lucidly, vigorously, succinctly and logically" written. He said the taste of the Whig editor George H. Colton was "rather unexceptional than positively good" but would no doubt improve with more experience. N. P. Willis of the *Evening Herald*, he said, was "out of his element" as an editorialist but unequaled as a writer of sketches.[18]

Publication of Poe's poetry in journals, some of which he edited, show him constantly revising in the last decade of his life, before his death of delirium in Baltimore in October 1949.

His poem "To Helen" appeared in the March 1836, issue of the *Southern Literary Messenger* as follows:

Helen, thy beauty is to me
    Like those Nicean barks of yore
That gently, o'er a perfumed sea,
    The weary, wayworn wanderer bore
    To his own native shore.

On desperate seas long wont to roam,
    Thy hyacinth hair, thy classic face,
Thy Naiad airs have brought me home
    To the beauty of fair Greece,
And the grandeur of old Rome.

Lo! in that little window-niche
    How statue-like I see thee stand!
    The folded scroll within thy hand—
Ah! Psyche from the regions which
    Are Holy land!

By the time the poem appeared in *Graham's Magazine* in September 1841, the closing lines of the second stanza had become the familiar "To the glory that was Greece— / To the grandeur that was Rome." The "little" window-niche in the first line of stanza three had become "shadowy" and he would later change it to "brilliant." In both the *Messenger* and *Graham's* versions, Helen had a simple "folded scroll" in her hand, but Poe later made it a more evocative "agate lamp."

Three versions of "The Raven," all published at about the same time, show like differences. In the February 1845 *American Review,* the poet proclaims that "no sublunary being" would be likely to encounter a bird named "Nevermore." In the February 8, 1845, *Broadway*

Journal and the March 1845 *Southern Literary Messenger,* the arcane "sublunary" being had become a simpler "living human being." One of the six repetitions of the refrain "Quoth the Raven, 'Nevermore'" in the *Review* version was changed in the *Messenger* to "Then the bird said 'Nevermore,'" the form that survives in most editions. The *Journal* and *Messenger* versions also have the speaker "startled," instead of "wondering" as in the *Review,* at the Raven's iteration of the one word. Both the *Review* and *Messenger* versions call the forgetfulness drug invoked by Poe "Nepenthe," but in the *Journal* the capital letter is correctly changed to lower case.[19]

The editor's note in the May issue of Godey's said that Poe had been ill, but that the magazine had received "a new batch of the Literati, which show anything but feebleness either of body or mind." However he may have neglected his journalistic duties, there was obviously no faltering in the care that Poe took with his poetry.[20]

The historical scholar Vernon Louis Parrington, who tended to see art through the prism of politics, was correct by his lights when he declared, "The problem of Poe, fascinating as it is, lies quite outside the main current of American thought." Looked at as a poet instead of a problem, Poe embodied in his best work "the curt, the terse, the well-timed" that he prescribed for successful journalism.[21]

5 "Unhappily Smitten with the Love of Rhyme"

As a poet, Leigh Hunt is better known for his friendship with Keats and Shelley than for his slight, clever verses. As a journalist, he was on the front lines in the fight for freedom of England's press, and he went to prison for it for two years.

Hunt's leading article in the *Examiner* for March 22, 1812, an unsparing criticism of the country's then Prince Regent, later King George IV, came to be known for the epithet "Fat Adonis of Fifty." That isn't exactly what it said, but it was a turning point for a press that until then had shied from any but the mildest criticism of the monarchy. Possibly Hunt inherited his passion for free speech. By his account, his father, Isaac Hunt, the son of a Church of England vicar of the same name in colonial Barbados, issued "scurrilous and scandalous pieces" against persons of importance after being sent to college in Philadelphia in 1757. The younger Isaac's outspokenness led him to expressions of loyalty to King George III just as sentiment for independence was about to erupt into the American Revolution. He was stoned by a mob, barely escaped tarring and feathering, and was briefly jailed, but escaped to Barbados on a merchant ship owned by his father-in-law. After making his way to England, he was joined by his wife, the former Mary Shewell. James Henry Leigh Hunt, the youngest of several children, was born to them on October 19, 1784, at their home in Southgate, near London.[1]

Leigh Hunt's mother was the daughter of prosperous Philadelphia ship owner Samuel Shewell, a man who entertained Benjamin Franklin and Thomas Paine in his Philadelphia home. Life with the improvident Isaac must have been a shock. Failing in a try at the practice of law, the boy's father scraped together an uncertain living as a preacher noted for dramatic sermons. He had hopes of becoming a bishop, but financial mismanagement led him to a debtor's prison instead. Leigh Hunt recalled that "the first room I have any recollection of is a prison."

In 1791, after receiving a Loyalist Pension of one hundred pounds, Isaac Hunt indulged in pamphleteering, offending one of his father-in-law's sometime house guests with a work called *Rights of Englishmen: An Antidote to the Poison Now Vending by the Transatlantic Republican, Thomas Paine*. He once took his son Leigh to both houses of Parliament, and the boy was struck by the "personally insignificant look" of the Lords. Although still a loyal subject, Isaac Hunt found his pension inadequate and, reported his son, "grew deeply acquainted with prisons, and began to lose his graces and his good name." He died in 1809, aged fifty-seven.[2]

Young Leigh was sent to school at Christ-Hospital, an institution that Coleridge had attended before him. He found himself among other "sons of poor gentry," as well as "the sons of tradesmen of the very humblest description" and the occasional boy from a noble family. It was, he said, "a medium, between the patrician pretension of such schools as Eton and Westminster, and the plebeian submission of the charity schools." He was assigned to the institution's grammar school, which placed such exclusive emphasis on writing that when he left the school in 1799 at the age of fifteen he did not know the multiplication tables. Already, however, he was writing verse. One of his earliest poems celebrated the Duke of York's "Victory at Dunkirk," which, to his chagrin as well as the duke's, turned out to have been a defeat.[3]

The youth first broke into print with a collection of verses published in 1801 by his father, then still a fairly prosperous clergyman, under the appropriate title *Juvenilia*. The book was good for his ego, as it sold well and got him feted as a prodigy. Later, with more mature judgment, he saw it as "a heap of imitations, all but absolutely worthless." In 1804, Hunt began writing essays for an evening paper, *The Traveller*, and "could not behold the long columns of type, written by myself, in a public paper, without thinking there must be some merit in them." His pay was five or six copies of the paper.[4]

His older brother, John, instead of going to school, had been apprenticed to a printer, an event that would affect the course of Leigh Hunt's life. In 1805, John started a paper called the *News,* and Leigh became its drama critic. He commenced a policy that he would claim to follow when his criticisms extended to the world outside the theater. It had been the practice for critics to belong to the theatrical set, dine well at the tables of actors and playwrights, and accordingly give them favorable reviews. As Hunt succinctly put it, "It was thought a feather in the cap of all parties; and with their feathers they tickled one another." Hunt took no free tickets and avoided the company of the theatrical folk, as he would later say he avoided that of the political.[5]

This practice, coupled with his natural talents, earned him a reputation as one of the leading theater critics of his day. It also aroused the ire of theatrical luminaries unused to such treatment. In his first review, of a performance of Shakespeare's *Much Ado About Nothing,* he complained of the "prominence of mouth" that actor William Thomas Lewis displayed in attempting to portray surprise in the role of Benedick. He described Mrs. H. Johnson as demonstrating "the mere disgusting malice" of "a North American cannibal" in her portrayal of Beatrice. Of the popular Christmas pantomimes at Drury Lane and Covent Garden, he said, "A spectacle in which little is understood and nothing gained is unworthy serious criticism." Reflecting on all this years later, Hunt wrote, "Good God! To think of the grand opinion I had of myself in those days, and what little reason I had for it." Of one actor, he said, "I knew almost as little of the drama as the young Roscius himself." Still, remembering the actor's performance, he added, "Luckily, I had the advantage of him in knowing how unfit *he* was for his office."[6]

On January 3, 1808, the first issue of a London Sunday paper, the *Examiner,* appeared. The paper would deal, said its prospectus, with "Politics, Domestic Economy, and Theatricals" in its sixteen double-column pages. John Hunt was the publisher, and he made his brother editor. In his biography of Leigh Hunt, the poet Edmund Blunden wrote, "Besides inventing political parables and social studies, this young man seemed capable of enlivening an audience with the literary and dramatic news presented in a style of confidence and vitality." Hunt moved easily into the drama critic's chair. As for the rest, he said: "In politics, from old family associations, I soon got interested as a man, though I never could love them as a writer. It was against the grain that I was encouraged to begin them, and against the grain I ever afterward sat down to write, except when the subject was of a very general description, and I could introduce philosophy and the belle-lettres."

Hunt told the *Examiner*'s prospective readers that he would continue to review theatrical productions "and as the Public have allowed the possibility of IMPARTIALITY in that department, we do not see why the same possibility may not be obtained in POLITICS . . . the EXAMINER has escaped from the throng and bustle, but he will seat himself by the wayside, and contemplate the moving multitude as they wrangle and wrestle along." He granted that the readers might be skeptical of such promises, and no doubt many were, not without reason. Although Hunt claimed to not even know any politicians, the record shows that he regularly corresponded on political issues with the Whig parliamentarian Henry Brougham. In 1815, Brougham even wrote to congratulate the poet on the defeat of Bonaparte, against whom Hunt had inveighed as an editor.[7]

By his own account, Hunt spent most of his week at the *Examiner* writing poetry and reading, and then sat up late at night working on his editorial duties much like a student cramming at the last minute for an exam. One of his editors said that his journalistic writings were "produced, so to speak, from hand to mouth, on the emergency of the moment, in obedience to the clamorous necessity of the occasion . . . his face becoming flushed as he wrote, and his whole nervous system visibly agitated," in contrast to the "utmost composure" in which Hunt himself said he wrote his verse. He had no political works on his bookshelves, only poetry and essays. About this time, he wrote a poem called "Politics and Poetics or, the Desperate Situation of a Journalist Unhappily Smitten with the Love of Rhyme." The poet complains of:

> The foul fiend, who—let it rain or shine,
> Let it be clear or cloudy, foul or fine,
> Or freezing, thawing, drizzling, hailing, snowing,
> Or mild, or warm, or hot, or bleak and blowing,

Or damp, or dry, or dull, or sharp, or sloppy,
Is sure to come—the Devil, who comes for copy

and then exclaims, "Off, cares, and wants, and threats, and all the race / Of foes to freedom and to laurelled leisure! / To-day is for the Muse, and dancing Pleasure."

Before the *Examiner* was launched, Hunt had found a job clerking at the War Office. By then he had brushed up on arithmetic enough that he could do the job adequately, but he had little interest in it and soon resigned to avoid a conflict with his newspaper duties. In November, 1808, the paper had a regular sale of twenty-two hundred, and the Hunts were optimistic it would reach three thousand by Christmas. John Hunt told his brother that "he had no doubt but we should be getting eight or ten guineas *apiece* every week in a year's time."[8]

Hunt's resignation from his War Office post came shortly after the *Examiner,* then only ten months old, had its first brush with the law. An artillery major named Hogan, described by Hunt as "a furious but honest Irishman" who had been in the army seventeen years, published a pamphlet under the title *Appeal to the Public, and a Farewell Address to the Army.* He charged that the Duke of York, as commander-in-chief, had unjustly refused him promotion while advancing others, and added that as a British officer, he scorned "to owe the king's commission to low intrigue or petticoat influence!"[9]

The "petticoat influence" phrase was a reference to the duke's mistress, Mary Anne Clarke. The *Examiner* printed an account of the affair, in which Hunt assailed the army as a corrupt institution "never to be moved but by its lust for women or its lust for money" and described the duke as "the promoter and foster father, if not the begetter, of these corruptions." The words got him prosecuted. A Welsh member of Parliament then brought Mrs. Clarke before the House of Commons. She testified that she "had a thousand pounds" from one man to secure him a promotion. The duke resigned his command and the prosecution was dropped.[10]

Less than a year later, the government again charged the *Examiner* with libel. At the time, King George's mental decline was becoming increasingly obvious, and there was talk of having George, Prince of Wales, take over his duties as Prince Regent. The article that gave rise to the libel charge did not deal mainly with the king, but with a change of ministries in the government. However, after discussing the prospect of a regency, Hunt wrote: "What a crowd of blessings rush upon one's mind, that might be bestowed upon the country in the event of such a change!—Of all the monarchs, indeed, since the Revolution, the successor of George the Third will have the finest opportunity of becoming nobly popular." That was the part considered libelous.

The pro-government *Morning Post* responded: "Never, surely, was anything more calculated to insult the good sense, or *horrify* the *pure* and amiable nature of his *Royal Highness;* nor was anything more calculated to call forth the *indignation* and execration of a *loyal* and *admiring* People, upon the *Wretch* who is capable of broaching an idea at once so repugnant to the feelings of the illustrious *Heir Apparent* and to the ardent wishes of every good and (also) virtuous subject."

The brothers stood their ground. Writing in the *Examiner,* Leigh Hunt noted that two actions had been brought against them "to grace the close of each year. I say, *to grace,* not out of mere defiance to power or any disrespect to law, but because the object of both these actions was to overpower the most manifest truths respecting the most disgraceful measures." James Perry, the proprietor of the London *Morning Chronicle* was also charged with libel, merely for reprinting the article's concluding words. Perry's trial came first, and after he had pleaded his own case the presiding judge, Lord Ellenborough, instructed the jury to find in his favor. Once again, charges against the Hunts were dropped.[11]

They were charged for the third time in 1810 after reprinting a portion of an editorial from a country paper, the *Stamford News,* describing English military flogging as "that most heart-rending of all exhibitions on this side of hell." The paper, edited by the radical journalist John Scott, was a new arrival in Lincolnshire, established the year before as a counterpoint to the staid *Stamford Mercury,* "the articulate voice of eastern England."

The Hunts turned to their friend Brougham as their attorney. Their case was not an easy one. A few months before, the firebrand editor

William Cobbett had been sentenced to two years in prison and fined a thousand pounds for a similar attack on flogging. Brougham was reported to have "no hope of a verdict" of acquittal. Nevertheless, the Whig lawyer, better known for his courtroom oratory than his grasp of the fine points of the law, let out all the stops. He pictured to the jury the plight of soldiers forced "to see their comrades tied up, and to behold the flesh stripped off from their bodies, aye, bared to the bone!" Had not men who felt strongly about such a matter, he asked, "a right to express themselves in proportion . . . to the strength of the feeling it excites in them?" The jury acquitted the Hunts after deliberating for an hour and forty-five minutes. Four days later, Brougham defended John Drakard, the proprietor of the *Stamford News,* at his trial in the county town of Lincoln for the original, and longer, article, written by his editor, Scott. Drakard, unlike the Hunts, was convicted. England, the last country in Europe to retain flogging in the armed services, abolished the practice in 1868.[12]

One reason for the different outcomes of the two trials may have been the makeup of the juries. Ten of the jurors in the Hunt trial in Westminster were drawn from what was known as a common jury pool, made up of ordinary freeholders. Only two were special jurors, men with the rank of esquire or higher, or bankers or merchants. Half of the Drakard jury was made up of special jurors, more likely to side with the government and, in a rural town, likely to influence the commoners. The Hunts did not, in any event, get off scot-free. Under the prevailing law, they had to pay court costs even when acquitted. The costs came to more than ninety-nine pounds, a sizable amount at the time, for their first trial alone.

During the Hunts' trial, the attorney-general, Sir Vicary Gibbs, "a little, irritable, sharp featured, bilious-looking man," asked them why they did not "speak privately on the subject to some member of Parliament" instead of airing it in their newspaper. At Drakard's trial, the presiding judge, Sir George Wood, told the jury that "parliament was the place for the discussion of the laws of the country, not newspapers." It was an increasingly common view. From 1808 through 1810, Gibbs filed forty-two complaints against publishers for libel, compared with fourteen that had been filed in the preceding seven years. In a March

1811 parliamentary debate Lord Folkestone charged the attorney general with prosecuting "for everything that may be said against the political friends of the minister of the day" while passing over "The grossest and most indecent observations which can possibly be made against the highest persons of the community, unless those persons happen to coincide in political opinion with the Government for the time being."[13]

The charge that led both of the Hunts to prison grew out of an annual Irish celebration held on St. Patrick's Day in 1812 at the Freemasons' Tavern in London by the Benevolent Society of St. Patrick. A toast to the former Prince of Wales, elevated to Prince Regent a year before, evoked hisses from the revelers, who felt he had not lived up to promises to Catholics. The *Morning Post,* assailing such "ungenerous, unmanly conduct," responded with a poetical encomium saluting the prince as "the *Glory of the People* . . . the *Protector of the Arts* . . . this *Maecenas of the Age* . . . an *Adonis in loveliness*" and similar flatteries. This was too much for Hunt. In the March 22 *Examiner,* he wrote that the casual reader of the Tory paper would have no way to know that "this *Adonis in Loveliness,* was a corpulent gentleman of fifty. In short that this *delightful, blissful, wise, pleasurable, honourable, virtuous, true* and *immortal* Prince, was a violator of his word, a libertine over head and ears in debt and disgrace, a despiser of domestic ties, the companion of gamblers and demi-reps, a man who has just closed half a century without one single claim in the gratitude of his country, or the respect of posterity." In verse, Hunt wrote a mock coronation soliloquy in which the regent declares:

> I know where
> A fat, a fair,
> 　　Sweet other self is doting:
> I'd reply
> With wink of eye,
> 　　But fear the newsman noting.[14]

Hunt obviously knew that in his editorial he was treading on dangerous ground, for on March 16, the day before the Irish meeting, he told Henry Crabb Robinson, "No one can accuse me of not writing a libel, everything is libel, as the law is now declared, and our security lies only in their shame." To Robinson, Leigh seemed "an enthusiast, very well intentioned, and I believe prepared for the worst." The worst soon came. This time, the Hunts faced a jury made up entirely of special jurors. Three decades later, Hunt recalled that he "declined an offer brought me by the friend of a friend of the Prince Regent (on the Prince's part) to drop proceedings against the *Examiner* if I would promise to take no notice of him in the future." Brougham said there were two such offers, both refused by the Hunts.[15]

After a six-month delay sought by the prosecution in order to seek the more favorable jury, the Court of King's Bench convened on December 10, 1812. The *Examiner* was described as the most popular weekly in the country, "especially among high political men," with a circulation of seven to eight thousand by 1812, and the Hunts' trial drew a crowd. The *Times* reported that "The Hall was so much crowded at a very early hour that it was impossible to open the doors of the Court to the public indiscriminately, and there were consequently many places in the Court, although many more candidates that would have filled them (were) in the Hall."

Solicitor General Richardson asked that the alleged libel be read in court, a practice not always followed. "If that bare reading did not convince every dispassionate, cool, thinking, honest man, that it was a most atrocious libel, no man could be convicted of such a libel by any subtlety of reasoning or nicety of argument," Richardson said. Brougham responded that Hunt's only motive had been to expose the absurdity of the *Post*'s rhymed eulogy and that "The defendants, having been formerly prosecuted for warmly expressing their hopes of the Prince Regent's administration, are now called upon for expressing the bitterness of their disappointment, that these hopes have not been realized." Leigh Hunt, he told the jurors, was far from a firebrand, but "a retired, studious man . . . with the habits of one who assorts with books rather than with men."

In charging the jury, Lord Ellenborough asked them to "decide today whether we were in future to live under the dominion of libel, or the control and government of the law; for against all the law and its pro-visions had this libeler set his whole front at defiance." When the jury retired, Brougham was called away from the courtroom on other busi-ness, but he already knew that there was "scarcely a chance" of acquit-tal. After deliberating for about a quarter of an hour, the jury returned a verdict of guilty in the case of John Hunt. When the foreman was asked how the jury found on the charge against Leigh Hunt, "he hesitated, and looked to his fellows; but soon answered, 'equally guilty,'" the *Times* reported. The crowd, the reporter said, "waited the event of the verdict, and dispersed very peaceably."[16]

On February 13, 1813, Leigh Hunt put on a new suit and his best hat and gloves and went to court to be sentenced, carrying with him a satirical book by a Dutch poet. Hunt and his brother pressed each other's arms when the judge pronounced their punishment: two years in separate prisons and a fine of five hundred pounds for each of them. At the end of their terms, each must put up another five hundred pounds to guarantee five years of good, presumably nonlibelous, behavior. Oth-erwise, they must remain imprisoned. As Hunt remembered it, the two brothers did not speak before being taken away in hackney coaches: Leigh to Surrey Gaol in Horsemonger Lane, and John to Coldbath Fields Prison in Middlesex.[17]

Establishment supporters were quick to applaud the sentences. The *Satirist, or Monthly Meteor,* declared libel one of the worst of crimes and said the Hunts' whole career had been a "course of libelling." The *British Review, and London Critical Journal* said the Hunts' attacks on the Prince Regent jeopardized the right relation "between sovereign and subject." Even Leigh Hunt's fellow poet, Robert Southey, said persons convicted of libel should be sent to penal colonies, where they would be "out of the way of pity and mischief." Irish poet Thomas Moore, how-ever, saluted the imprisoned journalists for "The pride that suffers with-out vaunt or plea, / And the fresh spirit that can warble free, / Through prisons bars, its hymn of liberty."[18]

Others tried to come to the rescue. Shelley, who had met Leigh Hunt briefly during the latter's early days at the *Examiner,* visited him in prison and launched a subscription campaign to raise money to pay the brothers' fines. For some reason, the campaign came to nothing, but in September 1814 Brougham told Leigh Hunt that one of the jurors had repented and was anxious to pay the fine. Brougham urged the Hunts to consider the offer, but they declined. In his autobiography, Hunt did not identify the juror but said that before the trial few persons had been "more zealous or liberal" than the generous juror in the Regent's behalf.[19]

It would make a dramatic story to say that conditions at the Surrey Gaol were as harsh as those eloquently described by Oscar Wilde in *The Ballad of Reading Gaol,* but the truth is somewhat different. Hunt spent his first month in a garret that he found "a malignant insult to my love of liberty," climbing on a chair to look through a high window at prisoners in chains taking their exercise. The prison doctor found him in poor health, however, and on March 16 he was moved to a ground floor apartment in the infirmary, where he could have his wife and children with him. He papered the walls with pictures of roses, screened the barred windows with Venetian blinds, set up his bookcases, and played host to the likes of Lord Byron, Lamb, Lamb's fellow essayist William Hazlitt, and Thomas Moore. To Lamb, there was "no room at all like it anywhere, except in a fairy tale." At times, Hunt took his guests for games of battledore and shuttlecock, or strolls in a small garden that went with his room.[20]

Once established in this new home, Hunt resolved to finish his long romantic poem *The Story of Rimini,* which he had begun the previous summer. In addition to poetry he continued to contribute weekly articles to the *Examiner.* His brother, from two rooms freshly painted for him in his Middlesex jail, also performed editorial chores.

On his first day in his infirmary apartment, Leigh Hunt wrote that "a few weeks ago," which could have been either before or after he entered the prison, he committed "a miserable blunder . . . upon a matter of every-day knowledge." The mistake embarrassed him and prompted reflections on his role in the world of journalism, and whether he was miscast in it.

It is true, I have hitherto confined myself, as a journalist, to very general politics, and principally to the ethical part of them, to

Leigh Hunt, author of "Abou Ben Adhem," served two
years in prison on conviction of libeling England's then
Prince Regent, later King George IV. His cell was an
apartment, where he set up his bookcases and continued
writing. Sketch of Hunt by unknown artist from *Leigh
Hunt and His Circle* by Edmund Blunden (New York:
Harper and Brothers, 1930).

the diffusion of a liberal spirit of thinking, and to the very broad-
est view of characters and events, always referring them to the
standard of human nature and common sense; but although this
may be enough for a general reformist, and is calculated to do,
and, I believe, has done, some good among the better minds of
the public, yet it is far from sufficient for a particular one,—for
one who undertakes, or should undertake, to improve, from a
full knowledge of what is imperfect,—one, who ought to have

completely studied the differences of things, and to come to his great work with a knowledge suitable to his intentions.[21]

Leigh and John Hunt were released from prison on February 3, 1815, and Leigh went to live in a house near John's, in a suburban neighborhood then near the open fields. The two, who had wordlessly pressed each other's arms when they were sentenced, embraced in tears when they met again. A month earlier, Leigh had welcomed to the *Examiner*'s columns a poem by Charles Lamb, telling readers that "poetry is not so easily obtained, and compared with the usual run of newspaper articles, is like a precious liqueur, which is seldom and charily drank." Two days after his release from the Surrey jail, it was back to politics. The proprietors, he wrote, were unrepentant after "two years' imprisonment . . . for differing with the *Morning Post* on the merits of the Prince Regent." Nevertheless, Hunt's attention turned increasingly to poetry. He finished *The Story of Rimini*, which was praised by Byron and other friends, condemned by the *Examiner*'s enemies, and soon dismissed by critics. In 1816, John Keats came to live with the Hunts, but the great poet, mortally ill and depressed, quarreled with his host and soon left. Hunt visited Coleridge, white-haired at fifty and living with the Gillmans in Highgate, and "fancied him a good natured wizard, very fond of earth."

The newspaper, meanwhile, fell on hard times. In 1818, its average weekly circulation was 4,000; a year later, it had dropped to 3,200. That year, John Hunt retired to the country, leaving the management of the paper to his imaginative but financially inept brother. By 1821, circulation was down to 2,750. John kept his oar in, writing in a letter to the editor that the House of Commons contained "a far greater portion of public criminals than public guardians." Again, he served two years in prison for libel. In August 1821, Leigh wrote that the paper was rapidly nearing the point where it would not pay for its own expenses.

On October 21, Hunt's signature appeared for the last time in the *Examiner,* and he joined Shelley in Italy, taking his family along. The plan was that he, Shelley, and Byron would publish a paper, the *Liberal*. Shelley drowned, Hunt and Byron had a falling out, and only five issues of the paper ever appeared. In 1837, after his return to England, Hunt established a journal called the *Monthly Repository,* a title that showed how far he had moved from political activism. The journal would be a storehouse of literature, not an examiner of government foibles. Leigh Hunt's days as a reluctant journalistic crusader were over. Until his death in 1859 at the age of seventy-four, he devoted himself to poets and poetry.[22]

On September 25, 1853, Charles Dickens sat pen in hand at his desk in the Villa de Moulineaux in Boulogne, as always enjoying the "range of view and air, most free and delightful." He had spent the summer in a rented house in the French seaside resort and in his summer home in Switzerland working on *Bleak House,* the capstone of his career as England's preeminent novelist.

On this day, he was writing to the widow of his old friend Richard Watson. In sketching Chesney Wold, the scene of much of the action in his novel, Dickens had drawn "many bits, chiefly about trees and shadows" from his observations of Rockingham Castle, the Watsons' home. Mrs. Watson herself was his source for many of the physical characteristics of Lady Dedlock.

It was not of them, though, that he was writing. As *Bleak House* unfolded serially in London, word circulated that the charming but selfish and irresponsible Skimpole, who at one point argues for turning a gravely ill child out into the cold because there would be "a certain sort of poetry" in his fending for himself, was based on Leigh Hunt. Hunt, who had lifted his glass to toast Dickens on his twenty-seventh birthday and found him "as pleasant as some of the best things in his books," was deeply hurt. Dickens revised the Skimpole portrayal and told his adviser John Forster, "I think I have made it much less like." In his letter to Mrs. Watson, he boasted of how like it originally was.

> Skimpole. I must not forget Skimpole—of whom I will proceed to speak as if I had only read him and not written him. I suppose he is the most exact portrait that was ever painted in words! I have very seldom, if ever, done such a thing. But the likeness is

astonishing. I don't think it could possibly be more like himself. It is so awfully true that I make a bargain with myself "never to do so any more." There is not an atom of exaggeration or suppression. It is an absolute reproduction of a real man. Of course I have been careful to keep the outward figure away from the fact; but in all else it is the life itself.[23]

The life itself. But was it? Certainly, Hunt was impractical. He graduated from school without knowing how to multiply. When he entered prison at the age of twenty-eight, he "had not yet learned to think of money." As soon as the *Examiner* was left in his hands, it foundered. But there is nothing to show that he was, like Skimpole, not only callous but a sponger who habitually borrowed money and did not repay it. Most people who knew him enjoyed his company, but some had doubts about the depth of his character. Hazlitt preferred Hunt's conversation "almost to any other person's, because, with a familiar range of subjects, he colours with a totally new and sparkling light." Historian Thomas Carlyle, with a more sober outlook than Hazlitt, was uncomfortable with Hunt because nothing could "persuade him that Man is born for another object here than to *be happy*."[24]

In his best known poem, "Abou Ben Adhem," Hunt showed himself so dedicated to being "one that loves his fellow men" that he has an angel pronounce it a virtue superior to the biblical "first and great commandment" to love God. At a party in 1832, one guest thought Hunt's "self-importance was ludicrous—talking of the persecution he had suffered—he observed that it had had great results." The twentieth-century historian Chester W. New considered Hunt "a thoroughly intolerant champion of liberty" who thought that "those who disagreed with him were the enemies of humanity, as were all those who offended his sense of the fitness of things." It is true that Hunt was proud of what he had done. In 1846, seeking a government pension, he said he had "lived to see almost all the measures for which I fought and suffered, secured one after the other."[25]

As a poet, he was sentimental and preachy. As a journalist he showed his mettle.

6 "The Crank of an Opinion-Mill"

If Leigh Hunt was a minor figure in the world of poetry and a more important factor in that of journalism, John Greenleaf Whittier is remembered as an oddity in both.

As a journalist, Whittier was far more interested in his Quaker faith and his religious and moral passion for the abolition of slavery than in the tools of his trade. Coleridge showed interest in those tools, criticizing some of his colleagues on the *Courier* for writing stories that were too long and not newsy enough. Hunt lacked the carefulness with facts that is vital in journalism but was concerned enough to acknowledge the fault and apologize for it. Whittier, on the other hand, told one editor that the "crowning excellence" of his paper was that it was *"anti-slavery* pure and simple" and "neither assails nor encourages other schemes of reform." He urged a fellow religionist to give his planned paper "a Quaker bearing—and see to it that nothing is printed inconsistent with our principles." In short, a paper was good if nothing was allowed in its columns that disagreed with Whittier's views. As for the editorial chores, Whittier the editor often left them to others while he was away at abolitionist meetings or on political business.

His view of the journalistic craft is expressed in his 1867 poem "The Tent on the Beach":

And one there was, a dreamer born,
　　Who, with a mission to fulfil,
Had left the Muses' haunts to turn
　　The crank of an opinion-mill,

Making his rustic reed of song
    A weapon in the war with wrong.[1]

Whittier's collected poems cover 298 two-column pages of small type, but only a handful of the nearly four hundred works in these pages is read today.

One of his most notable poems, "Snow-Bound," grew not out of his political activism, but out of life in the New England farmhouse in which he was born on December 17, 1807. Looking back on a long career in a world in which sweetness was often the farthest thing from sight, he concluded his poem with the memorable lines:

The traveller owns the grateful sense
Of sweetness near, he knows not whence,
And, pausing, takes with forehead bare
The benediction of the air.[2]

His career as a poet—and, indirectly, his career in journalism—began at the age of eighteen when William Lloyd Garrison, then the abolitionist editor of the Newburyport, Massachusetts, *Free Press,* accepted a sentimental poem Whittier had written and his elder sister, Mary, had submitted with only the letter "W" to indicate the author. Garrison found out who wrote it, drove fourteen miles to the Whittier farm and urged John Whittier to encourage his son's talent. The elder Whittier is said to have replied, "Sir, poetry will not give him bread."[3]

Garrison continued to publish poems by Whittier and, perhaps heeding the words of the young poet's father, urged the Reverend William Collier to hire him as editor of a paper he owned, the *National Philanthropist.* Collier made an offer, which Whittier accepted after some hesitation, but Collier assigned him instead to edit the *American Manufacturer,* a paper the cleric had established in Boston to celebrate the "American System." Whittier's duties included proofreading, book reviewing, writing news analysis as well as poetry, and serving as his own office boy. His compensation consisted mostly of free room and board with Collier and his family.[4]

On February 26, 1829, the young editor reported that the *Man-ufacturer* was doing well "thanks to the gullibility of the public." By May, however, after being "all day trying to write something for the next day's paper," he found it unreasonable to expect that "a fellow's ideas bubbled up on every publication day." Part of his problem, he admitted, was "habitual laziness." The *Philadelphia Album* praised his editorials, although conceding that they might be "somewhat too highly or rather poetically" worded. In August, Whittier resigned.[5]

He was editor of the *Essex Gazette* in Haverhill, Massachusetts, for the first seven months of 1830, leaving to become temporary editor of the *New England Weekly Review* in Hartford, Connecticut. By September he was permanent editor, and had to apologize to readers that the September 10 issue had little editorial content because he had been confined at home with "a tremendous cold." Nevertheless, he could write, "I now feel as if I could wrestle manfully in the strife of men. If my life is spared, the world shall know me in a loftier capacity than *as a writer of rhymes.*"

For a while, he thought he had such a capacity in his grasp. The politically prominent Caleb Cushing, locked in a Massachusetts congressional race that pitted him against two rivals, withdrew after concluding that he could not muster a majority. Whittier's name was put forward as a possible candidate, even though he would not reach the required age of twenty-five until December. The poet quickly maneuvered to bring about a stalemate that would prolong the contest and enable him to accept the nomination. "The truth of the matter is," he said, "the thing would be peculiarly beneficial to me,—if not at home, it would be so abroad. . . . It would be worth more to me *now,* young as I am, than almost any office after I had reached the meridian of life." It was probably Whittier's most candid statement of political ambition, but his strategy failed, and another candidate was elected. Whittier remained at his *Review* post until January 1832, although he took occasional leave for political jaunts. His ambitions suffered another blow in 1833. At his own expense, he printed a pamphlet he had written called *Justice and Expediency,* laying out for the first time his position in favor of immediate emancipation of the slaves. The pamphlet gained him wide notoriety in a country not ready for such views and caused cautious editors to reject his verse. The pro-abolition *Liberator,* however, published in 1834 his poem, "Our Countrymen in Chains." Abolitionist broadsides reprinting the poem were distributed throughout the rest of the 1830s, giving wide circulation to Whittier's rhetoric:

> What ho! Our countrymen in chains!
> The whip on WOMAN's shrinking flesh!
> *Our* soil yet reddened with the stains
> Caught from her scourging, warm and fresh!
> What! Mothers from their children riven!
> What! God's own image bought and sold!
> AMERICANS to market driven,
> And bartered as the brute for gold![6]

Despite this fiery language, Whittier generally followed a moderate and pragmatic course in abolition politics. Garrison, whom Whittier apostrophized in verse as the "Champion of those who groan beneath / Oppression's iron hand," was a sharp counterpoint. At an antislavery convention in 1833, the poet served on a subcommittee that succeeded in watering down a Garrison diatribe against those who favored colonizing the slaves in Africa instead of making them free Americans.[7]

By Whittier's account, he by then had "a large number of political friends" and was "on terms of intimate personal acquaintance" with editors of leading newspapers. Still, he could not afford to hire help for the family farm. He and his brother operated the farm together, and he eked out a living writing occasional literary articles. He sought, apparently unsuccessfully, a $150-per-month stipend for six months from the American Anti-Slavery Society to help him in his abolitionist work. While working for the cause, he did not neglect his own political ambitions. In the fall of 1834, after serving as secretary of antislavery groups he organized in Haverhill and Essex counties, he was elected to the Massachusetts House of Representatives. More than ever, he was in the thick of the fight. In September 1835, while traveling with the British abolitionist George Thompson, he was the target of rocks and debris thrown by a New Hampshire mob trying to tar and feather his companion. A few weeks later, it was stones and rotten eggs, pelted by townspeople while he was attending an antislavery meeting in Newburyport.[8]

Early in 1836, Whittier declined an offer to edit a projected newspaper in Philadelphia, citing heart trouble and his desire to devote himself fully to the "struggle now going on between Slavery and Freedom." In May, he resumed the relative quiet of the editor's chair at the *Essex Gazette*. Even here, his forceful abolitionist editorials offended Whig readers and brought about his exile from editorial writing. He had considered buying a half interest in the paper, which had so far paid him only ninety dollars and his expenses, but he thought better of it when word reached him that some Whigs had told the publisher "that he must get rid of me." He resigned at the end of the year, saying he believed his editorials would cost the paper only two or three subscribers in town and few if any out of town and would attract some antislavery readers. In February 1837, he was back at the legislature, this time as a lobbyist for resolutions seeking an end to slavery in the District of Columbia and the right of jury trial for fugitive slaves. In the spring, he was approached about a post editing an abolitionist newspaper in Portland, Maine, but the backers failed to get enough subscribers. That summer, he was appointed one of the secretaries of the American Anti-Slavery Society. He anticipated that this would be a temporary arrangement until he found an opening in Portland or Philadelphia. Working at the organization's New York headquarters, he directed a national petition campaign, drafted abolitionist propaganda and helped edit an abolitionist organ, the *Emancipator*.[9]

On March 15, 1838, his name appeared on the masthead of the *Pennsylvania Freeman*. The Pennsylvania Anti-Slavery Society had bought the Philadelphia weekly from pioneer antislavery publisher Benjamin Lundy, who had called it the *National Enquirer*. The Anti-Slavery Society not only changed its name but, with Whittier at the helm, steered a more aggressive course than the ailing Lundy. In the second issue as the *Freeman* it published the poet's "The Farewell of a Virginia Slave Mother to Her Daughters Sold into Southern Bondage," a tearjerker with the refrain, "Gone, gone—sold and gone, / To the rice-swamp dank and lone." In an editorial, he took a more thoughtful tack, telling his readers: "Were our anti-slavery organizations to cease tomorrow, the anti-slavery FEELING would still live on and gather strength. It bears about with it the indestructible vitality of Truth. It appeals with certainty of success to best emotions and sympathies of our nature. To arrest its progress there must be a change affected in the very elements of the human mind."[10]

In two years as editor of the *Freeman,* Whittier was absent on abolitionist or political business about half the time. His devotion to the cause was soon to be put to an acid test.

Supporters of philanthropic and reform organizations, mostly abolitionists, had raised the then-substantial sum of $43,000 to build three-story white-columned Pennsylvania Hall in Philadelphia, providing an auditorium and office space. Dedication ceremonies in May lasted several days, with an anti-abolition mob of fifteen hundred throwing stones through windows and shouting "hang Whittier." Following his usual custom, Whittier had gone to New York to attend the annual national *Anti-Slavery Society* meeting and had left others in charge of the *Freeman.*[11]

The society was split into feuding factions. Should they pursue their ends through political or other means? How should they deal with those who favored colonization of the slaves? Whittier presented a resolution designed to get them all working together but could not get it passed. Disappointed, he left the convention early. But the discord in New York was nothing to what he found in Philadelphia. The *Freeman* had moved its office into Pennsylvania Hall during his absence, and some of his manuscripts were there. On May 17, the mob broke into the hall and set it afire, using copies of the *Freeman* for kindling. As the building burned, Mayor Daniel Neall refused to call out police. City firemen arrived but aimed their hoses at surrounding structures only. While the flames still raged, Whittier disguised himself as a looter, with a long white coat and a wig, and rescued his prized writings. Moments later, the hall's motto, "Virtue, Liberty and Independence," was effaced, and the roof fell in.[12]

It was not long before Whittier was again an absentee editor, visiting New York and going on to Boston for the New England convention of

John Greenleaf Whittier, author of "Snow-Bound," rushed into this burning building to retrieve papers from the office of the *Pennsylvania Freeman,* of which he was editor. Courtesy of the Historical Society of Pennsylvania.

abolitionists, where he opposed bringing up the issue of votes for women. Many in the abolition ranks opposed even the presence of women at their conventions, telling them, as one writer paraphrased it, that their participation tended to "make the whole matter seem little, and below the attention of men."

William H. Burleigh, a fellow writer of antislavery verse, conducted the *Freeman* until Whittier's return in June. In the August 2, 1838, issue, Whittier denounced the burning of Pennsylvania Hall as the "Base and Contemptible" act of business interests more concerned with economic than moral issues. "The Pennsylvania Hall," he wrote, "was destroyed for the benefit of the Southern trade—a 'business transaction'—a commercial speculation,—the result of mercantile forecast and prudent calculation of profit. SHAME, SHAME upon this vile bartering of humanity for gold! This sacrifice of principle to the sordid and base spirit of gain."[13]

The burning of the hall continued to fester. Colonization supporter R. J. Breckinridge told a gathering of the faction that the hall was built in support of illegal intermarriage between the races. A grand jury was called and received petitions against rebuilding the structure, one probably from Breckinridge. Someone, probably foreman Elliott Cresson, forwarded the petitions to the court with approval, arguing that "the 'peace, tranquility and safety' of the community will be endangered by its reconstruction." Whittier, forced by illness to return to the home he had established in Amesbury, Massachusetts, wrote in a letter to the editor that it might be better to let the charred walls remain "as a monument and a warning." The structure was never rebuilt.[14]

Early in 1839, Whittier's name came up as a potential editor for a new weekly to be called the *Massachusetts Abolitionist*. By April, he felt well enough to return to the *Freeman*. Under the heading "The Editor at His Post," he urged abolitionists to present a united front. Nevertheless, in an editorial a few weeks later, he cautioned against countenancing mob violence, as some in the abolition ranks appeared to be doing. "Let the instigators of mobs beware," Whittier wrote. "What if it should be ascertained that it is as easy to destroy a bank as a Hall of Free Discussion! that deeds of warranty and mortgage are as combustible as anti-slavery papers: that the hoarded heaps of the capitalist are as accessible as the 'incendiary documents' of the Abolitionist?"[15]

Whittier had been too optimistic about his health. At the end of June, he told readers that he must allow his cousin, Moses A. Cartland, to take at least temporary charge of the *Freeman*. By July 25, he was back at his desk praising "the man who, alone and without sympathy, stands firmly up against popular prejudice" while "meeting, wheresoever he turns, an eye of hatred or contempt."[16]

On October 30, an Anti-Slavery Society committee invited Cartland to be the new editor. "The Freeman is now established on the basis of Abolition alone," said Whittier. Cartland declined the position, feeling he wanted to be free to express differing views. Whittier withdrew from the field with a farewell editorial on February 20, 1840, and Charles C. Burleigh, brother of William, became editor. Poe, also working in Philadelphia at the time as editor of the *Gentleman's Magazine*, summed Whittier up shortly after the latter's departure: "Mr. Whittier is a fine versifier so far as strength is regarded independently of modulation. His subjects, too, are usually chosen with the view of affording scope to a certain *vivida vis* of expression which seems to be his forte; but in taste, and especially in *imagination,* which Coleridge has justly styled the *soul* of all poetry, he is ever remarkably deficient. His *themes* are never to our liking."[17]

Although no longer with the *Freeman,* Whittier remained one of its avid readers, welcoming it in the morning "as I would the familiar face of an old friend." In April 1842, after the paper temporarily ceased publication, he lamented the apparent demise of what had seemed to him a weekly "connecting link between me and the Philadelphia abolitionists—recalling one of the pleasantest periods of my life."[18]

In 1841, Whittier helped edit the *Anti-Slavery Reporter,* an organ of the newly formed American and Foreign Anti-Slavery Society, which attempted once again to reconcile the religious and political wings of the abolitionist movement. Still, he said, he could not "depend upon my health for any vigorous exertion." From the sidelines he wrote editor Joshua Leavitt praising the paper for "the kindly and Christian tone of its articles, combined with firmness of principle."[19]

In July 1844, Whittier became editor of the *Middlesex Standard,* an organ of the Liberty Party, which was organized at Albany four years earlier as an abolitionist alternative to the Whigs and the Democrats. The *Standard* failed to bolster the Liberty Party vote, and after the November elections, a coeditor was named in an effort to broaden the paper's appeal beyond antislavery ranks. Whittier, as always devoted to an abolition-only stance, resigned in March 1845. He then helped edit an Amesbury weekly, the *Essex Transcript,* transforming it into an antislavery organ.[20]

The small-town New England editor soon found a wider platform for his views. In 1847, Whittier became corresponding editor for the *National Era,* a weekly published in Washington. For a person whose income had never surpassed five hundred dollars a year, the post was a stroke of good fortune both professionally and financially. In 1847 alone, the *Era* published ninety-three of his prose articles and fifteen poems, and the paper was the main outlet for his writings for a decade.[21]

The only one of Whittier's many antislavery poems to earn a place among American literary classics appeared in May 1850. The poet had long admired Massachusetts senator Daniel Webster and considered him an eloquent ally in the battle against slavery. On March 7, 1850, however, imploring senators to "Hear me for my cause," Webster spoke in support of a compromise, designed to keep the Union intact, that included harsh penalties for helping a slave to escape or interfering with a runaway's recovery. Northern legislators and individual citizens, Webster said, had failed "to perform, fully, their constitutional duties" in regard to the escaped slaves. "In that respect," he said, "it is my judgment that the South is right and the North is wrong." Whittier, in what he later called "one of the saddest moments of my life," read Webster's speech and wrote a "stern and sorrowful rebuke." He called it "Ichabod!" after a passage in the Old Testament book of Samuel in which a newborn child is named I'-cha-bod, the Hebrew for "no glory," because "The glory is departed from Israel" with its defeat by the Philistines, who stole the ark containing the Ten Commandments. The poem appeared in the *National Era* on May 7, 1850.

So fallen! so lost! the light withdrawn
    Which once he wore!
The glory from his gray hairs gone
    Forevermore!

Revile him not—the Tempter hath
    A snare for all;
And pitying tears, nor scorn and wrath,
    Befit his fall!

O, dumb be passion's stormy rage,
    When he who might
Have lighted up and led his age,
    Falls back in night.

Scorn! Would the angels laugh, to mark
    A bright soul driven,
Fiend-goaded, down the endless dark,
    From hope and heaven!

Let not the land once proud of him
      Insult him now,
Nor brand with deeper shame his dim,
      Dishonored brow.

But let its humbled sons, instead,
      From sea to lake,
A long lament, as for the dead,
      In sadness make.

Of all we loved and honored, naught
      Save power remains,—
A fallen angel's pride of thought,
      Still strong in chains.

All else is gone; from those great eyes
      The soul has fled:
When faith is lost, when honor dies,
      The man is dead!

Then pay the reverence of old days
      To his dead fame;
Walk backward, with averted gaze,
      And hide the shame![22]

Whittier the editorialist and Whittier the poet had come together triumphantly, but until his death in 1892, poems of rural life in New England would predominate. A two-volume edition of his poetry, in blue cloth covers with gilt lettering, was issued in 1857 and placed him, by the popular standards of the day, in the pantheon along with Emerson and Longfellow. To the latter, he seemed to have grown "milder and mellower." As for journalism, the *National Era* ceased publication in 1860, but by then Whittier had found a new outlet in the *New York Independent*. After John Brown's raid at Harper's Ferry, he pleaded for an end to violence but placed the blame for it on the South and slavery. In a mawkish poem, he pictured Brown standing at the gallows for his crime whose "bold, blue eye grew tender, and . . . old harsh face grew mild" as he stooped to kiss a black child. In the 1870s, he was still writing for the Amesbury *Villager,* but his fame was nationwide. On his eightieth birthday in 1877, newspapers printed special editions and school children celebrated. The author of "Snow-Bound" and "The Barefoot Boy" had taken the place of the stern antislavery moralist of "Our Countrymen in Chains" in the consciousness of his countrymen.[23]

7 "The Reputation of a Refined Poet"

By the most generous reckoning, Coleridge's off-and-on career in journalism lasted for about twenty-five years. Walt Whitman was an editor in Brooklyn and New York for a decade. Rudyard Kipling was a reporter and editor in India for a little less than seven years. By contrast, William Cullen Bryant was editor-in-chief of the *New York Evening Post* for half a century. Yet the names of Coleridge, Whitman, and Kipling spring to mind, and Bryant's does not, when one thinks of poets who have doubled as journalists.

The reasons are not hard to find. The shelf life of poetry is longer than that of journalism, but time has not been kind to Bryant. "The journalist has been forgotten in the poet," the cultural historian Vernon Louis Parrington said in the 1920s. But as Parrington wrote those words, the poet also was on his way to relative obscurity. As early as the 1840s, a critic in the *Democratic Review* placed Bryant "not in the first, or second, but in the third or fourth rank" among American poets. In 1890, the English writer and parliamentarian Justin McCarthy noted that Bryant's philosophical poem "Thanatopsis" and other works "used to be the delight of many observers." Used to be. In 1888, Whitman told a friend that all of Bryant's late poetry was "poorer than indifferent," and although he admired the poet-editor's earlier work he did so with reservations.[1]

Bryant came to journalism because he needed a job. Raised in Cummington in western Massachusetts, Cullen, as he was known in the family (after a noted Scottish physician, William Cullen), came early to poetry. "Thanatopsis," which drew its title from the Greek for a

102

view or contemplation of death, was begun when he was sixteen or seventeen. It was revised over the years and emerged in its final form in 1815, when the poet was twenty. It was still taught by American teachers in the 1930s and 1940s, when the author of this book was in school, but current fashion disdains the tendentious morality exemplified by its closing lines:

So live that when thy summons comes to join
The innumerable caravan that moves
To that mysterious realm, where each shall take
His chamber in the silent halls of death,
Thou go not, like the quarry slave at night,
Scourged to his dungeon, but, sustained and soothed
By an unfaltering trust, approach thy grave,
Like one who wraps the drapery of his couch
About him, and lies down to pleasant dreams.[2]

Bryant's father, Dr. Peter Bryant, a physician and surgeon who was fond of Alexander Pope and the Roman poet Horace, taught his son to "write only when I had something to say." Poetry, however, would not make him a living. If the field of journalism was considered, it was rejected as not holding enough promise. In the end, he read law in a lawyer's office, was admitted to the Massachusetts bar and practiced in Plainfield and later in Great Barrington.[3]

Poetry was his first love, and five preliminary fragments of "Thanatopsis" were accepted by editor Edward T. Channing for publication in Boston's *North American Review* in September 1817. Bryant also wrote critical articles for the same publication. His work was well received, and in 1821 he was invited to write and deliver the Phi Beta Kappa ode at Harvard's commencement. He was twenty-six years old, and it was the first time he had been to Boston. As he approached the city he marveled at "the rows of lamps along the great western avenue, and beyond them those of the Cambridge and Charleston bridges."[4]

Bryant, increasingly unhappy as a country lawyer, trained his sights on New York City and became editor of the monthly *United States*

Review and Literary Gazette. The promised salary of one thousand dollars a year was twice what he made in law practice. Still, experience indicated that yet another literary magazine might not survive long. "I have given up my profession, which was a shabby business, and I am not altogether certain that I have got into a better," Bryant wrote his friend Richard Henry Dana. Much of his work was reviewing new books, which he found "not the literary employment most to my taste, nor that for which I am best fitted." Nevertheless, with a wife and young daughter, he found the salary "a matter of some consequence."[5]

A runaway horse was the cause of Bryant's switch from monthly journalism to daily journalism, which would be his career, not always to his liking, for the rest of his life. William Coleman, editor of the *Evening Post,* one of New York's leading newspapers, was out for a spin in his buggy when the horse bolted and threw him to the ground. The injured editor needed help putting out the paper and offered Bryant a position as his assistant. Bryant knew the *Post,* as his father had subscribed to it, and accepted the offer at a salary of fifteen dollars a week. He was looking ahead, however. He told his wife, Frances, who was staying in Great Barrington until they found a home in New York, that Coleman and his partner each earned an estimated fifteen thousand dollars a year from the paper. "This is better than poetry and magazines," he wrote. He seemed at first to like the job, telling her, "I have got to be quite famous as the editor of a newspaper since you were here, and some of my friends . . . are quite anxious that I should continue." He enclosed a copy of the newspaper's account of the Columbia College commencement, and marked the paragraphs he had written. One passage showed his care with language, noting that some of the orators at the ceremony seemed not to understand the distinction between "will" and "shall."[6]

Bryant, still working part time for the *Review and Literary Gazette,* wrote to Dana, "I drudge for the Evening Post and labor for the Review, and thus have a pretty busy life of it. I would give up one of these if I could earn my bread by the other, but that I cannot do." Dana cautioned him to avoid the "vile blackguard squabble" of politics, and he responded, "I do not like politics any better than you do; but they get only my morning, and you know politics and a belly-full are better than poetry and starvation." His duties were routine at first, but he seems to have begun fairly early to write the liberal editorials that would make his reputation. The editorials were unsigned, but one of them on February 12, 1827, attacking a bill designed to curb wool imports, seemed to Bryant's biographer, Charles H. Brown, to be "typically Bryantesque." The editorial's writer declared, "The members of Congress wear fine broadcloths, . . . and those among them who support the new tariff have friends among the noisy and hungry manufacturers besieging the doors of Congress whose activity may have some influence on their own popularity at home.—What do these members care for the consumers of cheap woolens? Their own interests are safe, and they will be able to buy fine clothes about as cheap as ever, and their manufacturing friends will get rich and send them again to Congress."[7]

In addition to his accident injuries, Coleman had lost the use of his legs in a series of paralytic strokes in 1819, and his health was further diminished when a minor public official, angered by something the paper wrote about him, beat him severely with a cane. In July 1829, when Coleman suffered another stroke and died, Bryant succeeded him as editor. The man he chose for an assistant, William Leggett, moved to daily journalism, as had Bryant, from a literary review, in Leggett's case the New York weekly *The Critic*. Like Bryant, he wrote poetry, although little of his survived. In other respects, their backgrounds were vastly different. In 1825, when Bryant was nearing the end of his labors as a small town lawyer, Leggett was leading a mutiny against the tyrannous captain of the *U.S. Cayne* in the Mediterranean. He was ordered dismissed but the order was remitted because he had been held so long in jail while awaiting the court-martial. On April 26, 1826, he resigned his midshipman's commission.[8]

As Bryant may have anticipated, Leggett was as fiery in the editorial column as on the quarterdeck, perhaps more so than the editor had anticipated. In 1834, after acquiring a one-quarter interest in the *Evening Post* and taking Leggett into partnership, Bryant left for a two-year sojourn in Europe. The paper had flourished under his editorship. He had purchased a new press that printed twenty copies a minute and expanded the number of columns per page from six to seven. In his absence, Leggett

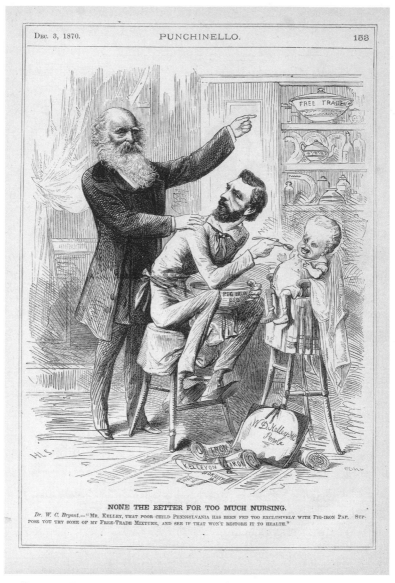

Dec. 3, 1870.　　PUNCHINELLO.　　153

NONE THE BETTER FOR TOO MUCH NURSING.

Dr. W. C. Bryant.—"Mr. Kelley, that poor child Pennsylvania has been fed too exclusively with Pig-Iron Pap. Suppose you try some of my Free-Trade Mixture, and see if that won't restore it to health."

William Cullen Bryant, author of "Thanatopsis," was editor of the *New York Evening Post* for half a century. This December 3, 1870, cartoon from the weekly paper *Punchinello* shows him encouraging free trade. Collection of the New York Historical Society.

antagonized advertisers with vituperative attacks on the U.S. banks, support for the early labor unions, and defense of the free speech rights of abolitionists. Bryant, himself a champion of free speech and free soil but in more refined tones, found on return that the *Post* had suffered financially. While the more temperate Bryant struggled to get the paper back on its feet, the tempestuous Leggett grew more restive. On November 1, 1836, Leggett's partnership was dissolved and he issued a prospectus for a weekly political newspaper, the *Plaindealer,* to be "distinguished by such boldness and directness as the title chosen implies." Bryant saw him off three days later with a handsome editorial praising "his ardour in the cause of truth, his detestation of oppression and unjust restraint in all their forms . . . and the manly, unstudied eloquence which riveted the attention and persuaded the judgment of the reader." On Leggett's death some years later, the poet saluted "His love of truth, too warm, too strong / For Hope or Fear to chain or chill."[9]

Walt Whitman was six years old when Bryant arrived in New York from Massachusetts. By the time Bryant died in 1878, they had known each other for more than thirty years as editors, lovers of long walks, and uneasy admirers of each other's poetry. While Whitman was at the *Brooklyn Eagle,* Bryant "several times came over, middle of afternoons, and we took rambles, miles long, till dark, out towards Bedford or Flatbush." The young Whitman, who was never to leave North America, was entranced with Bryant's "clear accounts of scenes in Europe—the cities, looks, architecture, art."[10]

Even before that, however, Whitman had expressed reservations about Bryant as an editor. In an editorial in the *Aurora* on March 26, 1842, that assessed rival New York newspapers, he wrote: "Perhaps the best paper as regards abstract merit, is the EVENING POST. This daily is unexceptional, what there is of it; but the reputation of a refined poet, and the course that must be pursued in order to make a readable paper, clash with each other. To our mind, and we have not hesitated ever to express the opinion, Bryant is the best poet who writes in the English language. His fame will endure as long as Americans retain a love for the beauty of sentiment or delicacy of style. From what we now say, however, let no one infer that we think the *Post* what a newspaper ought to be; our opinion is very different from that."[11]

Whatever he thought of Bryant's poetry, Whitman seems to have found too much "delicacy of style" and perhaps too much of the poet's beloved Europe in the *Post*'s editorial columns. "Very few really good papers are published in New York," he wrote. "They *cannot* and *do not* come out with that fiery enthusiasm in the cause of truth and liberty—that vigor of advocacy—that energy and boldness and frankness which will ever mark the apostle of the new system—the system which teaches far different doctrine from the rusty, cankered, time-honored, anti-democratic philosophy that looms up in Europe, and is planting its poisonous seeds too widely among us." At the time, the two editors were expressing sharply conflicting views on aid to parochial schools—Bryant calmly pointing out that although the state legislature had acted to permit such aid, he saw no chance that it would ever be disbursed, while Whitman ranted about "dregs of foreign filth" and "refuse of convents." Differences in style also bothered Whitman. He found the *Post* one of the "almost hopeless cases" because of its use of "our" instead of "or" in ending words such as "labor."[12]

About Bryant's poetry, Whitman's judgment wavered. In 1846, he declared that his assessment of his fellow editor as the best poet in the language "smacks so much of exaggeration that we are half a mind to alter it." Six years later, he still ranked Bryant first among the four most prominent American poets of the day—"Bryant, Emerson, Whittier, Longfellow, in that order." By 1888, however, he was saying, "Old men are too apt to insist upon being in the swim after their vitality is departed. It was so with Bryant." He thought Bryant's translation of Homer "damnable . . . so stiff, so bad, it hardly seems anything could be worse." Whitman said that Bryant, for his part, "was afraid of my work: he was interested, but afraid," and told him, "I will admit that you have power—sometimes great power," yet "would never admit that I had chosen the right vehicle of expression." Whitman demurred. "I have often tried to think of myself as writing *Leaves of Grass* in Thanatopsisian verse," he said. "Of course I do not intend this as a criticism of Bryant—only as a demurrer to his objection to me. Thanatopsis is all right in Thanatopsisian verse: I suppose Bryant would fare as badly in *Leaves of Grass* verse as I would fare in Thanatopsis verse."[13]

In 1868, Whitman recalled Bryant telling him he had "'the whole wolf pack' on my heels," and saying, "As you have challenged the whole world I don't suppose you are surprised or resentful when you find the whole world out against you with its hounds." When Justin McCarthy, visiting Bryant in New York, asked him about Whitman, Bryant "shook his head, and professed himself no great believer in Walt Whitman." Naturalist John Burroughs, attending Bryant's funeral with Whitman, got the impression that the friendship of the two was "before Walt wrote poetry—after that Bryant was cold and distant."[14]

Whitman's disdain for Bryant's strength as an editor has not been widely shared. Vernon Louis Parrington, looking back from the standpoint of the 1920s, saw Bryant as a "democrat who spoke for American liberalism" and "for fifty years sat in judgment on matters political and economic as well as cultural, who reflected in the *Evening Post* a refinement of taste and dignity of character before unequaled in American journalism." Bryant was an ardent Jacksonian Democrat who turned into a free-soil Republican and was an early supporter of Lincoln for the new party's presidential nomination. He stood for free speech when an abolitionist press was attacked by a Cincinnati mob and when the Reverend Elijah P. Lovejoy, editor of the antislavery paper *The Observer* was murdered in Alton, Illinois. "The right to discuss freely and openly, by speech, by the pen, by the press, all political questions, and to examine and animadvert upon all political institutions, is a right so clear and certain, so interwoven with our other liberties, so necessary, in fact to their existence, that without it we must fall at once into despotism or anarchy," he wrote.[15]

In Bryant's fifty years with the *Post*, it became one of America's leading newspapers and its editor a leading citizen of New York. "He presided at important civic meetings; and the erect figure of the aged editor-poet, his noble features, and flowing white beard marked a character respected by his fellow-citizens and all Americans," Frank Luther Mott wrote in his classic history of American journalism. By 1870, Bryant was ready to go into semiretirement and pursue the translation of the *Iliad*

and *Odyssey* that drew Whitman's disdain. His son-in-law, Parke God-
win, took over supervision of the paper, assisted by a series of managing
editors. Bryant still plied his oar, however, making sure that the paper
continued to support the Republican party in presidential elections. On
May 29, 1876, he collapsed after speaking at the dedication of a bust of
the Italian liberator Giuseppe Mazzini in Central Park. For weeks, the
Evening Post published regular bulletins on his condition. He died on
June 12. Whitman, visiting with friends at their home on Fifth Avenue,
saw the announcement of Bryant's funeral and "felt a strong desire to
attend." He was not alone. An hour before the funeral, a throng gathered outside the Church of All Souls. Once inside, they filled all the pews
and stood in the aisles, the balcony, and the lobby. Whitman found the
church "dim, even now, at approaching noon" as New Yorkers said
goodbye to "the good, stainless, noble old citizen and poet."[16]

8 "The Exhuming of Buried Reputations"

Park Benjamin was not one of America's great poets, and the several newspapers he edited were not New York's best. They were, however, probably the largest.

The pages of Benjamin's *New World,* on which Whitman worked as a printer in his early days in New York, were sometimes more than four feet long and eleven columns wide. More commonly, they were two feet across and nearly a yard from top to bottom. In heavy black type that could be seen across the street, its masthead proclaimed, "No pent up Utica contracts our powers / But the whole boundless Continent is ours." The *Constellation,* a New York weekly that Benjamin edited late in his career, was advertised as "twice as large as the *New York Ledger.*" One issue measured seventy-two by one hundred inches.[1]

Benjamin, born in British Guiana in 1809 to a sea captain who traded New England cattle, lumber, and flour for sugar, coffee, and rum, contributed poetry as a youth to the *New England Magazine,* a forerunner of the *Atlantic Monthly.* Later, he became its owner and editor. By 1834, he was in New York, serving as an assistant to Horace Greeley at his newly formed weekly the *New-Yorker.* From there, he moved to a partnership with Rufus Griswold at the largely literary weekly *Brother Jonathan* and its daily counterpart, the *New World.*[2]

A major part of Benjamin's journalistic business was the highly competitive trade of pirating English works as soon as they arrived by steamer. Harper & Brothers, the book publishers, were already in the business, sending messengers to board incoming packets and rush the sheets to the print shop, where every compositor was put to work.

111

Peveril of the Peak, one of Sir Walter Scott's popular Waverly novels, was in New York bookstores in a pirated edition twenty-one hours after the ship tied up to the wharf. Not to be outdone, Benjamin hired his own hands to board the ships, worked typesetters night and day, and had the literary works on the streets within twenty-four hours as extra editions of the *New World* and *Brother Jonathan.* Newsboys shouted, "Extry! Dickens' new novel! Only ten cents a copy!" Benjamin told his readers, "You are not so green as to give a dollar for what you can get for eighteen pence or a shilling—not you!"[3]

Benjamin's biographer, Merle Hoover, wrote that he "might have become a poet of distinction if destiny had permitted him to enjoy a life of freedom and leisure." That may be, but, as even the generally admiring Hoover acknowledged, Benjamin never got farther than being a minor poet of "careful workmanship and finish." His work is well represented by a stanza from a poem about a lake he frequented in his youth:

'Twas my delight to sit upon thy shore,
    And hear thy billows breaking at my feet;
Not, like the ocean's, with incessant roar,
    But, like a sea-shell, low-voiced, hushed and sweet[4]

As usual, there were conflicts between the poetry and the journalism. When Benjamin, fresh out of Washington College (later to be Trinity College) became editor of the Norwich Spectator in Connecticut and it failed after ten issues, editor George D. Prentice of the *New England Weekly* observed—inaccurately, as it turned out—that the youth was "altogether too much of a poet to wear the editorial fetter for any great length of time." Walt Whitman, as a fellow New York editor, took a dim view of Benjamin's poetic talents, writing derisively, "sets himself up as a poet!" Whitman declared that the sonnets Benjamin frequently wrote and published in his own pages were, despite being limited to fourteen lines, "proverbially great in the way of sleeping draught." On the other hand Edgar Allan Poe, who, whatever his merits as a poet, was usually a perceptive literary critic, wrote, "As a poet, he is entitled to far higher consideration than that in which he is ordinarily held. He is skilful and passionate, as well as imaginative. His sonnets have not been surpassed. In short, it is as a poet that his better genius is evinced—it is in poetry that his noble spirit breaks forth, showing what the man is, and what, but for unhappy circumstances, he would invariably appear."[5]

One of the unhappy circumstances was a childhood illness that left Benjamin with an atrophied and shrunken leg that may have exacerbated a natural testiness. He seems to have quarreled with practically everyone he worked with. His career took him from magazine to magazine and newspaper to newspaper on the crowded New York scene, and most of his associates found him difficult. Only a few issues into the history of the *New World*, he and his founding partner, Rufus Griswold, parted company. He was caustic not only in personal relations but in the editorial columns, where he was, said Poe, "too frequently biased by personal feelings—feelings now of friendship, and again of vindictiveness." Nevertheless he could be charming when he needed to be, as when gathering New York's rowdy newsboys around him for pep talks, fueling them with hot coffee, and equipping them with placards such as, "We Have Met the Enemy and They Are Ours."[6]

Benjamin's combative style comes out most clearly during the great newspaper war of 1840, in which politicians, clergymen, stockbrokers, and managers of party newspapers joined forces against James Gordon Bennett and his independent *New York Herald*. The clergy didn't like Bennett's irreligion, and the politicians and their allies didn't like the idea of a newspaper being independent of any political party. They all had one objection in common: the *Herald* was far too successful. Benjamin, then editing the *Evening Signal*, had another grievance. Bennett had accused him of plagiarism and referred to his lameness as a "curse by the almighty." He responded by calling the *Herald*'s editor an "instrument of mischief" and a "venal wretch" guilty of "daily lies and libels" as well as "most shocking displays of contempt for the most sacred mysteries of religion." All in all, the war may have helped the *Herald*, which continued to thrive but became more restrained in its news and editorial columns.[7]

In his later years, Benjamin took to the lecture circuit, reading poems on such subjects as "Modern Intellectual and Popular Amusements"; "The

Park Benjamin edited several of New York's largest (in page size) newspapers. Courtesy of Library of Congress.

English Language, How Used and Misused"; "Domestic Life"; and, not surprisingly, "The Press." The poems were, in effect, editorials in verse.[8]

On July 17, 1861, Edmund Clarence Stedman, a twenty-seven-year-old correspondent for the daily *New York World,* rode with the Union army onto the field where the first battle of Manassas would shortly be fought, and wrote to his wife, "I never enjoyed a day so much in my life . . . it was exciting and dramatic beyond measure." The next day, he reached Blackburn's Ford, a strategically important crossing of Bull

Run, where a Union brigade came under Confederate fire and lost eighty
men, and one of its regiments fled in panic. Stedman recorded the experience in his diary: "My first battle. . . . Under fire from beginning to end.
Helped to right the first gun. Came out safe. My telegraphic dispatch
beat the other papers."[9]

The young correspondent's excitement in being at the scene of battle
is reflected in the seventeen exclamation points of a poem he wrote later
and called "Cavalry Song":

Our good steeds snuff the evening air,
    Our pulses with their purpose tingle;
The foeman's fires are twinkling there;
    He leaps to hear our sabres jingle!
       HALT!
Each carbine sends its whizzing ball:
Now, cling! clang! Forward all,
    Into the fight!

Dash on beneath the smoking dome,
    Through level lightnings gallop nearer.
One look to heaven! No thoughts of home:
    The guidons that we bear are dearer.
       CHARGE!
Cling! Clang! Forward all!
Heaven help those whose horses fall!
    Cut left and right!

They flee before our fierce attack!
    They fall, they spread in broken surges!
Now, comrades, bear our wounded back,
    And leave the foeman to the dirges.
       WHEEL!
The bugles sound the swift recall:
Cling! Clang! Backward all!
Home, and good night![10]

A more sober assessment of the battle is found in a dispatch in the *World* for July 24, bylined "FROM OUR SPECIAL CORRESPONDENT," who was Stedman, and datelined "Washington, Monday, July 21."

At 2 o'clock this morning I arrived in Washington, having witnessed the great conflict near Manassas Junction, from beginning to end, and the gigantic rout and panic which broke up the federal army at its close. I stayed near the action an hour or two later than my associates, in order to gather the final incidents of the day, and fully satisfy myself as to the nature and extent of the misfortune.

And now in what order shall I describe the event of yesterday? Even now, how shall one pretend to give a synthetic narration of the whole battle. . . . I only know that at sunset last evening, generals, colonels, and majors were all retiring, devoid of their commands, no more respected or obeyed than the poorest private in the broken ranks. I know that a grand army, retreating before superior numbers, was never more disgracefully or needlessly disrupted and blotted, as it were, out of existence in a single day. This is the truth, and why should it not be recorded?[11]

This time Stedman did not "beat the other papers" by getting his dispatch in first. Uriah Painter of the *Philadelphia Inquirer* was a day ahead of him, getting his story into print on Tuesday, July 23. Stedman's, however, was the more detailed, taking up all of page one and continuing at length inside, with an accompanying dispatch about the battle's aftermath. Stedman told it all, the heroism and the panic, from the "thousands of comrades in arms going forward to lay down their lives in a common cause" to the "colonels, captains, lieutenants, and even generals" who "spent their time at the hotels and in other public places" after the battle. Although his editor had been after him to send "livelier letters with news that never got through by telegraph," his account of First Manassas was so popular with readers that it was published in pamphlet form with a note saying it was "not so bad for a greenhorn of twenty-seven."[12]

Stedman, born in Hartford, Connecticut, in 1833, began writing poetry at an early age and while at Yale won the sophomore prize in English composition for a long poem, "Westminster Abbey." Shortly afterward, he was expelled for rowdy behavior and neglect of his studies. He was interested enough in journalism to ask Horace Greeley, during a trip to New York, if there were any openings on the *Tribune*. Greeley said there were not. The ex-student then bought a half share in a Norwich, Connecticut, weekly, also called the *Tribune,* and became its editor. The paper failed to make headway and closed in June, 1853. At age twenty, Stedman became copublisher of the *Mountain County Herald* in Winstead, Connecticut. By 1854, he was gaining modest recognition as a poet, placing "Amavi," a poem in the style of Tennyson, in *Putnam's Monthly.* Work on a provincial newspaper began to pall, and he decided to divide his time between business and literature in New York.[13]

Explaining his decision to his mother, Stedman wrote:

Why did I leave off editing? Because, as I told you, there were five days of small business, and one day of editing. . . . I did not like the reputation of being "E. C. Stedman, Esq., the talented young editor of the *Bungtown Gazette*"—a reputation fast spreading. The man who has the reputation of a *good second rate actor* can never touch the Audience like a "Star" even if he play *as well.* . . . And so I found that money-grabbing was the principal part of country editing, and not a moment's time for heavy writing. I thought I might as well be at something that would give me a little time to write for myself, study, etc., and so came to New York to do *business* eight hours a day, I thought, instead of twelve, and have my evenings to cultivate higher "literary associations" than editing a country paper never so well could procure for me.[14]

Stedman had his eye on being a "Star" in the literary firmament. Unlike many poets, however, he had talent for business. He managed a clock store until its warehouse burned down and then became a real estate agent and broker. He didn't like that any better than being a country editor. "I growl at business because I have a *right* to—being now a businessman and doing as well as any of them, at their dirty, sordid, but alas! alas! alas!—sadly necessary pursuit. . . . If I can bring any genius to bear, and do it more quickly and genteely [*sic*] than others, why, so much the better, and then good-bye to it forever."

The end, at least temporarily, came sooner and differently than he thought. In the brokerage business, 1858 was a bad year, and Stedman found himself back in the newspaper world. He placed a series of satirical verses, for which he was not paid, in the *Tribune* and was offered a position on the staff. At last, he was in the newsroom he had angled to break into as an expelled student.[15]

His duties ranged from covering an execution in New Jersey, an assignment he described as "shameful," to sitting in for the city editor. To supplement his scanty earnings, he served as a correspondent for Chicago papers. In April 1860, his first collection of poems was published by Charles P. Scribner, and *Harper's Monthly* acclaimed it as "the promise of a brilliant future." On July 16, 1860, he was made editor of the *Tribune*'s weekly edition, and three weeks later he went to work as day editor at the *World* for twenty-five dollars a week.[16]

As a published poet and a rising journalist, Stedman became an occasional customer at Pfaff's Cave, a popular cellar restaurant in Manhattan, where he shared a large table against the far wall that was reserved for the literary set.[17]

The outbreak of the Civil War also brought Stedman to Washington. Eager to be close to the action, he took a night train from New York to the capital on April 14, 1861. Two weeks later he was recalled to New York to step in for an overworked editor. He did not stay long. On May 24, Union troops crossed the Potomac River and occupied Alexandria, Virginia. When twenty-four-year-old Elmer Ellsworth, a Chicago patent attorney serving as a colonel, saw a Confederate flag flying from the Marshall House hotel, he climbed to the roof and cut it down. The hotel proprietor, Donald Jackson, killed Ellsworth with a shotgun blast and was himself killed by Ellsworth's men. The Union had its first hero, and Stedman was on his way to Washington to cover a state burial with President Lincoln as chief mourner.[18]

Edmund Clarence Stedman was an
American banker and a successful
Wall Street broker. He was also one
of the leading poets of his time.
Courtesy of Library of Congress.

Although he secured a position as a Justice Department pardon
clerk and resigned from the *World* because of its pro-southern editorial
policy, he continued to serve as a *World* correspondent with the
approval of the paper's editor, Manton Marble, and of attorney general
Edward Bates. He covered General George B. McClellan's peninsula
campaign and the Battle of Ball's Bluff, and accompanied General Nathaniel
P. Banks on a foray up the Potomac in the vain hope that he
would cross the river into Virginia.[19]

Stedman was not the only poet to enter the lists as a war correspondent.
Epes Sargent, who combined verse writing with editing the *Boston
Evening Transcript,* had a go at it. In the South, Henry Timrod, known
at times as "The Laureate of the Confederacy," covered the Confederate
retreat from Shiloh for the *Charleston Mercury,* but "staggered homeward,
half-blinded, bewildered, with a dull mist before his eyes, and a
shuddering horror at heart." Timrod suffered from tuberculosis, and a
friend, Rachel Lyons, felt that the hardships of a correspondent's life
"told heavily on his sensitive soul and delicate frame."[20]

In September 1863, Stedman went to work for a banking firm, Samuel Hallett and Company, and decided he would return to journalism only as a last resort. In that year, he turned down offers of editorships in Louisville and Pittsburgh. From then on he devoted himself to business and poetry, earning a reputation not only as a poet but as a critic and anthologist. Poe, Whitman, and Ralph Waldo Emerson, he said, were "those of our poets from whom the old world has most to learn." In an anthology of American poetry, he devoted thirteen pages to Whitman, more than to any other poet.[21]

In his three-volume work *Main Currents in American Thought,* Vernon Louis Parrington found room for Benjamin and Stedman along with Whitman and Poe. "I have not wished to evaluate reputations or weigh literary merits," Parrington wrote, "but rather to understand what our fathers thought, and why they wrote as they did. . . . The exhuming of buried reputations and the revivifying of dead causes is the familiar business of the historian, in whose eyes forgotten men may assume as great significance as others with whom posterity has dealt more generously."[22]

When Emerson edited a poetry anthology, *Parnassus,* in 1875, he included Edmund Clarence Stedman. He did not include Walt Whitman.

9 "Every Quality That Made Reporting a Misery"

As a journalist, Stephen Crane was described by a colleague as a young man who hated to ask questions, wrote too slowly, and in general seemed poorly equipped for the job.[1] Not much of a recommendation.

On the other hand Richard Harding Davis, one of the flotilla of correspondents who covered the Spanish-American War, said that Crane "would seem to have distinctly won the first place" among them. Although the flamboyant Davis later said that he didn't really like the diffident Crane, he wrote just after the war that the novelist turned reporter was preeminent in "his power to make the public see what he sees." Crane himself said that although he was thankful for his great success with *The Red Badge of Courage,* "I am much fonder of my little book of poems." As the author of a classic novel about a war that ended six years before he was born, as the war correspondent whose compassion for soldiers in the ranks invites comparison with the Second World War's Ernie Pyle, and as the poet who wrote that "war is kind," or that it is not, Stephen Crane deserves attention.[2]

Like Coleridge and Hunt, Crane was the son of a clergyman. His father, The Reverend Doctor Jonathan Townley Crane, held Methodist pastorates in Newark, where Crane was born in 1871, and later in Port Jervis, just across the New Jersey border into New York. The youth was introduced to journalism at the age of sixteen, when he went to Asbury Park on the Jersey shore as a summertime correspondent for his older brother, Townley, whose diligence as shore correspondent of the *New York Tribune* had got him nicknamed "The Shore Fiend." Young Crane covered such events as a baby parade, a tennis tournament, and meetings of the Seaside Assembly, an educational gathering on Chautauqua lines in adjacent Avon-by-the Sea. After three summers, his brother got him a job as Syracuse correspondent for the *Tribune,* and he enrolled briefly at Syracuse University. Here, a fraternity brother noticed his extraordinarily readable penmanship in an essay he had written. Crane replied that he had taken care with his handwriting ever since learning that typesetters' pay depended on how rapidly they could read, and thereby compose from, a reporter's copy. Others, too, would note how legibly Crane wrote.[3]

By 1892, he had gone to New York seeking a literary career but temporarily gave it up to work for his brother again. Crane's mother, a devotee of camp meetings after her husband's death, had religiously covered activities in Ocean Grove, just south of Asbury Park, which called itself "The Summer Mecca of American Methodists," for the *Tribune* and the *Philadelphia Press.* Her son, never much of a hand at just-the-news reporting, took a less pious approach, telling the *Tribune*'s readers, "The somber-hued gentlemen who congregate at this place in summer are arriving in solemn procession, with black valises in their hands and rebukes to frivolity in their eyes." Describing a member of a visiting troupe of entertainers, the young reporter wrote, "he, or she, wore orange stockings, with a bunch of muscle in the calf. The rest of his, or her, apparel was a chromatic delirium of red, black, green, pink, blue, yellow, purple, white, and other shades and colors not known." A report on a troubled carnival told how "residents of Ocean Grove came and said that the steam organ disturbed their pious meditations on the evils of the world," leading to the organ's suppression by the police. Of a founder of Asbury Park, he wrote, "It warms his heart to see the thousands of people tramping over his boards, helter-skeltering in his sand and diving into that ocean of the Lord's which is adjacent to the beach of James A. Bradley."[4]

This kind of writing drew some criticism from *Tribune* editors, but it was a story that appeared in the paper on August 21 that really got Crane into trouble. Members of the Junior Order of United American Mechanics of New Jersey had held their annual "American Day" parade at Asbury Park. Crane described the parade as "probably the most awkward, ungainly, uncut and uncarved procession that ever raised cloud of dust on sun-beaten streets" and "an assemblage of the spraddle-legged men of the middle class." This was, in Kipling's phrase, "something more than ordinary journalistic prose," and it hit the *Tribune* at a bad time. The newspaper's editor and owner, Whitelaw Reid, was the Republican candidate for vice president in a presidential election to be held in less than three months. Rival newspapers described the story as an insult to the American working man, a member of the Junior Order denounced it in a letter to the editor as "uncalled-for and un-American," and the newspaper said editorially that it contained "sentiments both foreign and repugnant to The Tribune." Everybody tried to avoid responsibility. Townley Crane said he was at a funeral. Willis Johnson, the editor who let the story slip by, said he was preoccupied by a flood of news and distracted by remodeling work in the newsroom. Johnson, a friend of the Crane family, advised Stephen that "ordinary news reporting was not a good place for subtle rhetorical devices"—a bit of advice that Crane seems to have ignored. In the end, the affray probably had little to do with the fact that the ticket of Benjamin Harrison and Whitelaw Reid was defeated in November and Grover Cleveland became president.[5]

An unbiased reading of Crane's story suggests that the solid citizens of Asbury Park may have had more to complain about than the visiting mechanics. For all his amusement at their lack of parade-ground skills, Crane said, "The visitors were men who possessed principles," in contrast to the "bona fide Asbury Parker (who) is a man to whom a dollar, when held up to the eye, often shuts out any impression he may have had that other people possess rights." Besides, the mechanics' "hands were bent and shoulders stooped from delving and constructing," whereas "Asbury Park creates nothing. It does not make; it merely amuses."[6]

Although some accounts suggest that Stephen's employment simply terminated with the end of the summer season at the beach, it appears that both Cranes lost their jobs. Author Hamlin Garland, who had become friendly with Stephen, said the young reporter came to him and said, "Well, I've got the bounce." Garland read what Crane had written and asked, "What did you expect . . . a medal?" Townley was fired by mail.[7]

Back in New York, Crane was finding that "of all human lots for a person of sensibility, that of an obscure free lance in literature or journalism is, I think, the most discouraging." On the side, he started writing what he at first referred to as "lines" and later called poetry. The work reminded Garland of Emily Dickinson, some of whose poems Crane had heard William Dean Howells read during a visit to the elder writer's home for tea. Garland encouraged Crane and wanted to get a leading New York publisher for his work, but the critic John D. Barry was also impressed and sent the collection to an avant-garde house in Boston, Copeland & Day. At last, publication of *The Black Riders and Other Lines* was announced on May 11, 1895.[8]

A month later Crane, recuperating in Port Jervis from a bout of the digestive trouble that plagued him throughout his short life, had heard that the book was "making some stir." By November 10, the poet was feted at a dinner given at a Buffalo hotel by the Society of the Philistines, founded by the essayist and publisher Elbert Hubbard. The following May, Hubbard's *Roycroft Quarterly* published seven new poems by Crane, including the graceful "I have heard the sunset song of the birches." In the same issue there was a jibe by fellow newspaperman Arthur Lucas expressing "profound admiration for a man who, casting to the winds rhyme, reason, and metre, can still write poetry." Crane was "getting very ably laughed at," as he recalled later when he found himself reading "long extracts from English newspapers" with favorable reviews and "for the first time in my life I began to be afraid—afraid that I would grow content with myself."[9]

The poems were indeed unconventional for an era in which Stedman could outrank Whitman. The title poem of *The Black Riders* read in its entirety:

> Black riders came from the sea.
> There was clang and clang of spear and shield,
> And clash and clash of hoof and heel,
> Wild shouts and the wave of hair

In the rush upon the wind:
Thus the ride of sin.

Still to come, after the writer of *The Red Badge of Courage* had seen
war at firsthand, were the lines:

Do not weep, maiden, for war is kind.
Because your lover threw wild hands toward the sky
And the affrighted steed ran on alone,
Do not weep.
War is kind.

Hoarse, booming drums of the regiment,
Little souls who thirst for fight,
These men were born to drill and die.
The unexplained glory flies above them.
Great is the battle-god, great, and his kingdom—
A field where a thousand corpses lie.

Do not weep, babe, for war is kind.
Because your father tumbled in the yellow trenches,
Raged at his breast, gulped and died,
Do not weep.
War is kind.

Swift, blazing flag of the regiment,
Eagle with crest of red and gold,
These men were born to drill and die.
Point for them the virtue of slaughter,
Make plain to them the excellence of killing
And a field where a thousand corpses lie.

Mother whose heart hung humble as a button
On the bright splendid shroud of your son,
Do not weep.
War is kind.

The irony that bedeviled Crane as a reporter was serving him well in his "lines."[10]

Meanwhile Crane haunted what was then New York's newspaper row, the offices of the *Tribune, Times, Sun* and *World* in a seedy neighborhood not far from the brothels and dance halls of the Bowery. In an unsigned article in the *Tribune* on June 10, 1892, he wrote of how the red-haired driver of a broken-down Bowery van, engaged in a sort of competitive road rage with the van's conductor, "began to yell, and ki-yi, and whoop harder than the worst personal devil encountered by the sternest of Scotch Presbyterians ever yelled and ki-yied and whooped on the darkest night after the good man had drunk the most hot Scotch whiskey." It was the first of many such sketches of the underside of what have been called the Gay Nineties. In 1894, Garland called them to the attention of magazine publisher S. S. McClure, who assigned Crane to visit a coal mine in Scranton, Pennsylvania. At the mine, Crane heard of a recent accident that occurred during a visit by a party of coal-brokers. In telling the story, he concluded: "I confess to a dark and sinful glee at the description of their pangs; a delight in for once finding coal-brokers associated in hardship and danger with the coal miner. It seemed to me a partial and obscure vengeance. And yet this is not to say that they were not all completely virtuous and immaculate coal-brokers! If all men who stand uselessly and for their extraordinary profit between the miner and the consumer were annually doomed to a certain period of danger and darkness in the mines, they might at last comprehend the bitterness and misery of men who toil for existence at these hopelessly grim tasks."

Despite Crane's emphatic qualification, the editors at *McClure's* thought this was too hard on big business. When Crane saw the edited version of his article, he said, "The birds didn't want the truth after all." The passage did not appear in print until a memoir by artist Linson K. Corwin, who illustrated the piece and to whom Crane gave his manuscript, was published in 1958. The reporter's experience may well have been in the poet's mind when he wrote that "A newspaper is a collection of half-injustices / Which, bawled by boys from mile to mile, / Spreads its curious opinion / To a million merciful and sneering men." There is ambiguity here. The cynicism is tempered; the injustices are only half unjust and the readers are sneering yet merciful. The same ambiguity is seen only a few lines later: "A newspaper is a court / Where everyone is kindly and unfairly tried / By a squalor of honest men." Crane found his newspaper colleagues both kind and unfair, both squalid and honest. Lazer Ziff, in his history of 1890s America, reached the same conclusion, saying the newspaperman's "daily life was conducted in an atmosphere in which semi-truths were consciously or unconsciously constructed and whole truths were systematically suppressed by men who sympathized with the victims of this injustice."[11]

One of Crane's New York sketches was a gripping account in the *New York Press* of November 25, 1894, of a fire in a tenement, complete with a policeman dashing into the flames in a vain effort to rescue a hysterical mother's baby. The only trouble is that the fire never took place. It was fabricated by Crane. This was a practice apparently tolerated in journalism more readily than it would be a century later. In 1981, Janet Cooke of the *Washington Post* had her Pulitzer Prize taken away and lost her job for fabricating an account of an eight-year-old heroin addict; the Sunday editor of the *Press*, Edward Marshall, called Crane's story "one of the best things that he or any other man ever did." Crane's account of the spread of the flames is indeed both a vivid example of nineteenth-century newspaper writing and a sample of the skills that served him in his naturalistic fiction and poetry.

> The blaze had increased with a frightful vehemence and swiftness.
>
> Unconsciously, at times, the crowd dully moaned, their eyes fascinated by this exhibition of the strength of nature, their master after all, that ate them and their devices at will whenever it chose to fling down their little restrictions. The flames changed in color from crimson to lurid orange as glass was shattered by the heat, and fell crackling to the pavement.

Some lines in Crane's *Black Riders*, published a year later but probably written earlier, depict fire in similar language but with different insights:

There was a man who lived a life of fire.
Even upon the fabric of time,
Where purple becomes orange
And orange purple,
This life glowed,
A dire red stain, indelible;
Yet when he was dead,
He saw that he had not lived.[12]

As early as August 25, 1892, Crane was contemplating a writing trip into the West and South, partly to get rid of a persistent cough, and tried to sell the American Press Association on the idea. It would be January 1895, however, before he left on the trip, commissioned by the Bacheller Syndicate, which had serialized *The Red Badge* in truncated form. By then, Mexico was added to the itinerary. But Crane's first stop was Nebraska, which had been buffeted by a summer of drought, a winter of devastating blizzards, and scandals over greed and corruption in distribution centers. The *Lincoln State Journal* greeted him with the words, "Mr. Crane's papers have asked him to get the truth, whether his articles are sensational or not, and for that reason his investigation will doubtless be welcomed by the business interests of Nebraska."[13]

From the capital, Crane traveled two hundred miles to the small north central Nebraska town of Eddyville, "in the heart of the stricken territory," and hired a wagon driver to take him forty-five miles through the country during a storm that coated the team of horses with snow and ice. His story was written in a bedroom where the temperature was one and a half degrees below zero. Outside, it was eighteen below. The story was datelined "Eddyville, Dawson Co., Neb., Feb 22."

The vast prairies in this section of Nebraska contain a people who are engaged in a bitter and deadly fight for existence. . . .

The cry for aid was heard everywhere. The people of a dozen states responded in a lavish way and almost at once. A relief commission was appointed by Gov. Holcomb at Lincoln to receive the supplies and distribute them to the people in want.

The railroad companies granted transportation to the cars that came in loaded with coal and flour from Iowa and Minnesota, fruit from California, groceries and clothing from New York and Ohio, and almost everything possible from Georgia and Louisiana. The relief commission became involved in a mighty tangle. It was obliged to contend with enormous difficulties. . . .

Meanwhile, a certain minority began to make war upon the commission at the expense of the honest and needy majority. Men resorted to all manner of tricks in order to seduce the commission into giving them supplies which they did not need. Also various unscrupulous persons received donations of provision from the East and then sold them to the people—at a very low rate it is true, but certainly at the most obvious of profits. . . . The commission was obliged to make long wars upon all these men who wished to practice upon the misery of the farmers. . . .

. . . there is now looming the great catastrophe that would surely depopulate the country. These besieged farmers are battling with their condition with an eye to the rest and success of next August. But if they can procure no money with which to buy seed when spring comes around, the calamity that ensues is an eternal one, as far as they and their farms here are concerned. They have no resort then but to load their families in wagons behind their hungry horses and set out to conquer these great distances, which like walls shut them from the charitable care of other and more fortunate communities. In the meantime, they depend upon their endurance. . . .

It was the best journalism Stephen Crane ever did.[14]

Back in Lincoln, he spent several days waiting for the payment that the syndicate had told him it would send. An hour before midnight of the day before he left, he showed up at the *State Journal* office while Willa Cather, a University of Nebraska junior working part time for the *Journal,* was writing her review of a play. Crane's money still had not come, and he was "out of sorts and deeply despondent." Like many others, the future novelist was unimpressed with the personal appearance of the gaunt, unshaven, and shabbily dressed writer. In fact, she thought he looked more disreputable than tramp printers she had seen "come up the *Journal* stairs to hunt a job." But she had read and admired the syndicated *Red Badge,* and Crane was the first author she had met. He did little to encourage her literary ambitions. Sitting on the ledge of a window that had been opened because of the oppressively warm night, "Crane began to talk, began to curse his trade from the first throb of creative desire in a boy to the finished work of a master." After reading her some lines from *The Black Riders,* he spoke of his "double literary life; writing in the first place the matter that pleased himself, and doing it very slowly; in the second place, any sort of stuff that would sell."[15]

From Lincoln, Crane proceeded to Hot Springs, Arkansas, to New Orleans at Mardi Gras, to Texas, and over the border to Mexico. He seems to have been still suffering from the depression Cather detected in Lincoln. The western experiences planted the seeds that grew into two great short stories, "The Bride Comes to Yellow Sky" and "The Blue Hotel," but nothing he wrote at the time matched the vigor of "Nebraska's Bitter Fight for Life." On March 12, from a San Antonio hotel room, he wrote to a friend, "I would tell you many strange things I have seen if I was not so bored with writing of them in various articles."[16]

Crane may have cheered up when he reached New York. Publication of *The Red Badge of Courage* in book form in 1895 was his first big break, and made him something of a celebrity at the Sign o' the Lanthorne, a sort of press club on Williams Street. He frequently came to lunch, climbing a hanging iron ladder to the flat of a hardware merchant's stable yard and entering a door with an old ship's lantern hanging from a wrought iron bracket. He whiled away time chain smoking and playing poker with the likes of Richard Harding Davis and Irving Bacheller, proprietor of the Bacheller Syndicate. On Saturday nights, the members held literary banquets, sitting on mahogany window seats and lounges upholstered in red leather while members read stories for criticism by the light of lanterns of various designs. Crane got some ribbing about his odd poems, but it came from friends. They wanted him to write a story with a reporter as a hero, but he declined. Once, Mark Twain showed up for lunch. It was, said Garland, "a bit of Colonial New York which had perilously survived."[17]

Late in 1895, American news organizations sent reporters to Cuba to cover a revolt against Spanish rule that was being led by José Martí. Crane joined them late in November, representing Bacheller. The trouble was that, after they reached Florida, it was hard to get to Cuba because of a U.S. naval blockade. Some gun-runners got through, taking arms to the rebels, but reporters languished in Jacksonville. Crane struck up a love affair with Cora Stewart, the proprietor of a thinly disguised brothel. She would later be known as Mrs. Crane, although they did not marry. Cora was still married to an English colonialist in Africa who for religious reasons would not agree to a divorce. Finally, Crane secured passage on one of the gun-running ships, the *Commodore*. On the night of January 12, he was seated half asleep in the pilot house when the chief engineer dashed up the stairs to tell Captain Edward Murphy that something was very wrong in the engine room. Crane was quickly commandeered to go there and help bail with buckets, and overheard talk about pumps being out of order. Overcome by the heat, he went back up on deck, where he heard the order to lower lifeboats.[18]

Crane ended up in a ten-foot dingy with the captain, a cook, and an oiler named Billy Higgins, whom he had met in the engine room. The four watched in silence as the *Commodore* lurched to one side, then the other, and then sank, swamping rafts that other men clung to. In his dispatch to the syndicate, Crane telescoped the fifteen-mile crossing to the shore into two paragraphs, ending as the boat capsized in the surf at Daytona and the three survivors "saw Billy Higgins lying with his forehead on sand that was clear of the water, and he was dead." The rest of the thirty-hour ordeal he saved for his short story "The Open Boat," beginning with four men so intent on the giant waves they faced that "none of them knew the color of the sky" and ending as "the wind brought the sound of the great sea's voice to the men on shore, and they felt that they could then be interpreters." Crane got a ride back to Jacksonville on a navy tug, the *Three Friends*, and returned to New York after failing to find another way to reach Cuba.[19]

It was an era when newspapers, not for the last time, hired celebrities to boost circulation. One of the novelist's journalistic colleagues, Charles Michelson, said of him: "He hated to ask questions, got no glow of adventure in landing a news story, resented the importance of policemen, and was insulted at the ruthlessness of copy readers, who slew his words under the necessity of getting a painfully written column into two inches at press-time. His writing pace was slow from a newspaper standpoint, and a copy boy at his elbow on the deadline infuriated him. In short, he had every quality that made reporting a misery."[20]

Nevertheless, the author of *The Red Badge* was a catch. Samuel S. Chamberlain, managing editor of William Randolph Hearst's *New York Journal,* signed him up to cover Greece's impending war for the independence of the Greek island of Crete from Turkish rule. Crane persuaded Chamberlain to send Cora along with him as a fellow correspondent. She filed dispatches from the field, revised and possibly dictated by Crane. Independently, Crane obtained a contract with the McClure syndicate, which served other American newspapers and London's *Westminster Gazette.* "I have changed all my plans and am going to Crete," he said.[21]

In London en route to Greece, Crane encountered Richard Harding Davis, who like him was a novelist as well as a correspondent. Davis was much more in the Victorian vein, and Crane had previously described him as having "the intelligence of the average saw-log." The meeting, however, went well. Davis was host at a luncheon in Crane's honor at the Savoy, attended by James Barrie, the author of *Peter Pan,* and other popular writers of the day. The next day the two correspondents crossed the English Channel together. Davis avoided meeting Cora, describing her as "a bi-roxide blonde who seemed to be attending to his luggage for him."[22]

Once in Greece, Crane first saw action with the Greek army in Epirus. In a dispatch after returning to Athens, he said that practically every man in the Greek capital "is arming to go and fight the Turks." Five times in the dispatch, he referred to himself with the personal pronoun "I." The *Journal* ran it on the front page along with other dispatches from Greece, including one by "Imogen Carter," the pen name of Cora,

Stephen Crane was hired to cover the Spanish-American
War, largely on the strength of his success with his Civil
War novel *The Red Badge of Courage*. Here he is at
work on the Navy tug *Three Friends*, on which he trav-
eled to and from Cuba. Photograph by Frances Cabane
Scovel Saportas, 1898.

relating her problems in getting to the front as a female correspondent.
Greek troops under the inexperienced Crown Prince Constantine were
soon in retreat, but achieved a short-lived victory at the village of Velestino. Crane traveled to Velestino with Davis and other correspondents
but, like most of the others, assumed that the Turks would not return. He
and Cora found accommodations in Volos, a small seaport town twelve

miles west of Velestino. As a result, Davis and John Bass, the chief *Journal* correspondent, were the only American reporters on the scene as the battle opened on May 4. Crane arrived the next day, as the poorly officered Greek troops were in full retreat. As Davis told it, "Crane came up for fifteen minutes and wrote a 1300 word story on that. He was never near the front but don't say I said so. He would have come but he had a toothache which kept him in bed." Actually, Crane was suffering from the dysentery to which he was subject. Davis believed it was the presence of Cora that really kept him from the battle. In his dispatch, filed from Volos on May 10, Crane blamed the defeat on "reverses or something of the sort in other places." He had missed the crucial battle of the brief war. "Willie Hearst has made a bad bargain," he wrote.[23]

In sharp contrast to the irony of his later "War Is Kind," Crane described the roar of musketry at Velestino as "the most beautiful sound of my experience, barring no symphony," while conceding that another point of view "might be taken from the men who died there." "From a distance it was like a game," he wrote. "There was no blood, no expression, no horror to be seen." The dispatch prompted a parody in the *New York Tribune* of eight days later:

> I have seen a battle.
> I find it is very like what
> I wrote up before.
> I congratulate myself that
> I ever saw a battle.
> I am pleased with the sound of war.
> I think it is beautiful.
> I thought it would be.
> I am sure of my nose for battle.
> I did not see any war correspondents while
> I was watching the battle except
> I.[24]

After Greece, there was an interval in England, where a friend gave Stephen and Cora the use of an Elizabethan manor house in Surrey.

Cora fondly described Stephen as "the squire at Brede Place," playing host frequently to "some poor-in-luck-or-health chap." Joseph Conrad, whom he met at the time, took a dimmer view: "I didn't visit them often. They were always surrounded by a gang of near-authors and grafters from London." The ailing Crane had grown a beard, but his eyes, Conrad recalled after the American writer's death, were "the eyes of a poet."[25]

The English idyll was interrupted on the night of February 15, 1898, when the American battleship *Maine* was blown up in Havana harbor. Two days later, word spread that the Americans suspected foul play. Two months later, Congress passed a war resolution and President William McKinley signed it.

Crane had sailed for New York in April, leaving behind an anxious Cora, who wrote a newspaper acquaintance that Stephen was to be "a correspondent in the U.S. Spain row." After all, said Crane, this war would be fought in English. Besides, he wanted to write a book about it. While he was at sea, the *New York World* cabled an offer for his services. Arriving in New York, he tried to enlist in the navy, was rejected because of his health, and accepted the newspaper's offer.[26]

In May, he was again aboard the tug *Three Friends,* which was continuing the navy's blockade of the Cuban coast. Fellow correspondent Frank Norris observed him "wearing a pair of duck trousers grimed and fouled with all manner of pitch and grease and oil," using a suitcase on his lap as a desk and holding a bottle of beer between his feet to keep the rolling boat from spilling it. This time, he was not late for the fighting, going ashore with the marines to cover their amphibious landing at Guantanamo in early June and witnessing at least one skirmish between Theodore Roosevelt's Rough Riders and Spanish troops. In Greece, he had celebrated the beauty of war; in "War Is Kind," he would evoke the tragedy of it; in Cuba he mostly observed men working hard at boring tasks, "all that digging and smoothing which gains no encrusted medals." "The infamous pettiness of it all!" he exclaimed. It did not last long. By August, he was back in New York.[27]

Staff correspondents covering the war saw a distinct difference between themselves and those, like Crane and John Fox, author of *The*

Trail of the Lonesome Pine, who were recruited for their literary fame. The "trained seals," said Davis, were "interested in what was most dramatic and picturesque," such as the image of Roosevelt's Rough Riders singing "Fair Harvard" in the rifle pits. Staff men, on the other hand, saw it as their job "to treat the whole campaign as a series of events, to describe it as they would a political convention. . . . The last words of a dying soldier were not important to them. His name, spelled correctly, and the letter of his troop, were to their employers of the highest value."[28]

For the Puerto Rican campaign that was the last phase of the Spanish-American War, Crane left the *World* and reported for the *Journal.* Charles Michelson's description of him, during a tugboat crossing from Pensacola to Ponce on the island's southern coast, makes clear the perilous condition of his health. He "looked like a frayed white ribbon," wrote Michelson, with "once square shoulders crowded forward by the concavity of a collapsed chest."[29]

When the brief campaign was over and they were headed home, Michelson noted that at no time "on the long, comfortable, easy voyage back to New York did anybody see Stephen make a note. Perhaps nothing differentiated his way from the newspaper way of recording impressions so clearly as this." Crane, he said, was working in his mind on "Wounds in the Rain," the volume of short stories he would write. "The plots, even the words, cropped out in . . . desultory conversations."[30]

The book was published in 1900. Crane, who had returned to England, died on June 5 of that year in a tuberculosis sanitarium in Germany.

10 "It Is Only Ignorance Which Is Boredom"

Christopher Grieve's parents, like Whittier's, found a boy on their hands who seemed more interested in poetry than in anything else. Like Whittier's also, they feared he would never make any money at it. Christopher didn't let it bother him. As Hugh MacDiarmid, he did not become rich, but in the eyes of his admirers he fulfilled his boyhood conviction "that I was going to be a famous poet."[1]

MacDiarmid, to use the pen name he adopted early in his long life, was born August 11, 1892, in the village of Langholm in Scotland's Borders region, about five miles from the boundary of England, the country with which he would wage lifelong literary war, "For I am not an Englishman, but utterly different / And I throw Scotland's challenge at the English again." The villagers and the country people around them spoke broad Scots, the language in which MacDiarmid would write much of his poetry, buttressing it with what the twenty-first-century Scottish poet Robert Crawford called his "trolling of dusty Scots dictionaries." MacDiarmid himself spoke of his "delight in Scots words, finding them in the dictionary."[2]

His father was the local postmaster, and they lived in one of a cluster of buildings that housed the post office. Upstairs was the Langholm Library, with more than twelve thousand books. "I had constant access to it, and used to fill a big washing-basket with books and bring it downstairs," MacDiarmid recalled in his memoirs. Despite the "religiosity, the puritanism" against which he rebelled, his parents did not interfere with his reading, whether it was Sir Walter Scott or Emma Lazarus. By the time he was fourteen, he said, he could go up those stairs at night

and find any book he wanted to in the dark. Out in the countryside were
pleasures he recalled years later and turned into a tribute to a fellow
Scottish Nationalist who had served as a Communist member of Parliament and "one of the finest MPs I have known in my lifetime":

> . . . I remember as a boy
> Searching a wide Borders moor, acres of purple heather,
> Looking for white heather—and suddenly
> I saw it, hundreds of yards away,
> Unmistakable—so in the hosts of men I've known,
> William Gallacher shines out
>
> . . . .
> A sprig of white heather in the future's lapel.[3]

MacDiarmid was, he said, "fed on out-and-out Radicalism and Re-
publicanism when still a child." Both parents were trade unionists. "If
an election was on, the local paper would be full of clever rhyming—all
sorts of pungent and provocative lampoons." John Laidlaw, a cousin
on his father's side, was "a great controversialist in witty verse, and had
a sardonic turn of expression and a faculty of biting invective which I
greatly admired." No wonder the boy's aspirations turned toward literature and journalism.[4]

John Laidlaw's brother, Robert, also a dabbler in verse, was enlisted
to teach MacDiarmid shorthand when he was twelve, apparently in
preparation for a possible career in journalism. When the boy reached
fourteen, schooling in Langholm ended, in accordance with Scottish law.
Two years later he was sent off to the Broughton Higher Grade School
and Junior Student Center in Edinburgh to train as a teacher. His parents, having rejected writing as financially risky, were even more opposed to MacDiarmid's second choice of becoming either a gamekeeper
or a gardener.[5]

The principal teacher of English at Broughton, thirty-seven-year-
old socialist George Ogilvie, had started a school periodical, *Broughton
Magazine,* after his arrival at the school in 1904. He welcomed MacDiarmid when the "quiet, sensitive figure with sharp features, pointed chin

and a great mop of unruly hair" arrived four years later at the age of sixteen with "a Border accent you could cut with a knife." Within a year, MacDiarmid joined the Independent Labor Party, in which he would be active for many years. He also became editor of the magazine, writing editorial columns for the first time. His taste for such work was whetted by a visit to the Edinburgh Public Library, where he read a journalist's memoir "full of splendid stories of literary and journalistic characters in New York." He was scooping up books as avidly as in the Langholm Library, and it got him into trouble. There was a burglary at the school and several reference volumes belonging to Ogilvie were stolen. One student pleaded guilty and was placed on probation. Another was arrested, but charges against him were dismissed. Somehow MacDiarmid was implicated. On January 27, 1911, he left school "on grounds of health and mistaking his vocation."[6]

Less than a week after MacDiarmid left Broughton, his father died of pneumonia at the age of forty-seven. With James Grieve's death, MacDiarmid felt no longer bound by his agreement to go into teaching. "I was drawn to journalism because I already knew the greatest lesson of journalism—that it is only ignorance which is boredom, and that everything is interesting and important if only you learn enough about it," he said. Ogilvie, not put off by whatever MacDiarmid's role in the book caper was, helped him find work with the Edinburgh *Evening Dispatch*. Here again, there was book trouble. Part of MacDiarmid's work was reviewing, and he was fired for selling books that the newspaper claimed belonged to it. MacDiarmid contended he was "legally entitled to retain the Review books in question and to dispose of them as I thought fit." Accordingly, he said, he sold them to secondhand shops so he could pay for the typing of freelance articles, as he never did learn to use a typewriter. He wrote his friend Ogilvie that the *Dispatch*'s chief reporter, Isaac Donald, with whom he was at odds, "did a very cruel and worse, a very stupid, thing" by magnifying the matter in describing it to the management.[7]

In October 1911, MacDiarmid moved to Wales to work as a reporter on the *Monmouthshire Labour News,* the weekly organ of the South Wales Miners Federation in Ebbw Vale. He found himself in the midst of a series of riots by miners suffering hard times as a result of mine and railway strikes. The first and most serious of these had occurred on August 11, when the town of Tredegar was invaded by marchers who wrecked and looted eighteen shops owned by Jews. According to Home Office files made available to a researcher seventy years later, the presiding magistrate in the case reported that some Jews had "been purchasing slum dwellings and, it is freely rumored, considerably raising the rents."[8]

Over the next few days, there was similar rioting in a number of nearby towns. Although the riots occurred two months before MacDiarmid joined the *Labour News* staff, he wrote to Ogilvie as though he had covered either these or similar disturbances. "They gave me my first taste of war corresponding: and I narrowly escaped being bludgeoned more than once," he said. "I heard the Riot Act read thrice in one night (in different towns, of course) and saw seventeen baton charges. My attack on the police, for their conduct during these riots, sent up the sales of the paper considerably."

At least one authority has suggested that MacDiarmid may have been referring to other riots, directed at the Irish. However, the reporter's letter to Ogilvie said that his own investigation and that of local authorities revealed "an almost inhuman system of rack-renting and blood-sucking on the part of the Jews in the district."[9]

Whatever riots he may or may not have covered, MacDiarmid had a lively time in Ebbw Vale. "It's like living on the top of a volcano down here," he wrote. "I have had three triple murders this last fortnight and have two strikes in hand now," as well as "inquests, colliery accidents and Federation meetings." MacDiarmid quickly ran into hostility because of his radicalism and admitted tactlessness. His articles offended Miners Federation leaders who served on the paper's editorial committee, including Tom Richards, the Labour member of Parliament for West Monmouthshire. "Re-organisation of paper afforded convenient opportunity of dispensing with my services," he told Ogilvie. His frequent drunkenness, which was to be a problem all his life, may also have contributed.[10]

After an interlude in Langholm, MacDiarmid found work on the *Clydebank and Renfrew Press,* "a cushy job, but poorly paid." He landed a better paying one in Cupar, as assistant editor of the *Fife Herald, St. Andrew's Citizen,* and *Fife Coast Chronicle,* three papers under a single ownership. His brother, Andrew Grieve, a civil servant with the Inland Revenue office in Cupar, had put in a good word to get him the job, and by his own account he enjoyed it immensely and "worked harder than I should have believed it possible for me to do." He later said he liked working on weekly local newspapers "because in that way one is involved in every element of a community's life and gets to know practically everybody in the area." He also continued his frequent drinking bouts and learned to dictate stories by telephone from the shorthand notes of colleagues who had passed out. For this or other reasons, he fell afoul of one of his bosses and moved to the *Forfar Review* after the feud developed into "a rupture beyond repair." The boss may have been the one with a birthmark on his cheek whom he described in the opening stanzas of his poem, "MacDiarmid's Curses."

Here in the hauf licht hoo I've grown!
Seconds but centuries hae flown
Sin I was a reporter here
Chroniclin the toon's sma beer
Tinin' the maist o' life to get
The means to hain the least wee bit.

Pars aboot meetins, weddins, sermons, a'
The crude events of life in the raw
Vanish like snowflakes on the river. . . .
Dans le flot sans honneur de quelque mon mélange . . .
On wha's black bank I stand and shiver;
Nakit!—What gin the boss, as weel he micht,
Comes in and switches on the licht?

The Twentieth Century at Eternity
Gapes—and the clock strikes: Tea!
And sombrous I arise
Under his silly eyes

And doon the stairs, the devil at my back.
I doot the morn I'll get the sack!

"What was I da'en sittin' in the dark?"
"Huntin' like moses for the vital spark,
—A human mole
Wi' a hole for a soul?"
"I sud think o' my wife and faimly"
I listen to him tamely.

"Cut oot this poetry stuff, my lad. Get on
Wi' advts. And puffs, and eident con
the proofs; it's in you gin you care
to dae't and earn (your master) mair.
Furth Fortune fill the fetters!
Apply yersel' to what's worth while
And I'll reward ye: that's my style."

"Yessir, I'm sorry. It'll no'
Happen again. The clock was slow
And I was slower still, I'm sorry,
In gettin' back again afore ye
To sicna state as fits the job
O ane wha's brains you lout to rob."[11]

In 1915, a year after the outbreak of World War I, MacDiarmid enlisted in the Royal Army Medical Corps, serving with the rank of sergeant. His first overseas posting was to the Greek port of Salonika, in a marble-floored general hospital staffed by Scots doctors and nurses. One of his duties was to be caterer of the officers' mess, watching for such things as tarnished silverware and "slow, slovenly, or uneven dishing up on the part of the cooks." The job helped him, he said, to develop an eye for details. By 1918, he was back in Wales, as he had come down with cerebral malaria and had been sent to a concentration center near Rhyl. In June, while still on home leave, he married Peggy Skinner, whom he had met while she worked as a proofreader's assistant at the newspaper office in Cupar.[12]

After being pronounced well enough to return to service, MacDiarmid was again assigned as a caterer, this time at Blackpool on the Irish Sea, and then was sent briefly to Dieppe, where the wet, muddy, and cold weather depressed him. Late in 1918, he was assigned to the Sections Lahore Indian General Hospital at Marseilles, established to treat the psychological problems of Indian and other Asian soldiers who had fought on the Western Front. "We had always several hundred insane there, and the death rate was very high," he recalled fifty years later. At that time, the duty—peacetime duty because the war had ended before he arrived—had compensations that lifted his spirits. He and three other noncommissioned officers shared "a delightful little flat in a fine old chateau set on a cliff on the outskirts of the city," he told Ogilvie. In his letter to his former teacher, he wrote glowingly of red and yellow rosebuds and slowly ripening oranges "along the old walls in the strong sunshine."[13]

In this setting, MacDiarmid began writing poems in both Scots and English, getting some of them published in literary magazines, and completing the largest part of a book of mixed poetry and prose, *Annals of the Five Senses*. All were published under his given name, as by C. M. Grieve. "My plans for after the war are all cut and dried," he wrote to Ogilvie. He had a number of books in mind and all that remained, he thought, was the writing—something that often turns out to be more difficult than the thinking. While still in uniform, he traveled in France, Spain, and Switzerland, cultivating literary acquaintances—on one occasion talking with Czech playwright Karel Capek on a tour of a Zuider Zee reclamation project.[14]

Demobilized in 1919, MacDiarmid moved to Montrose on the North Sea for a job as a reporter on the *Montrose Review*. Seeking more time to devote to poetry, he soon left the paper and decided to try his hand at teaching after all. He accepted an offer to tutor the two daughters of the head stalker at Kildermorie, a deer forest and lodge near Loch Ness. His poem "The Following Day," an unorthodox view of the Passion of Christ, was set in a "remote shooting lodge" based on Kildermorie.

In April 1921, he returned to the *Review* at an increased salary but regarded the job as a dead end requiring only "brute endurance, solid slogging, and routine experience." Besides, his wife did not like living in Montrose. He sought work on the editorial or literary staff of the *Scotsman* in Edinburgh, a city more to Peggy's taste, but the old business of the books that he sold at the *Dispatch* came back to haunt him. There would be no job for him at the *Scotsman*.[15]

Early in 1922, he was elected to the Montrose town council as an Independent Socialist. He also became active in the Scottish Free State movement, began addressing public meetings (and complaining about his coverage by the press), and took part in "an incredible variety of newspaper controversies." On the literary side, he was involved in publication of three poetry periodicals. Publisher T. N. Foulis, who had accepted *Annals of the Five Senses,* went bankrupt, so he published the book himself.[16]

The *Annals* and his magazine appearances were making the name C. M. Grieve known in literary circles. In one of his periodicals, a short-lived monthly poetic miscellany called *The Scottish Chapbook,* the name M'Diarmid first appeared in August 1922, over a short drama and a group of Scots lyrics. Two issues later, editor Grieve acclaimed M'Diarmid's work as "peculiarly interesting because he is, I think, the first Scottish writer who had addressed himself to the question of the extendability (without psychological violence) of the Vernacular to embrace the whole range of modern culture—or, in other words, tried to make up the leeway of the language." The Scottish poet Edwin Muir dismissed the *Chapbook* as mostly poor work but said it was "redeemed by the occasional appearance of Mr. Grieve's prose" amid the poems of MacDiarmid, whom he apparently did not know was the same man.[17]

After the birth of his first child, Christine, on September 6, 1924, MacDiarmid renewed his search for employment, hoping to find "something where the drudgery might be less unadulterated than here" and with better prospects. Novelist John Buchan tried to find work for him in London, but Fleet Street was "in a bad way, owing to amalgamations, etc.," and his work on local papers did not fit him for metropolitan competition. He applied for an opening as keeper of the National Galleries of

Scotland after seeing it advertised in a newspaper, but, despite "whipping up all the influence I possibly can," was unsuccessful. One friend whom he consulted told him he was "the last man in Scotland the Trustees are likely to favor." "I can't get out of Montrose, do what I will, but I loathe my work here," he wrote to Ogilvie in May 1925.[18]

MacDiarmid's second volume of poetry, *Sangschaw,* was out that year to cautious acclaim. Writing in the American magazine *The Saturday Review of Literature,* Muir described the best of the poems as "strangely felicitous" and said the "composite language" in which he wrote "may turn out to be a fact of great importance to Scottish letters." Muir later recanted his early praise and wrote that "a Scottish writer who wishes to achieve some approximation to completeness has no choice except to absorb the English tradition," as he had done. This, in the words of Muir's wife, Willa, "prompted a literary vendetta against Edwin Muir which went on for years." Muir's poetry was excluded from the *Golden Treasury of Scottish Poetry* that MacDiarmid edited in 1940.[19]

It was 1929 before MacDiarmid escaped from Montrose. The Scottish novelist Compton Mackenzie had established a magazine, *The Gramophone,* dealing with the then infant phenomenon of radio. Mackenzie invited the poet to come to London as editor of a companion journal, *Vox,* intended to specialize in radio criticism. Arriving in London in September, MacDiarmid wrote, "My lines have fallen in very pleasant places." He and Peggy found a house they liked and he "could not be associated with a more congenial lot of fellows" than he was in the magazine's ample Soho Square quarters. Peggy, he told Mackenzie was "the most competent typist in the office." This was important for the nontypist MacDiarmid.[20]

Very soon, he was finding London less pleasant. Three months after he settled in, he fell head first from the top deck of a London bus and suffered severe concussion. There was no fracture, probably, he speculated "owing to my great cushion of hair." Next, Peggy left him to live with Billy McElroy, a London coal merchant of cultural interests with whom MacDiarmid had been friendly and whom he had consulted about his financial affairs. On top of that, *Vox* collapsed after only fourteen weeks. MacDiarmid argued that "at least a year should be allowed to get a weekly on its feet—and I feel it has largely 'gone by default.'" Once again, he was looking for work and trying to tide himself over by freelancing. A potential opening as London correspondent of the Aberdeen *Press and Journal* disappeared as soon as the editor learned MacDiarmid was a Scottish Nationalist.[21]

After a month or two of unemployment, he caught on as publicity officer of the Liverpool Organization, writing leaflets and articles to boost the commercial interests of England's Merseyside region. His feelings about the job were mixed. He told his old schoolmaster Ogilvie that he had "an excellent office," was pleased when he got a raise from a poor starting salary, and liked the fact that "what I do is entirely dependent on my own initiative." To fellow writer Neil Gunn he was more candid: "I have fallen on evil days: and my lot is to have illustrated articles on technical subjects in the Overseas edition of *The Ironmonger,* the *London Chamber of Commerce Journal,* the *Hamburger Nachrichten,* etc.—signed articles, damnie! . . . I am not in some way doing myself justice."[22]

In addition to publicizing Merseyside businesses, MacDiarmid did a bit of press-agent work with an odd twist for his latest book *To Circumjack Cencrastus.* In a letter to his publishers, Blackwood & Sons, he wrote, "The incomprehensibility of the title will perhaps have its own publicity value and in any case I believe that a very extensive press campaign in connection with the book is being organized by some of my friends and that this will have the effect of concentrating public interest upon it." Whatever his friends were up to, it is obvious that MacDiarmid led the charge. In the *Scots Observer* for October 2, 1930, three weeks before the book's publication, he wrote, under the byline "Pteleon":

There is much in Hugh MacDiarmid's new long poem, *To Circumjack Cencrastus* which most people will deplore and a great deal that, surely, no one can justify. There is a super-abundance of needless personalities—scurrilous vilification of great Scotsmen past and present with whom the poet happens to disagree for political or other reasons or for none to all appearances except gratuitous ill-will. . . . Anti-English sentiment of the most virulent kind abounds, and along with it violent depreciations of British Imperialism and a rank hatred of America.[23]

Despite his disdain for the English literary establishment, MacDiarmid continued to make influential connections in London. By July 1931, he was "carrying the war into the enemies' camp" with a six-thousand-word essay on "English Ascendancy and British Literature," accepted for *The Criterion* by editor T. S. Eliot. He denounced "the sorry imperialism which has thrust Gaelic and dialect literatures out with the pale" and ranked himself among those who "see no reason why the whole English tradition from Shakespeare to the present day should not be as completely lost to British, and world, consciousness as Ancient Gaelic Literature was little more than half a century ago."[24]

In 1931, MacDiarmid and Peggy were divorced. He met his second wife, Valda Trevlyn, in London. Their son, Michael, was born in 1932. His drinking, by his own admission, "interfered with the diligent discharge of my duties" in Liverpool, and he was soon looking for a job— "anything," he said, "that has nothing to do with selling things." "Can I get deeper doon than this / Amang the world's inanities?," he asked in verse. In 1933, "down and out . . . with no money behind me at all, broken down in health, unable to secure remunerative employment of any kind," he moved to the island of Whalsay in the Shetlands. "I'm glad to be away from political movements, newspapers, and all the rest of it for a while," he told a friend. In fact, his newspaper days were over. A physician acquaintance offered him at nominal rent a four-room cottage on a hillside with a marine view. Here, he concentrated on poetry and tried "leading the simple life of an island fisherman" by going out with a Shetland herring fleet on a sailing vessel.[25]

Still, there was "cold and damp and darkness" on the island, and MacDiarmid missed "being 'on the spot'" where "anything might be happening." Whalsay was "so near and yet so far" from the life he had led. In 1935, he suffered a nervous breakdown. He left the Shetlands in 1942 and did war work in Clydesdale engineering shops, transferring to the merchant service a year later after sections of copper fell on him and cut both his legs severely. Starting as a deck hand, he became first engineer on a ship servicing British and American navy vessels in the Clyde Estuary. In 1945, he registered as unemployed in Glasgow. Writing of himself under his given name as C. M. Grieve, MacDiarmid said that ever since his wartime duty, he had "with an interval as a post-office sorter, had to endure the ignominy of being unemployed" because "he is a 'dangerous man' and there is no job for him in Scotland today."[26]

MacDiarmid was "dangerous" because in 1934 he had joined the Communist Party of Great Britain and because of his radical views on Scottish nationalism. The two were in conflict through much of his life. He had been one of the founders of the National Party of Scotland in 1928. In 1930, he said that his days as a socialist propagandist were over and "on the whole I think I can best be described as a 'crusted old Tory.'" In 1933, though, the Scottish nationalists expelled him, and he pronounced himself perfectly satisfied, saying that "if there is any further to the left I can possibly go I am going it." It is not surprising that before the communists would accept him as a member he was asked to describe his position and replied, "Just put me down as a muddled intellectual." That was good enough for a while, but in 1938, he was expelled from the party for nationalist deviation. He rejoined the National Party in 1942 but left it for good six years later.[27]

In 1951, he and Valda moved into a derelict but rent-free cottage near Biggar, about forty miles northwest of his boyhood home at Langholm. With the help of some admiring students from Edinburgh University, it was made comfortable and the living room lined with photographs, drawings, and paintings of MacDiarmid. By that time, there were plenty of them. Such works as *Scots Unbound, Stony Limits* and his three *Hymn to Lenin* poems had made him a celebrated poet, rewarded with a government pension. His work had been translated into many languages. He had lectured in Russia and western European countries and in China.[28]

In 1962, at an International Writers Conference in Edinburgh, MacDiarmid rattled some cold-war sensibilities when he restated his commitment to communism. In 1967, he visited the United States, where he sipped whiskey with poet Archibald MacLeish, the son of a Scottish immigrant, at his farm home in western Massachusetts. He found MacLeish,

The Scottish poet and journalist Hugh MacDiarmid wrote poems in a mixture of the dialect he heard spoken during his childhood in Scotland's Borders region and words found in "dusty Scots dictionaries." *Hugh MacDiarmid* by Duncan Glen. Reprinted by permission of the British Council.

who had also worked as a journalist, passionate enough about things Scottish, but his poetry "not my kind."[29]

The honors and travels continued with visits to Italy, Ireland, and Canada. On September 9, 1978, as MacDiarmid lay ill with cancer in a hospital in Edinburgh, he was awarded an honorary doctorate of literature by Dublin University. Four days later, he died. He was buried in Langholm, the town where as a boy he had resolved he would be a famous poet.

11 "As He Learned to Know It Day by Day"

More than the work of any other poet in this book, the poetry of Carl Sandburg is of a piece with his journalism. His political and social views saturated both. His interview with the accused Big Bill Haywood clearly showed his sympathy with the champion of labor. From his poems also, you could always tell whose side he was on.

The reporter who wrote that "railroad firemen got beaten, soaked, trimmed to a finish" in a 1915 wage arbitration was the poet who wrote twenty years later of a veteran railroad engineer who directs in his will that "they should burn his body / as a piece of rolling stock / beyond rehabilitation or repair."[1]

Railroads were in Sandburg's blood. His Swedish immigrant father, August Sandburg, worked as a blacksmith's helper in the railroad yards in Galesburg, Illinois. Carl was born on January 6, 1878, on a bed with wooden slats and a corn husk mattress in a three-room house near the tracks, where the family lived until August Sandburg saved the money to buy a larger home in a better part of town.[2]

In his early teens, Carl got a job as a delivery boy for the *Galesburg Republican-Register,* taking papers to a table as they came off a flatbed press, folding them three ways and then folding them crossways so he could hit his customers' front doors. In the rival *Galesburg Evening-Mail,* he read Washington columnist Walter Wellman and "wondered what it would be like to live in Washington and have a job where you went out every day and looked in here and there at the Government and then wrote about it, making plain to millions of people what was going on."[3]

Because the Sandburgs could not afford high school, Carl left the public school system at age fifteen, after the eighth grade. He worked at odd jobs, including delivering Chicago papers. When he was eighteen, in 1896, his father got him a railroad pass to Chicago. He walked from the railroad station to the *Daily News, Tribune* and *Inter-Ocean* buildings because he had "carried and sold so many of their papers that I wanted to see where they were made."[4]

His pass apparently didn't get him farther than Chicago, so he rode the rails in boxcars, got arrested in McKees Rocks near Pittsburgh, and spent ten days in the Allegheny County Jail for traveling on a train without a ticket. Back in Galesburg, he worked as an apprentice housepainter.[5]

His apprenticeship didn't last long. While Stephen Crane was des-ultorily covering the Spanish-American War's Puerto Rican campaign, Sandburg was briefly soldiering in it. As soon as he read the news of the battleship *Maine* explosion on February 8, 1898, he signed up with Company C of the Sixth Illinois State Militia and donned its Civil War–style uniform, blue with brass buttons. He landed at Guanica on the island's southwestern coast on July 30 and began a twenty-mile march to Ponce. Fifteen days later, the war ended. Sandburg thought standing guard a farce, but he disagreed with Richard Harding Davis's contention that the Sixth Illinois had it easy. If there wasn't any enemy to fight, there were plenty of mosquitoes, heat, and mud.[6]

Back home again, Sandburg was honorably discharged. In 1899, he enrolled in Lombard College, a Universalist institution later taken over by Galesburg's other school of higher learning, Knox College, where one of the Lincoln-Douglas debates had been held. It was at Lombard that Sandburg decided he would do a lot of "fooling around with pens, pencils and paper." He started by becoming editor of *The Cannibal,* the college yearbook, and then editor of the *Lombard Review.* One of his first editorials was a black-bordered eulogy on the death of President William McKinley, which he later found "stilted and perfunctory." He also sold advertising for the *Review* during summer vacation. He consid-ered entering advertising and even took a short course in copy writing.[7]

Other interests intervened. In 1904, Sandburg wrote a column un-der the head "Inklings and Idlings" in the *Galesburg Evening Mail,* and his first book of poems, a collection of conventional sentimental verses called *In Reckless Ecstasy,* was published by Asgard Press. The press was owned by Philip Green Wright, a professor of English at Lombard. The book's title was drawn from words of the English romantic novelist Marie Corelli. Sandburg's poems were also published in two Chicago magazines, *Tomorrow* and *The Lyceumite,* both of which listed him as assistant or associate editor.[8]

Galesburg was a Republican town, and Sandburg's father took him as a child to a downtown torchlight parade for the Grand Old Party's candidates. At eighteen he announced, to his father's dismay, that he had become a Democrat. There were more shocks to come. By 1907, August Sandburg's son was sending submissions to the editorial page of the *Daily Socialist* in Milwaukee. In December of that year, he moved to Wisconsin as an organizer for the Socialist party. While in the office of Victor Berger, a Socialist congressman from Wisconsin, he met Lilian Steichen, a sister of photographer Edward Steichen. She was visiting their parents in Milwaukee and had been asked by Berger to translate some of his German editorials into English. She and Sandburg were married in June 1908.[9]

Both Sandburgs changed their given names about this time. Sandburg had been baptized Carl, but the name was anglicized to Charles and he was called Charley. His wife was Lilian officially but had been called Paula by her parents, and it was the name her husband favored. Carl, for his part, believed the Scandinavian version of his name would go over better with the immigrants he was trying to organize. Besides, Paula liked it.[10]

After a year of marriage, the new husband decided it was time to supplement poetry writing and socialist organizing with something that paid better. After failing to get a job at either the *Milwaukee Sentinel* or the *Free Press,* he found work writing advertising copy for Kroeger's Department Store at twenty dollars a week. "It will be a better job than reporting," he told Paula. Six weeks of writing window show cards and twice-weekly bargain day circulars was enough, however, and he jumped at an offer to write features and an occasional news story for the *Milwaukee Journal.* After some clashes with "a nervous city editor," he took a two-week vacation relief job as an editorial writer at the *Milwaukee Daily News*. Finally, a job opened at the *Sentinel*, but he soon returned to the *Journal*, nervous editor notwithstanding, as a court reporter and editorial writer. In his off-hours, he wrote articles for *LaFollette's Weekly* under the heading "Dear Bill" at ten dollars a piece. The byline "By Carl Sandburg" first appeared on a Lincoln's birthday story in February 1910 for Berger's weekly *Social-Democratic Herald*. Within three decades, Sandburg would have completed a monumental multivolume biography of the sixteenth U.S. president.[11]

On March 22, 1910, August Sandburg died. Carl, estranged from a father who disapproved of his radical politics, did not attend the funeral. When Emil Seidel became Milwaukee's first Socialist mayor that year, he named Sandburg as his secretary. Seidel was defeated for reelection in 1912 by a coalition of Republicans and Democrats. Sandburg had already left the mayor's staff to help raise funds for a projected Socialist daily. This led to the establishment of the *Milwaukee Leader* with Berger as editor and Sandburg as a labor reporter and author of a "Bunts and Muffs" column.[12]

By that time the Sandburgs had their eyes on Chicago. A pressman's strike had shut down all of the city's papers except the Socialist *Chicago Evening World*, which announced plans to expand and fill the void. The *World*'s plan worked for a while, with circulation booming to six hundred thousand. But when the strike was settled, the Socialist paper found itself no match for the establishment dailies. By Christmas 1912, the paper had folded, and Sandburg, now the father of an eighteen-month-old daughter, was out of a job. After the strike ended, he tried for a position at the *Tribune* without success. He also tried out-of-town papers. Early in 1913, he was hired by Negley D. Cochran, editor of a new daily founded by the innovative journalist E. W. Scripps. Scripps wanted the *Day Book*, to be free of dependence on advertisers. As Sandburg put it, the paper took "no advertising and therefore tells the truth." Cochran said much the same thing about the *Day Book*. "Those who got hold of it found all the news in it, but boiled down to the bone . . . but we played up the news that the other Chicago newspaper didn't print," such as fatal elevator accidents in State Street stores. For twenty-five dollars a week,

Sandburg covered city politics, crime, and labor issues, working out of the paper's basement office at the corner of Congress and Peoria streets. The *Day Book* put out two editions a day, six days a week, selling at first for a penny, as the other Chicago papers did. When the outbreak of World War I sent the price of newsprint skyrocketing, the *Day Book* became the first paper in the city to raise its price to two cents. Scripps had an old press rebuilt to produce a thirty-two-page paper with pages eight and seven-eights inches long and six and one-eight inches wide. Each copy equaled about four pages of a broadsheet newspaper. One woman canceled her subscription because the paper was too small to wrap her husband's lunch in. From his vantage point at the more conventional *Chicago Daily News,* Ben Hecht regarded the *Day Book* as "a daily newspaper of a most unprofessional look and equally strange content . . . full of news stories about the sins of Capitalists and the gallantry and wisdom of labor leaders." The experiment lasted from September 1911 to July 6, 1917, when it fell victim to wartime economies.[13]

In his early days at the *Day Book,* Sandburg submitted two articles on industrial accidents to *System: The Magazine of Business* and suddenly found himself a business journalist. Editor Daniel Casey not only accepted the articles but offered their writer a job as associate editor at thirty-five dollars a week. A seemingly secure job at a ten-dollar-a-week increase in pay was too good to turn down. But Sandburg was uncomfortable. "One of the terrible things I saw being worked out," he said, was "time and motion studies and a standardization reaching into workers' lives to the point where you could tell what any operative is doing at any minute of the day by consulting the card graphs of the efficiency engineers." Soon Sandburg's superiors found his view of industrial safety too harsh on management. His boss told him, "Your imaginary qualities and abilities lead toward the poetic rather than the selling." With these gentle words in the autumn of 1913, Carl Sandburg was fired.[14]

He was not quite through with business journalism, though. As a stopgap he took a job with the *American Artisan and Hardware Record,* writing a column, "Random Notes and Sketches," under the name Sidney Arnold. Soon he was back at the *Day Book,* which had about tripled its circulation to fourteen thousand but did not raise his salary.[15]

Poet Carl Sandburg and colleagues at work in the basement office of the *Chicago Day Book*, a miniature newspaper founded by E. W. Scripps. Sandburg is second from the left. Courtesy of University of Illinois Library, Rare Book and Special Collections Library at Urbana-Champaign.

Under his own name, Sandburg sent a group of poems to *Poetry*, a Chicago magazine with fewer than fifteen hundred subscribers that had been founded in 1912 by Harriet Monroe, an art critic for the *Chicago Tribune*. Alice Corbin Henderson, a poet and critic who was an associate editor of the magazine, opened Sandburg's envelope, was impressed by the poems' vigor and promptly advised Monroe to publish them. The editor, a sedate woman from a prominent Chicago family, may have been a little daunted by Sandburg's description of her city as "Hog Butcher for the World" and "Stormy, husky, brawling / City of the Big Shoulders," but she published nine of the poems in the March 1914 issue anyway. "Chicago," which had been rejected by *American* magazine, became one of Sandburg's best-known works, although he thought his "Windy City," with its "monotonous houses . . . mile on

mile / Along monotonous streets out to the prairies," was a better portrayal of the Midwest metropolis. The Sandburgs got a check for seventy
dollars—almost equal to three weeks' pay—and "Chicago" later won
the magazine's two-hundred-dollar Helen Haire Levinson Prize. The
poet Sandburg was on his way.[16]

From London, Ezra Pound, the magazine's European editor, wrote
Monroe, "Good luck, glad to see Sandburg. I don't think he is very
important, but that's the sort of stuff we ought to print." *Poetry*'s chief
rival in the literary magazine field, the *Dial,* was less encouraging. Writing of "Chicago," the journal's reviewer complained, "The typographi-
cal arrangement of this jargon creates a suspicion that it is intended to
be taken seriously as some form of poetry," but "No possible definition
of poetry could admit this botch."[17]

At the *Day Book,* Sandburg provided day-to-day coverage of an
Amalgamated Clothing Workers strike, paying regular visits to lawyer Clarence Darrow, who was representing the union. His beat also
included working conditions for railroad and hotel workers, the city
bus transportation system, and labor-law violations. One memorable
day, he set out for the Loop to interview a juvenile court judge. Walking through Grant Park, he noticed the way fog was settling over the
harbor. In the judge's outer office, he took a pencil and scrawled words
on a piece of folded newsprint. The words became his celebrated haiku-
like poem "Fog."

> The fog comes
> on little cat feet.
>
> It sits looking
> over harbor and city
> on silent haunches
> and then moves on.[18]

When the United States's entry into World War I closed the pages of
the *Day Book,* editor Cochran was called to Washington by Scripps. Sandburg went to work for the National Labor Defense Council, organized

to protect the rights of striking workers. He also broke with the Socialist Party over its opposition to war measures of the Wilson administration. With no newspaper job in hand, he accepted an offer to write
editorials for William Randolph Hearst's *Chicago Evening American* at
one hundred dollars a week. At first, he seemed satisfied with the job
and with himself. "I had learned my craft," he said. Before long, Hearst
was beginning to dictate points of view to him. "My ways didn't fit
theirs," he decided.[19]

In August 1917, scholarly and bespectacled *Chicago Daily News* editor Henry Justin Smith had an hour-long talk with Sandburg and hired
him. The *Daily News* would become his newspaper home for many
years. Smith had a penchant for reporters with literary sidelines and already had on his staff Ben Hecht, later the coauthor of *The Front Page*. In
the society department, Mary Welsh of Bemidji, Minnesota, later a war
correspondent and Ernest Hemingway's fourth wife, was "extolling the
charms of women's hats" and dreaming of someday covering City Hall.
The journalistic literati liked to gather around polished wood tables at
Schlogl's, a nearby restaurant where they could dine on eel in aspic or a
special order of owl meat. Schlogl's prided itself on an aura of bohemian
glamour, but Mary Hemingway recalled the writers' gathering place as
"the grimy little bar across Madison Street from the office."[20]

One of Sandburg's first assignments was to cover the trial on sabotage charges of William D. Haywood, a leader of the Industrial Workers of the World, whose members were known to both their admirers
and their critics as Wobblies. He secured a jailhouse interview, which
appeared in the *News* on October 2, 1917. It is a fair example of his
reporting style. "Through a steel cage door of the Cook County Jail, Big
Bill Haywood today spoke the defiance of the Industrial Workers of the
World to its enemies and captors," Sandburg's story began. "Bill didn't
pound on the door, shake the iron clamps nor ask for pity nor make any
kind of a play as a hero. He peered through the square holes of the steel
slats and talked in the even voice of a poker player who may or may not
hold the winning hand. It was the voice of a man who sleeps well, digests
what he eats, and requires neither sedatives to soothe him nor stimulants
to stir him up."[21]

Haywood was convicted and sentenced to twenty years in prison but jumped bail and moved to Russia.

Much of Sandburg's work was editorial writing, and in July of 1918 he accepted an offer to do "factual reporting rather than think pieces" as eastern European correspondent of the Newspaper Enterprise Association (NEA), serving 320 newspapers with 4,500,000 subscribers. "I may write a true poem of the Ocean," he told Amy Lowell. After some delay in getting a passport, he arrived in Bergen on October 17 after a "foggy, soggy, loggy" passage aboard the S.S. *Bergensfjord*. He knew enough Swedish to get around and was thrilled at "hearing the speech of one's forefathers spoken by everybody and on all the street signs."[22]

Sandburg's career as a foreign correspondent was as brief as the Finnish revolution that was the main reason for the assignment. It was also marked by some journalistic behavior that was, at the very least, indiscreet.

Late in 1918, as Sandburg sat on a bench outside the Grand Hotel in Oslo, he was approached by a bearded man with shaggy black hair brushed back from his forehead. The man, a Byelorussian known as Mikhail Borodin, told Sandburg they had something in common. Both had lived in Chicago—Borodin, under the name Mitchell Berg, as proprietor of a school that taught English to immigrants. Borodin offered to be useful as a source of information. Finland had declared its independence from Russia in December 1917, but Russian troops were still garrisoned there. In January 1918, a German-backed faction took to the field to expel them. A rival socialist faction, with backing from Russia, attempted to take over the Finnish government, and civil war ensued. The war would end in 1919 with a victory for the anti-socialist faction led by Carl Gustav Mannerheim. About the time he met Borodin, Sandburg was asked by Sam T. Hughes, editor-in-chief of NEA, to help put together an informative article about the ruling Bolshevik party in Russia to correct what he said was widespread misinformation. "Do not omit the good things they do for fear of the conservatives in this country," Hughes said. Sandburg, distressed by reports of atrocities committed by Mannerheim's troops in Finland, relied on Borodin as one of his sources of information. In a story he filed about the Bolshevik shelling of Jaroslav, Poland, he identified his source as "Mitchell Berg, a former Chicago school teacher."[23]

What Berg-Borodin did not tell Sandburg was that he was a Bolshevik agent with the mission of getting propaganda into the United States. When it came time for Sandburg to return home after the end of the Finnish civil war, Borodin handed Sandburg a trunk full of printed material, which Sandburg intended to turn over to the University of Chicago. Just before his departure, Borodin asked him if he would also carry two bank drafts for five thousand dollars each, payable to Santeri Nuorteva, head of the Finnish Information Bureau in the United States. Borodin also gave Sandburg an English translation of a pamphlet by Lenin. This seemed innocuous enough, but Sandburg began to worry about the bank drafts and told the U.S. minister in Christiana about them, saying that "from such a distance, I was not sure what sort of service I might be rendering." The minister knew something Sandburg didn't: Nuorteva was also a Bolshevik agent. When Sandburg arrived in New York on Christmas Day, his baggage was searched by government agents, and he handed the two bank drafts over to Military Intelligence, refusing to say from whom they came.[24]

This was not the end of the matter. Customs officers confiscated all of his papers, including notes on his own interviews with "probably 200 people" and his clippings from Swedish and Norwegian socialist and labor newspapers, including "lots of dandy stuff." Officials of the War Work Committee, the State Department, the Federal Bureau of Investigation, and the U.S. Attorney for the Southern District of New York also got into the case. The bank drafts were considered a possible violation of the Trading with the Enemy Act. Officials in the government censorship office studied the printed and manuscript material in his bags. Sam Hughes wrote in his defense, "Isn't it fine for the Government to treat such a man like a dog of a traitor?"[25]

Even Hughes, however, was troubled about the bank drafts. If it had not been for the ten thousand dollars, he said, he "would have raised all kinds of hell today with Washington by telegram over that censorship business." On December 27, the authorities returned one suitcase to Sandburg but still held the Scandinavian newspapers and the Russian pamphlets, books, and papers. The matter hung fire until January 28, 1919, when it was settled as Sandburg signed an agreed-upon statement:

> I, Carl Sandburg, do hereby consent that the Military Intelligence, of the War Department, the Bureau of Investigation, of the Department of Justice, or the United States Attorney for the Southern District of New York may retain in their possession or in the possession of any one of them all of the books, pamphlets, newspaper clippings, magazines, magazine articles, manuscripts and other similar material brought by me into the United States from Christiana, Norway, on or about the 25th of December, 1918; and I do further consent that any of the agencies above-named may allow any department or agency of the United States government to have free access to such material and to use the information contained therein, and I do waive any and all rights that I have to protect or object to such retention and use of the said material.
>
> It is understood that all the said material will be returned to Mr. Sandburg, providing an investigation by the United States attorney or any of the other above-named departments shows that the said material if published or otherwise used, would not constitute a violation of the Espionage Law or any other law of the United States.[26]

No charges against Sandburg were ever pursued. He sent the material that was released to him to Hughes, providing information that he had already dispatched from Stockholm, but which had not reached Cleveland because of the slow wartime mail service. With the investigation of him dropped, he headed home to Chicago and then on to Cleveland. Headlines over his copy read, "BOLSHEVIKI, GREAT AND NEAR GREAT" and "KAISER'S FINNISH PALS SHOOT DOWN LABOR AND RADICAL LEADERS." His byline carried the legend "N.E.A. Staff Correspondent Just Arrived from Northern Europe with Pictures and Documents Never Before Published." Hughes had tentatively offered Sandburg a permanent berth with NEA, and Sandburg sent stories and ideas from

Chicago to Cleveland throughout most of the spring of 1919. Hughes and editor Leon Starmont began to question the poet's news judgment, especially when they received from him an interview with the English novelist John Galsworthy. "Carl, only one in a hundred knows anything at all about Galsworthy," Starmont wrote. In May, Hughes told Sandburg, "You are a great writer—your poems are sufficient evidence of that. You are a fine, keen thinker. But admitting all these things, you don't fit into the N.E.A. scheme of things." Starmont, hinting at Sandburg's Socialist connections, told him, "I don't believe you're as dangerous as some people would have us imagine, and I know we are not as stodgy as some folks would have you think."[27]

Sandburg was hired back as labor reporter at the *Daily News* after telling editor Smith, "There never was a time when demand was so keen from a large section of the newspaper-reading public for scrupulous, sincere accuracy" about the labor movement. His first job, however, was to write a series of stories on the plight of Chicago's African Americans, their number swollen from 44,103 in 1916 to 190,504 in 1919, with little accompanying increase in housing. The assignment plunged him into one of the biggest stories of his career. With their growth in population, African Americans spilled over from the city's segregated Black Belt into adjoining white neighborhoods and their parks and beaches. In consequence, the beaches were divided into areas where blacks could swim and areas set aside for the whites. On Sunday, July 27, with the temperature at an unusual ninety-six degrees, seventeen-year-old Eugene Williams, who was black, was swimming in a designated black area of Lake Michigan. Looking toward the shore, he saw four black men enter waters reserved for the whites. They refused an order to leave, and a stone-throwing fracas ensued. Williams, not a strong swimmer and afraid to go ashore, grabbed a railroad tie, which floated into white territory. Stones were thrown in his direction. The frightened youth abandoned his tie and tried to swim back into "black" water. When a white swimmer approached him, he panicked and went down. His body was recovered from the lake.[28]

Rioting broke out, and by midnight, twenty-seven black men and four whites had been beaten. Seven blacks and five whites had been stabbed. Four blacks and one white man had been shot. On Tuesday, the mayor called out the state militia to restore order. The rioting still spread. Many blacks lost their homes to vandals or arsonists. Only when a rain storm brought cooler weather did the violence abate. About a thousand people, mostly blacks, were homeless. Twenty-three blacks and fifteen whites had died. In a series of articles later published as a book, Sandburg wrote, "The riots furnished an excuse for every element of Gangland to go to it and test their prowess by the most ancient ordeals of the jungle. There was one section of the city that supplied more white hoodlums than any other section. It was the district around the stockyards and packing houses."[29]

In a poem dated July 29, 1919, and published in 1920 in his collection *Smoke and Steel,* Sandburg elaborated bitterly on the hoodlum theme.

I am a hoodlum, you are a hoodlum, we and all of us are a
    world of hoodlums—maybe so.
I hate and kill better men than I am, so do you, so do all of
    us—maybe—maybe so.
In the ends of my fingers the itch for another man's neck, I
    want to see him hanging, one of dusk's cartoons against the
    sunset.
This was the hate my father gave me, this was in my mother's
    milk. This is you and me and all of us in a world of hood-
    lums—maybe so.
Let us go on, brother hoodlums, let us kill and kill, it has always
    been so, it will always be so, there is nothing more to it.
Let us go on, sister hoodlums, kill, kill and kill, the torsos of
    the world's mothers are tireless and the loins of the world's
    fathers are strong—so go on—kill, kill, kill.
Lay them deep in the dirt, the stiffs we fixed, the cadavers
    bumped off, lay them deep and let the night winds of win-
    ter blizzards howl their burial service.
The night winds and the winter, the great white sheets of north-
    ern blizzards, who can sing better for the lost hoodlums the
    old requiem, "Kill him! kill him! . . . "

Today my son, tomorrow yours, the day after your next door
neighbor's—it is all in the wrists of the gods who shoot
craps—it is anybody's guess whose eyes shut next.
Being a hoodlum now, you and I, being all of us a world of
hoodlums, let us take up the cry when the mob sluffs by
on a thousand shoe soles, let us too yammer, "Kill him!
kill him! . . . "
Let us do this now . . . for our mothers . . . for our sisters and
wives . . . let us kill, kill, kill—for the torsos of the women
are tireless and the loins of the men are strong.[30]

The American journalist Lincoln Steffens, who as editor of the *New
York Commercial Advertiser* once invited job applications from "anyone
who, openly or secretly, hoped to be a poet," took note of Sandburg's
growing reputation. "Carl Sandburg reported all that he knew, as he
learned to know it day by day without a judgment, without a tear, without a laugh; he reported daily his daily news on the Chicago *Daily News,*
. . . and now behold, Carl Sandburg's stuff turns out to be poetry, Carl
Sandburg proves to be a poet."[31]

From covering racial turmoil, Sandburg moved to a beat as different as
one could imagine. In 1920, he became his paper's movie critic, reviewing
five new silent films each week. The assignment fitted in with his increasing role as a guitar-playing poet and lecturer, enabling him to tour exten-
sively with the *Daily News* financing much of the travel. In Hollywood,
he met Charlie Chaplin, whom he considered "a fellow dreamer." Again,
his poetry would mirror his journalism. In his motion picture column, he
described a sumptuous dinner at Chaplin's home, followed by charades. In
his poem "Without the Cane and the Derby (For C.C.)," he wrote of "the
marvelous urchin, the little genius of the screen," being "somebody else . . .
a man, gray shirt, bandana, dark face" for the entertainment of his guests.
As a columnist, he interpreted Chaplin's comedy, "Work," as a bit of non-
violent sabotage in which he "does a bum job of paperhanging and slathers
buckets of paste all over the gazaboes who took him for a mutt."[32]

By 1924, Sandburg was embarked on his Lincoln biography and
took issue with a fictionalized film portrayal of his subject in *The Iron*

Horse, an epic about the building of the transcontinental railway. He remained on the movie beat through the advent of the talkies, but his poetry and the biography were increasingly his preoccupation.[33]

In 1938, he turned down an offer of thirty thousand dollars a year to write a column for Hearst. In 1940, he reluctantly agreed to write a column for the *Chicago Times* about the war in Europe. His journalistic days were essentially behind him. In what he called "Notes for a Preface" to his *Complete Poems* in 1950, he wrote that "there was puzzlement as to whether I was a poet, biographer, a wandering troubadour with a guitar, a Midwest Hans Christian Anderson, or a historian of current events whose newspaper reporting was gathered into a book."[34]

It was a good self-analysis. Sandburg came to fame during the Great Depression, when his brand of socially conscious writing was much in vogue. As the detached, ironic manner of T. S. Eliot and his followers rose in critical esteem, Sandburg's fell. In 1960, critic Gay Wilson Allen predicted that "readers will either learn to distinguish the poetry from the propaganda and sentimentality or Sandburg's name will fade from the history of twentieth-century poetry." As the century neared its close, his work was being less and less read. A just estimate was that of Louis D. Rubin Jr.: "What is bad in Sandburg is not his poetics, but his sentimentality. And when he is good, it is not because he sings of the common people, but because he has an extraordinarily fine gift of language and feeling for lyric imagery."[35]

12 "For Time to Keep"

Carl Sandburg broke into journalism by going from newspaper to newspaper in Milwaukee, desperate for a job that paid more than poetry or socialism. Archibald MacLeish slipped into journalism because he and Henry Luce had been fellow members of Skull and Bones at Yale.

In many ways, the two poets could not have been more different. MacLeish's father, Andrew MacLeish, was a Scottish immigrant who made a fortune in the department store business and raised his family on a big estate called Craigie Lea in an affluent suburb of Chicago. Sandburg grew up in working-class Galesburg, the son of a Swedish immigrant earning a bare living as a railroad-yard worker.

Their literary styles differed also. Sandburg conceded that some of his poems were "rowdies and I can't change their rowdy ways." MacLeish could be privately rowdy, but his verse was as elegant as Craigie Lea. Yet both poets mingled politics with poetry in a way that was acclaimed during the Depression and World War II years and later fell from literary favor.[1]

Sandburg was fourteen years old and peddling papers in Galesburg when MacLeish was born on May 7, 1892, in Glencoe, Illinois. MacLeish entered Yale in 1915, one year earlier than Luce. In 1919, the future publisher took an advanced writing course taught by Henry Seidel Canby. MacLeish, who had graduated the previous year and was already beginning to make his way as a poet, was among recent alumni, along with playwright Philip Barry, who visited the class.[2]

Despite his modest successes in poetry, MacLeish, who had gone on to Harvard Law School, was seriously considering journalism as a career, outlining his view in a letter to his friend Dean Acheson. "I believe that in accomplishing in one's own time, journalism—editorial journalism—is a most effective vehicle," the young MacLeish wrote. "The right sort of paper would give its editors sufficient leisure to do substantial work in the field they were to cover & to give fair expression to their conclusions. And though such a paper might not have great power it would have power. The rare thing about it is that journalism offers a chance for thought & study & for the attempt to make one's conclusions current in the world which we call influence."[3]

The letter shows that MacLeish's ambitions tended toward the editorial sanctum of a newspaper office rather than the grubby day-to-day reporting that helped to shape Rudyard Kipling, Stephen Crane, and Hugh MacDiarmid. His introduction to journalism turned out, however, to be less grandiose. Luce, out of Yale and planning a news magazine to be called *Time,* turned to MacLeish to be part-time education editor. In the magazine's first issue, dated March 3, 1923, the education section led with a paragraph more characteristic of *Time*'s sentence-reversing style than MacLeish's usual silky manner: "Simultaneously with a discussion in the Yale Corporation of the desirability of retaining Latin and Greek as requirements for the B.A. degree, arrives in the United States, and in New Haven, Sir Frederick Kenyon, noted classical scholar and director of the British Museum."[4]

The poet, by this time married and working in Boston as a lawyer, was glad to get the extra ten dollars a week. The work was not arduous. Each week, *Time*'s headquarters in New York sent him a batch of newspaper clippings about education, and he rewrote them in *Time* style. Later, he would defend *Time*'s practice of lifting news from the newspapers, saying, "It takes brains and work to master all the facts dug up by the world's 10,000 journalists and put them together in a little magazine."[5]

His work as a *Time* man was short-lived. Before 1923 had ended, he was in Paris, concentrating on poetry. It was, he said, a hard decision. Law practice with the prestigious Boston firm of Choate, Hall & Stewart was "the most exciting indoor game in the world." Charles F. Choate Jr. had offered him a partnership. But he knew that what he really wanted was "to write, and by writing, I mean poetry. And never anything but poetry." He made the decision, he said, crossing the Boston Common in the snow. On September 1, with his wife, Ada, and their two children, he sailed for France. Taking advantage of a favorable exchange rate, they lived there for five years.[6]

In Paris, MacLeish met Ernest Hemingway. At the beginning of his self-exile, Hemingway tried to be a full-time literary artist and part-time journalist. It didn't work. In one eight-month period, he filed sixty-four thousand words to the Toronto *Star* while writing a handful of short stories and poems. Of Hemingway, MacLeish would write that he "Whittled a style for his time from a walnut stick / In a carpenter's loft in a street in that April city." Hemingway said at the time that he preferred the poetry of Evan Shipman, whose recognition did not long survive his stay in Europe, to that of MacLeish. A decade later, he said that MacLeish had "come on steadily" in the intervening years, while others had languished.[7]

In 1928, it was time for MacLeish and his wife to return to the western Massachusetts farm they had acquired. Again, however, Henry Luce beckoned. Establishing his second magazine, Luce was undecided over whether to call it *Power* or *Fortune*. He chose the second because his first wife, Lila, preferred it. At first the magazine was respectfully descriptive in its portrayal of American business. When an article on Texaco appeared in the second issue, some suspected incorrectly that the Texas Company had paid for it. Prosperous readers were delighted with the heavy, expensive "wild wove antique" paper on which it was printed. Three months before the first issue came out, however, the Great Depression had begun. As it deepened, the tone of the magazine became more critical, and it gathered as editors and contributors such liberals as Alfred Kazin, Dwight MacDonald, and John Kenneth Galbraith.[8]

Luce wanted writers and believed it would be easier to turn a poet into a business journalist than to make a writer out of a bookkeeper. He told his former *Time* education editor that he could pretty much decide for himself how much time he would spend on *Fortune* and still earn fifteen thousand dollars a year, a respectable sum for 1930. Despite protesting that "I know absolutely nothing about business," MacLeish took the job on those terms and sometimes worked as little as six months a year. Hemingway, scornful of "the romance of business," couldn't understand how his friend got mixed up with such an outfit. But MacLeish was deep into his book-length narrative poem, *Conquistador,* which would win him the Pulitzer Prize in 1932, and needed money to keep him going. Besides, working for *Fortune* was "the greatest box seat to watch the world."[9]

At one point, MacLeish seems to have considered being a political publicity man. At lunch with writer Matthew Josephson in the spring of 1932, he said he had recently been invited to work on campaign literature for the Young Republicans. According to Josephson, MacLeish asked him what he thought, and he said, "Why don't you go for it? Politics is going to be very important in the years ahead, and you might learn a few things." MacLeish, Josephson said, agreed that he ought to consider it seriously.[10]

He remained, however, with *Fortune.* Luce was looking for a style for his new magazine, something different from the eccentric and often ridiculed style of *Time,* with its frequent backward sentences. "He'd have me rewrite pieces over and over in an effort to find that special style," MacLeish recalled. "Of course, all I could do was write my own style." And he did. In a profile of financier Ivar Kreuger, who shot himself to death in 1932, the poet wrote, "The stair smelled as it had always smelled of hemp and people and politeness—of the decent bourgeois dust." The description of Kreuger's Paris apartment held echoes of the poem MacLeish wrote on his thirtieth birthday, during his Parisian stay: "By hands, by voices, by the voice / Of Mrs. Whitman on the stair, / . . . By voices, by the creak and fall / Of footsteps on the upper floor." Even his captions to Arthur Gerlach's photos for an article on manufacturing were something more than ordinary journalistic prose. "An aluminum fiddle is sister to a ruby," one began.[11]

Certainly, *Fortune* was the great box seat MacLeish relished. He was sent to London to write "a candid and detached profile of George the Fifth." He went out west in 1935 and wrote that men moving from east to west and dust blowing from west to east were "chapters from the same book. And the book is not Theodore Roosevelt's *Winning of the West.*

The book is a book which has never been written. Its title is *The Grass.*"
For an article on skyscrapers, he interviewed Al Smith, the former New
York governor and Democratic presidential candidate, and found him
"in an office carpeted in Kelly Green with a gigantic plaster model of
the Empire State Building on a table against the wall." He traveled to
Europe, Asia, and South America. In 1936, he wrote five-eighths of the
magazine's Japanese issue in two months' time. In a series collected by Alfred Knopf as a book called *Background of War,* every article but one was
MacLeish's work. He would come into the office at nine in the morning,
tell researchers what he wanted, and write until five. Once more, the poet
and the editorialist marched in tandem. Of General Francisco Franco's
uprising against the liberal democratic government of Spain, MacLeish
wrote in *Fortune,* "Against that kind of challenge democracy can defend
itself. Indeed it is precisely by that kind of challenge that democracy is
made strong." Of the victims in the bombed town of Guernica and other
battlefields of the civil war, the poet MacLeish wrote, "Because they are
dead, are dumb, because they are speechless, / Do not believe, / Do not
believe the answer will not come."[12]

Shortly after President Franklin D. Roosevelt's inauguration in
March 1933, Luce, who had voted for Herbert Hoover, accepted Mac-
Leish's suggestion that they go to Washington and visit the new president. Luce, as impatient as he was thrifty, paced the floor of the double
room he had booked for them in the Carlton Hotel until Roosevelt's
secretary, Missy LeHand, telephoned to say the president would see
them. By the time they left the White House, Luce had succumbed to
the Roosevelt charm, exclaiming, "My God! What a man!" Working on
an FDR profile, MacLeish interviewed his one-time Harvard professor
Felix Frankfurter and a number of the "big rich fellows in New York"
who, he told Frankfurter, were increasingly bitter toward the president.
In the article, he found Roosevelt "the greatest and certainly the most
portentous enigma in the contemporary world." By December 1935, as
Roosevelt prepared to run for his second term, MacLeish was writing
that "the case against FDR is considerably stronger than the Republicans have yet made it appear" and that "Mrs. Roosevelt has talked so
much and in so many places that her countrymen have begun to tire."[13]

Archibald MacLeish (right) was on assignment for
Fortune in Montana when this photograph with wheat
farmer Tom Campbell was taken. *Fortune*'s publisher,
Henry Luce, thought it was "easier to turn poets into
business journalists than to turn bookkeepers into writers." Image provided by the Archibald MacLeish Collection at Greenfield Community College, Greenfield,
Massachusetts, by permission of A. Bruce MacLeish.

MacLeish also found a place in *Fortune* for literary friends.

In December 1929, Hemingway wrote to Maxwell Perkins, his editor at *Scribner's*, that he was "trying to write an article on bullfighting as an industry for 'Fortune.' Archy MacLeish asked me for it—written in journalese full of statistics . . . they probably won't take it—am keeping it as dull as possible." Hemingway's prediction was wrong. The twenty-five hundred-word article, "Bullfighting, Sport and Industry," appeared the following spring. Hemingway got a thousand dollars for it.

Sandburg, walking into MacLeish's office on a trip to New York in 1933, found him in consultation with Luce. In the course of their conversation, they agreed that the magazine of business should accept a poem by the poet who had so often scourged business practices in both his poetry and his journalism. Sandburg sent them "Moonlight and Maggots," in which the speaker is warned that "The moon is a cadaver and a dusty mummy and damned rotten investment. / The moon is a liability loaded up with frozen assets and worthless paper. / Only the lamb, the sucker, the come-on, the little lost boy, has time for the moon." The lost boy answers, "The moon is a friend for the lonesome to talk with." Sandburg's eighty-five lines were the first poem ever published by *Fortune,* and the editors were uncertain what to pay. MacLeish at first suggested two hundred dollars, but the poet apparently held out for more, and was paid five hundred.[14]

An attempt to get Hart Crane into the magazine's pages was less successful. Crane's book-length 1927 poem *The Bridge,* hymning the Brooklyn Bridge that he saw from his apartment window as a "steeled Cognizance whose leap commits / The agile precincts of the lark's return," was winning lavish praise from such critics as Waldo Frank and qualified praise from the more conservative Yvor Winters. Crane told Frank that it was being reviewed by MacLeish in *Poetry,* but the review did not appear. In 1930, however, MacLeish regarded Crane as a likely prospect to write an article *Fortune* was planning on the George Washington Bridge, then nearing completion. Managing editor Parker Lloyd-Smith liked the idea and commissioned Crane to write not only the bridge article but a profile of J. Walter Teagle, president of Standard Oil.[15]

Crane needed the money, and he went to work with a will. He interviewed engineers, spectators, and workmen at the bridge site. He studied the design of the span and the spinning of the cables. He got together with MacLeish and they assembled an outline. He set aside all other writing to work on the articles. He turned down an invitation to the Yale-Harvard football game. He met with Teagle and "managed to keep the oil king talking far beyond the time allotted." But the poet who could evoke a city and its bridge so lyrically was unable to meet the demands of factual journalism. He submitted a rough draft of the Teagle article, but it was returned and never put into a final form. The project had to be abandoned.[16]

Increasingly, MacLeish was moving into areas of public policy that would bring disagreements with fellow liberals. The *New Republic* took issue with his review of *The First World War,* a picture book edited by Laurence Stalling, coauthor of the antiwar play *What Price Glory?* The review said the book was antiwar propaganda in which the dead who "believed in the things for which (or so they thought) they died" were absent. The same magazine published the poet's moving "Lines for an Interment," recalling the death of his own brother, Kenneth, in the war and asking ironically, "Hadn't they taught you the fine words were unfortunate?" Malcolm Cowley, then the magazine's editor, replied that it was time for himself, MacLeish, and others whose "relatives crashed in airplanes or died by machine-gun fire" to concede that "all of us fought in vain." MacLeish stood his ground, asking, "Is it perhaps conceivable that to die generously and in loyalty to a believed in cause is not, regardless of the success of that cause, regardless even of its validity, to die in vain?"[17]

In 1935, Fortune considered a series on American Jews. In a memo to Luce, MacLeish said he found some Jews who approved of the idea but "strong disapproval . . . particularly among wealthy Jews who argued a discussion of anti-Semitism would stimulate it." The series was reduced to one article and the emphasis on anti-Semitism in the United States abandoned because, MacLeish said, "it will be impossible to establish the point with factual certainty." Instead the premise was to be "the acute and highly self-conscious apprehension of the Jewish race in this country." Hearing that Frankfurter had attended meetings with fellow Jews on the subject, MacLeish solicited his views. In the end, the long article found that "current American anti-Semitism is feeble." Mac-Leish found the reaction to it among Jews not only generally favorable but "too good from the point of view of objective journalism. One or two at least should have yelled bloody murder."[18]

When editorial employees of *Time* organized a chapter of the Newspaper Guild in 1936, MacLeish was one of the chapter's sponsors and helped formulate its negotiating position. Luce did not penalize guild activists, but MacLeish was unable to persuade him to favor a union shop.[19]

MacLeish objected strenuously to *Time*'s coverage of the Spanish civil war "as though it were some sort of spontaneous cockfight between Whites and Reds in which both sides are equally guilty." In a January 1937 letter to *Time* foreign editor Laird Goldsborough, with a copy to Luce, he wrote, "I feel that *Time* has never presented the war in Spain for what it was—an inexcusable and unjustifiable act of aggression by reactionary forces against a popular government." Goldsborough responded with a memo to Luce not only defending *Time*'s coverage of the war but saying that while he enjoyed MacLeish's "suave writings," he thought that they and all other *Fortune* articles were far too long. MacLeish replied: "As to your final statement about the way in which *Fortune* stories ought to be written, I think perhaps the simplest comment for me to make is that if we will each of us confine himself to his own ball park the game will go on a little better. The theory that a full length, carefully integrated magazine article discussing a subject in full can be written like a Hearst story, with the wow in the first paragraph and the exegesis thereafter, is a theory which I shall resist as long as I write on *Fortune*."[20]

He was not, as it turned out, to do so much longer. In 1937, Harvard University received a bequest of about $1.35 million from Agnes Nieman, widow of Lucius Nieman, founder of the *Milwaukee Journal,* on which Carl Sandburg had briefly labored. Mrs. Nieman's will stipulated that the money be used "to promote and elevate the standards of journalism in the United States." Harvard president James Bryant Conant was dubious about the offer. He had been having trouble already fitting the recently established Graduate School of Public Administration into the university framework. He did not welcome the idea of establishing a school of journalism, which no Ivy League university except Columbia had yet done. So how was Harvard to go about elevating journalistic standards? Some journalists and Harvard professors were also skeptical. When a reporter doing a story about the business administration school asked its dean whether journalism would be included, the dean replied, "Good God, no. Journalism is nothing but the gift of gab." The *New Yorker*'s "Talk of the Town" writer said, "After all, William Randolph Hearst went to Harvard, and he couldn't elevate a standard if it was rigged up with pulleys."[21]

A better idea than a journalism school, Conant thought, would be to turn selected midcareer journalists loose at Harvard to study what they wished. When he approached MacLeish about directing the program, he found that the poet didn't like the idea of a journalism school either. After all, he had studied law and poetry, and look where he was. "I had just gotten to the end of my usefulness to *Fortune* and *Fortune*'s usefulness to me when Jim Conant showed up one day," he said. Even though the salary would be a third of what he was making, he resigned from *Fortune* and accepted the position of curator of the Nieman Collection of Contemporary Journalism. The curious title came about because a portion of the Nieman bequest was set aside, at the suggestion of Harvard's library director, to start a collection of microfilms of daily newspapers. MacLeish spent little time on the microfilm collection and in fact forgot that it existed.[22]

"We started from scratch," he said. "I did not know what I was going to do. What I was going to do nobody knew." Conant had anticipated little interest among journalists in the program, but soon found out differently. More than three hundred applied. Four reporters and five editorial writers were selected by a committee of journalists. "MacLeish was guide and counselor and helped us explore the resources of Harvard," said Louis M. Lyons, a *Boston Globe* reporter who was a member of the first group of fellows and later would succeed MacLeish as curator.[23]

In addition to such things as getting his charges reserved press seats at Harvard football games, MacLeish arranged weekly dinners for them at Joseph's, a restaurant on the second floor of the Boston Art Club. After martinis and double lamb chops, they heard from the likes of James Reston of the *New York Times,* Henry Luce, and columnist Walter Lippmann. Each dinner would focus on some topic in the news such as the Sacco-Vanzetti case, starting with journalistic shop talk and broadening into wider perspectives. There was also a weekly luncheon with members of the faculty. "The university was experimenting, and we were inevitably the guinea pigs," said fellow Frank Snowden Hopkins. "I think the Nieman experiment has let more air into Harvard than anything that has happened in this century," MacLeish said four decades later.[24]

By 1939, Herbert Putnam had been librarian of Congress for forty years, and some lawmakers felt their library needed new management to bring it up to date. Although the library is part of the legislative branch, the librarian is appointed by the president, and the law is silent about his tenure. It does not say that he is appointed for life, or for a fixed term, or at the pleasure of the president. It doesn't say anything. President Roosevelt asked Attorney General Francis Biddle for an opinion on whether he could fire the librarian. Biddle told him what he wanted to hear: he could. Putnam, who could read handwriting on walls if it was large enough, took the matter into his own hands and resigned. Roosevelt then cast about for suggestions. On May 11, 1939, Felix Frankfurter, whom the president had just appointed to the Supreme Court, recommended his former law school student MacLeish, saying the librarian of Congress should be "a man who knows books, loves books and makes books." MacLeish at first declined the post, saying he needed free time to write, but changed his mind and accepted after a second meeting with the president. Roosevelt assured him that time could be found for his writing. Whatever assurances he had been given, the fact was he wrote only one poem during his five years as librarian.[25]

No sooner had MacLeish won confirmation by the Senate and moved into the librarian's rococo office in the forty-year-old Library of Congress building than the president informed him that he was planning a government-wide information office. MacLeish was to run it in his spare time. It was, as MacLeish later said, a "completely foolish" idea. The *New York Herald-Tribune,* in the headline to an editorial about the agency, known as the Office of Facts and Figures (OFF), said, "Here's Where We Get OFF." The editorial appeared two months before the Japanese attack on Pearl Harbor. In a Washington column written after the attack, Thomas L. Stokes likened the agency to "a combined Ministry of Propaganda and Ministry of Information" designed to serve as "a sort of umpire to determine whether certain news should be published." MacLeish, who had told Secretary of the Interior Harold Ickes that he was concerned about the administration's lack of an effective propaganda machine, adopted the slogan "the strategy of truth" in defending the agency. He sometimes disagreed with Secretary of War Henry L. Stimson's views on the need for military secrecy, but Stimson found him open to persuasion. The agency was subsumed into the Office of War Information, headed by veteran radio commentator Elmer Davis, and MacLeish resigned in January 1943 after telling Davis that "my efforts to be useful have not, I think, had the results I intended."[26]

Later in 1943, MacLeish and Luce discussed the possibility of his going to London as a correspondent for Time, Inc. In the end MacLeish decided against it, saying again that he wanted to get back to his own writing. MacLeish resigned as librarian on November 8, 1944, and Roosevelt promptly nominated him to be assistant secretary of state for cultural and public affairs. The nomination was sent to the Senate floor on an eleven to ten vote after Republicans attacked him as a propagandist, unqualified for the office. The Senate confirmed the nomination, forty-three to twenty-five, with twenty-eight senators abstaining. He got a stronger endorsement from Chicago reporter Ed Lahey, who had been one of the first class of Nieman fellows. "Archie MacLeish has convinced a lot of Americans that this is really their State Department, and not the private preserve of the lads in the striped pants and the homburg hats," said Lahey.[27]

MacLeish, however, was finding that life in the Washington bureaucracy came with problems. On December 30, 1944, the *New York Herald-Tribune* published a story suggesting a quarrel between Michael McDermott, the department's press officer, and the new assistant secretary. "There is a certain indefiniteness as to the line of demarcation between Mac and myself and sooner or later the line will have to be drawn more clearly but there is no squabble, actual or potential," MacLeish wrote to a *Herald-Tribune* editor. Indeed, all was not well. On February 3, 1945, MacLeish reported in a memo, "The department's information practices are unsatisfactory. . . . Less information is put out than the country has the right to expect, and far less than the press desires." After a meeting with Associated Press diplomatic correspondent John Hightower and others, he suggested the news conference policy be revised to permit an hour-long meeting between the secretary and reporters. Four days later, *New York Times* correspondent Reston told him that both the public and friendly senators were in doubt about what was happening at the Dumbarton Oaks conference in Washington that shaped the United Nations charter.[28]

Details of the agreements made by Roosevelt, Winston Churchill, and Joseph Stalin during their February meeting at the Black Sea port of Yalta were also being kept from the public, to MacLeish's dismay. Shortly after the Yalta meeting, MacLeish pushed for public disclosure of all agreements at the forthcoming conference in San Francisco that officially established the United Nations. Interviewed by commentator H. R. Baukhage, he said, as paraphrased by Baukhage, that if the conferees take a "papa-knows-best attitude and crawl into a hole of secrecy and pull the hole in after them, it will be his finish." On March 12, Secretary of State Edward R. Stettinius visited President Roosevelt and assured MacLeish that the president wanted all plenary sessions and committee meetings to be open, and that was the policy adopted. On March 30, Bert Andrews of the *Herald-Tribune* called MacLeish at 6:15 P.M. to ask him about a rumor that he planned to resign over the Yalta issue. According to a memo that MacLeish drafted as soon as he got off the telephone, he told Andrews "that I was naturally disturbed as anyone would be running an information policy dedicated to the belief that the people were entitled to all the facts, but I did not intend to resign." He declined comment when Andrews asked him whether he had gone to the White House and urged that the information be released.[29]

Early in 1945, Adlai Stevenson moved into an office next to MacLeish's corner space in the State Department's quarters, then across 17th Street from the White House. Stevenson's assignment was to work with MacLeish "in matters relating to postwar international organization."

On April 12, 1945, as he recalled, Stevenson was standing by a window looking down onto 17th Street when the phone rang. MacLeish listened, then said quietly, "The President is dead." The poet, who had known Roosevelt since he and Henry Luce interviewed him a dozen years before, was stunned by the news, but for the moment there was work to be done. The White House sent word that it was the State Department's responsibility to prepare an official proclamation, and MacLeish was to write it. Stevenson helped him look up precedents, and the two of them worked together on drafts. The final proclamation, finished by MacLeish after Stevenson had left, concluded, "Though his voice is silent, his courage is not spent, his faith is not extinguished. The courage of great men survives them to become the courage of their people and the peoples of the world. It lives beyond them and upholds their purposes and brings their hopes to pass." MacLeish walked over to the White House with the proclamation and then went to his car. He broke down and sobbed when he reached his Alexandria home and was unable to control his emotion when making a broadcast statement for the State Department the following morning.[30]

The next day, he submitted his resignation to President Truman but said he remained "entirely at your disposition for any service you may wish me to render during this period of emergency." Truman asked him to stay on but accepted his resignation when he submitted it again on August 15. In that letter, MacLeish said that personal reasons had led him to "ask to be released from the government service over a year ago." The phrase indicated that he probably did try to resign after the Yalta meetings, as Bert Andrews had heard.[31]

MacLeish served as chairman of the United States delegation to the London Conference that founded UNESCO in 1945 and to UNESCO's first general conference in Paris the following year. From 1949 to 1962 he was Boylston Professor of Rhetoric and Oratory at Harvard.

Throughout his career, Archibald MacLeish rejected the idea that "the two extremes which will never meet, the East and West of our fractured world, are poetry and journalism." He scorned the notion that poetry "won't work in the world . . . the political world, the world, the historical world. That's something else and poetry should keep out of it." It was a note he sounded in both argumentative prose and declamatory poems, with mixed results.

In the poems written in the 1920s, he showed an astounding lyric gift. The poet who described himself as "obsessed with time" meditated on seventeenth-century poet Andrew Marvell's obsession with "Time's winged chariot hurrying near" and came up with his 1920s poem "You, Andrew Marvell," beginning:

And here face down beneath the sun
And here upon earth's noonward height
To feel the always coming on
The always rising of the night

To feel creep up the curving east
The earthy chill of dusk and slow
Upon those under lands the vast
And ever climbing shadow grow

And strange at Ecbatan the trees
Take leaf by leaf the evening strange
The flooding dark about their knees
The mountains over Persia change.[32]

As he moved into the 1930s and a career in journalism and government, the lyricism of the trees taking "leaf by leaf the evening" gave way to "America Was Promises" with its politically charged question and answer: "Promises to whom?" and "The promises are theirs who take them." The poem and its 1943 corollary "Colloquy for the States," were popular and taught in the schools in an era of depression and world war. When Carl Sandburg wrote that his friend MacLeish had "forsaken his Massachusetts farm to make propaganda for Freedom," he meant it as a compliment. The poems showed MacLeish's patriotism and liberalism in striking rhetoric to which readers responded.[33]

In the 1950s, out of government and out of journalism, MacLeish returned to the lyric vein with works such as "Words in Time."

Bewildered with the broken tongue
Of wakened angels in our sleep—
Then, lost the music that was sung
And lost the light time cannot keep!

There is a moment when we lie
Bewildered, wakened out of sleep,
When light and sound and all reply:
That moment time must tame and keep.

That moment, like a flight of birds
Flung from the branches where they sleep,
The poet with a beat of words
Flings into time for time to keep.[34]

As depression and world war faded into memory, the colloquy of the states about the "mean talk" bearing west across the Atlantic, and the poet's admonition that "America is promises to / Take," seemed written for another moment in time, as Leonard Woolf said of the journalism written for consumption at the breakfast table.

The leaves in "You, Andrew Marvell" and the birds in "Words in Time" were images that time might keep.

13 "Perhaps I Have Become a Mere Reporter"

In the spring of 1926, the city editor of the *Worcester (Mass.) Telegram* assigned a new twenty-one-year-old reporter to go over to Clark University in Worcester and interview "some sort of loony who had been playing around with fireworks."

The reporter, Stanley Kunitz, went on to a career as editor of the *Wilson Library Bulletin* and a writer of literary reference books for the H. W. Wilson Company. He also won the Pulitzer Prize for Poetry and served a term as the U.S. poet laureate.

Recalling his assignment decades earlier to interview Dr. Robert Goddard, the American space rocketry pioneer, Kunitz told an audience at the Library of Congress that "in a sense, flying to the moon has been one of my persistent metaphors."[1]

My wife and I were in the library's elegant Coolidge Auditorium that night listening to one of the most honored poets and perhaps the greatest reader of poetry of his time. As a poet, I was fascinated by his work and his cadences. As a journalist, I wanted to know more about the metaphorical uses that his interview with Goddard set in motion.

George LaBonte, librarian of the *Telegram,* and Mott Linn of the Clark University Library tried to find the interview but it could not be distinguished among the many unsigned articles about Goddard. Kunitz's reading, however, helped. He was then the library's consultant in poetry and made his remarks in introducing a reading of his "Flight of Apollo." The poem was published in the *New York Times* on July 20, 1969, the day the spacecraft landed on the moon. "Earth was my home, but even

there I was a stranger," Kunitz wrote. "I shall never escape from strange-
ness or complete my journey."

In his collected poems, I found an earlier work, "The Science of the
Night," in which the speaker addressed his beloved as she slept:

> You would escape me—from the brink of earth
> Take off to where the lawless auroras run . . .
> . . . .
> Through gulfs of streaming air
> Bring me the mornings of the milky ways
> Down to my threshold in your drowsy eyes;
> And by the virtue of your honeyed word
> Restore the liquid language of the moon.[2]

There was, then, a connection between the rookie reporter sent to
interview an eccentric professor and the poet who proclaimed "we move
/ in clouds of our unknowing / like great nebulae."

Kunitz's brief career at the *Telegram* began when he wrote a letter to
the paper's editor-in-chief, Captain Roland Andrews, during his sophomore year at Harvard. The letter said that its writer "thought the paper
could use somebody who knew how to write." The editor overlooked
this youthful impertinence and hired Kunitz as a vacation relief reporter.
After graduating summa cum laude, he started work on his master's
degree with the aim of becoming an English professor, but word soon
reached him that the Anglo-Saxon elite of the Ivy League school would
resent being taught by a Jew, no matter how bright. He headed back to
Worcester, where he had grown up, to become assistant Sunday editor,
literary columnist, and feature writer on the *Telegram*.[3]

From a series of features on Goddard, whom he thought he might
have been the first person to interview, Kunitz went on to an assignment involving figures who would make a very different mark in
American history. He was assigned to cover Judge Webster Thayer,
who presided over the trial of Nicola Sacco and Bartolomeo Vanzetti,
anarchists who were found guilty of killing a paymaster and his guard
during a robbery in South Braintree, Massachusetts. Kunitz, who years

later recalled Thayer as "a mean little frightened man," was among many in the United States and abroad who believed the two did not get a fair trial and were convicted because of their political beliefs. After the two were executed, Kunitz decided it was time to leave the *Telegram* for broader fields. He went to New York, hoping in vain to find a publisher willing to publish Sacco and Vanzetti's letters in the face of a public fearful of radicals.[4]

Alone in New York and out of work at the age of twenty-three, Kunitz was nearly broke when he landed a job editing the *Library Bulletin*. He spent most of 1929 in Europe, doing his work for the *Bulletin* by mail. In succeeding years, he turned out, alone or in collaboration, a steady stream of the Wilson company's biographical reference books: *Living Authors* in 1933, *The Junior Book of Authors* in 1934, *British Authors of the Nineteenth Century* in 1936, *American Authors, 1600–1900* in 1938, *Twentieth-Century Authors* in 1942, and *Authors Today and Yesterday* in 1952.

Kunitz's humiliating treatment as a Jewish graduate student at Harvard made him wary of the academic life, although he did later accept a number of teaching posts, beginning at Bennington in 1946. It was an era in which poetry was moving—some would say retreating, some advancing—into the academy. Of poets identified by profession in the April 1945 issue of *Poetry*, seven were academics and one was a former newspaperman. Poets in the fall 2004 issue of the *South Carolina Review* included ten professors, mostly in English departments, and one professional journalist. "More and more writers found teaching at least as congenial with writing as advertising, journalism, or a hundred other means of livelihood," the publisher, teacher and poet Alan Swallow wrote.[5]

Still, some of Kipling's "vulgar herd who 'write for the papers'" did also break into poetry.

Joyce Kilmer, author of the once-praised and now denigrated "Trees," was a feature writer for the *New York Times Sunday Magazine* and wrote a poem on assignment about the sinking of the *Titanic*. Kilmer also taught a course, "Newspaper and Magazine Verse," at the New York University School of Journalism. Shortly before he was killed in action on July 30,

1918, as an infantry sergeant in World War I, he wrote that his work after he returned to civilian life "may be straight reporting."[6]

At the age of seventeen, Dylan Thomas went to work for the *South Wales Daily Post* and its weekly sister paper, the *Herald of Wales*. He showed himself adept at writing literary articles, describing the nineteenth-century Welsh writer Lewelyn Prichard as one of those who "become known not as creatures of flesh and blood, living day by day as prosaically as the rest of us, but as men stepping on clouds, snaring a world of beauty from the trees and sky, half wild, half human." Thomas was glad to get the job and desultorily studied shorthand to qualify himself. One of his editors said his shorthand "did not become efficient enough to help him at a mothers' meeting." He recalled the experience some years later as a dreary round of calls at mortuaries and the homes of suicides. "Another two years and I'd have been done for," he wrote to a friend. He was, in fact, a very bad reporter. One of his troubles was that he would get the names of suicides wrong and misstate the information the mortuaries gave him. On one occasion he missed the death of a well-known local woman by failing to make a routine call at Swansea Hospital. In addition to being careless, he was at least occasionally mendacious, once writing a detailed account of a lacrosse match that turned out to have been canceled. In a piece about bohemian artist Nina Hamnett's autobiography *Laughing Torso,* he falsely reported that the book had been banned, bringing the threat, eventually dropped, of a libel suit. Understandably, Thomas, by then eighteen, was fired after fifteen months.[7]

The poet Hayden Carruth worked on the college daily at the University of North Carolina. Carruth enjoyed deadlines and considered himself a good columnist and editor but abandoned plans of going into journalism because he was too shy to go after the news or interview people. Like Coleridge, he "liked the idea of writing something in the afternoon and then seeing people read it the next morning."[8]

The era of the full-time journalist and poet may have lasted longest in the western United States.

Thomas Hornsby Ferril worked for the *Denver Times* in the early 1920s, doing "everything from the police beat to editorials," including service as the paper's drama critic. He also contributed poems to the newspaper, and in 1926 won the Yale Series of Younger Poets competition. Later he published and edited, along with his wife, Helen, the weekly *Rocky Mountain Herald,* writing a column under the pseudonym Childe Herald so that readers would not "identify me, the poet, with the irresponsible word-slinger doing a weekly column." His main source of income was industrial journalism, or public relations, for the Great Western Sugar Company. In a poem, he lamented the times "When I write an advertisement and believe it / And watch the people believing my advertisement."[9]

Ted Olson, also a Yale Series winner in the 1920s, worked for the *New York Herald-Tribune* and as news editor of the *Republican-Boomerang* in his home town of Laramie, Wyoming, before going on to a career with the State Department.[10]

Charles Levendosky doubled as the author of nationally honored books of poetry and as editorial page editor and columnist for the *Casper Star-Tribune* in Wyoming. He made a rule that he would never write a poem and a column on the same subject, but once he broke it. He had learned that criminologists say people leaving a room always leave some evidence that they have been there, and that they take some traces of the room with them when they leave. "I couldn't get the poem, so I wrote the column first," Levendosky said. In it, he asked what happens "when you walk through another person's life?" Speaking of himself in the third person, he wrote:

He always stacked the coins from his pocket, next to his comb and folded handkerchief, on the bureau before he went to bed—stacked them neatly according to size, from a peak of dimes down to a base of quarters. It was a ritual—before he removed his trousers. So the items wouldn't fall out of his pockets when he hung them up, he told himself. Looking back, he has to admit that such an act seems compulsively neat, even strange. Overly organized.

His father had been a professional gambler who could deal poker chips out to other players in stacks of five or 10 without looking—as sure of the count as he was certain that the deck was fresh. Father had given his son the old poker chips for play; the boy would stack them and count them and stack them, again.[11]

"And then about two weeks later the poem came to me," Leven-dosky said. I heard him read it at a book signing at the Denver Press Club. The poem, "All the Blue Rooms," told of a different relationship in a different way:

You may have already left a room,
but I felt your heat from where
you had stepped or sat. I would scan
a room and know you had been there.

You radiated a thermal field I was
tuned to. I could trace your movements
and often did, through a room, repeating
you. My heat upon yours. Thermal map

upon thermal map. Heat on heat. Red zones
slip into conjunction. Thermal overlap.
When we were together all reds bloomed.
We could tell what the other had touched

in a room and pick it up too. Such heat.
We yearned for conjunction. We burned. And
ached to burn in each other. We left our
combined heat in so many rooms. In so many

rooms where gradually thermal levels cooled
to blue. So many blue rooms. All the rooms
are blue now. Even the ones we stand in—
together. Blue rooms. Even the most sensitive

infrared sensors can no longer find our heat.
All the rooms have faded into blue. The blue
rooms we live in. The cold rooms within us.[12]

The journalist's memory of a routine of stacked poker chips that he copied from his father became the poet's blue rooms and yearning for conjunction.

At Lafayette College in Pennsylvania in 1934, the young poet and professor Theodore Roethke was assigned to handle the college's public relations. Roethke ranked the assignment third in importance as a part of his job, with teaching in first place followed by creative writing. Nevertheless, he said, it took up about half of his time to exploit "a large and constant flow" of local news items in Pennsylvania papers. He also took a part-time job as public relations counsel for makers of lamps and ice cream. Discouraged, the future Pulitzer Prize winner wrote, "Perhaps I have become a mere reporter."[13]

A reporter, not a writer. The two are different things, Roethke said. The novelist Warren Adler once questioned whether poets are writers at all. Yet newspaper stories and poems do have something in common: both are made of words. Words used in different ways. I used to say that I told the facts in newspaper stories and the truth in poems. I no longer believe this. The poet tries to capture what eludes the journalist, but there is a sense in which each can have something to teach the other. The concreteness that is important to journalism can help avoid the vagueness that sometimes afflicts poetry, and fresh metaphors can serve the newspaper writer as well as the poet.

NOTES

BIBLIOGRAPHY

INDEX

Notes

INTRODUCTION

1. Archibald MacLeish, "The Poet and the Press," *Atlantic Monthly,* Mar. 1949, 40.

2. Leonard Woolf, *Beginning Again: An Autobiography of the Years 1911 to 1918* (New York: Harcourt, Brace and World, 1964), 133.

3. Felix Frankfurter, letter to Archibald MacLeish, June 5, 1937, MacLeish Papers, Library of Congress.

4. Samuel Taylor Coleridge, *Essays on His Own Time* (London: William Pickering, 1850), 1:lxvii.

5. Rudyard Kipling, "The Benefactors," in *Rudyard Kipling, Complete Verse: Definitive Edition* (New York: Doubleday, 1989), 339–40.

6. Henry James, *The Novels and Tales: New York Edition* (New York: Charles Scribner's Sons, 1908), 12:ix; John Keats, "On First Looking into Chapman's Homer."

7. Lawrance Thompson, *Robert Frost: The Years of Triumph, 1915–1938* (New York: Holt, Rinehart and Winston, 1970).

8. Charles G. Ross, *The Writing of News: A Handbook* (New York: Henry Holt, 1911), 22.

9. Charles Norman, *Ezra Pound* (New York: Macmillan, 1960), 92.

10. J. F. Kobler, *Ernest Hemingway: Journalist and Artist* (Ann Arbor, Mich.: UMI Research Press, 1985), 1, 2.

11. R. L. Barth, ed., *Selected Letters of Yvor Winters* (Athens: Swallow Press/Ohio State Univ. Press, 2000), 173.

12. Woolf, *Beginning Again,* 133.

13. W. Dale Nelson, "Reporting about the Volcano," *Visions,* no. 19, 1985.

14. W. Dale Nelson, "Reporting about the Earthquake," *Red Rock Review,* Winter 2002, 39.

15. W. Dale Nelson, "With Jerry Falwell in Darkest Africa, or Forty Years as a Reporter for the Associated Press," *Connecticut Poetry Review,* 1996, 28.

1. "I WILL WRITE FOR THE PERMANENT"

1. A. Aspinall, *Politics and the Press, c. 1780–1850* (London: Home and Van Thal, 1949), 6, 71.

2. Valerie Purton, *A Coleridge Chronology* (London: Macmillan, 1933), 45; James Dykes Campbell, *Samuel Taylor Coleridge: A Narrative of the Events of His Life* (London: Macmillan, 1896), 107.

3. John Colmer, *Coleridge: Critic of Society* (Oxford: Clarendon Press, 1959), 28–29; H. D. Traill, *Coleridge* (New York: Harper and Brothers, 1899), 9, 78.

4. E. K. Chambers, *Samuel Taylor Coleridge: A Biographical Study* (Oxford: Clarendon Press, 1938), 41, 147; Mary Stuart, ed., *Letters from the Lake Poets, Samuel Taylor Coleridge, William Wordsworth, Robert Southey, to Daniel Stuart, Editor of the Morning Post and* The Courier, *1800–1838* (London: Privately printed, 1889), 200–201, 252, 258–59.

5. Coleridge, *Essays,* 1:105.

6. Stuart, *Letters,* 96.

7. Coleridge, *Essays,* 1:xci.

8. Chambers, *Samuel Taylor Coleridge,* 22.

9. James Gillman, *The Life of Samuel Taylor Coleridge* (London: William Pickering, 1838), 42; Campbell, *Coleridge: A Narrative,* 26.

10. Chambers, *Samuel Taylor Coleridge,* 39, 49, 69; Earl Leslie Griggs, ed., *Collected Letters of Samuel Taylor Coleridge* (Oxford: Clarendon Press, 1956), 1:160–61, 222.

11. Samuel Taylor Coleridge, *Biographia Literaria* (London: Oxford Univ. Press, 1907), 1:116–17.

12. Coleridge, *Biographia,* 252–53.

13. John Cornwell, *Coleridge, Poet and Revolutionary, 1772–1804: A Critical Biography* (London: Allen Lane, 1973), 125–26; James Dykes Campbell, ed., *The Poetical Works of Samuel Taylor Coleridge* (London: Macmillan, 1893), 64.

14. Chambers, *Samuel Taylor Coleridge,* 51, 53; Coleridge, *Biographia,* 1:114, 119; Cornwell, *Coleridge, Poet and Revolutionary,* 128–31.

15. Cornwell, *Coleridge, Poet and Revolutionary,* 313; Chambers, *Samuel Taylor Coleridge,* 53–54; Coleridge, *Biographia,* 119–20; Griggs, *Collected Letters,* 1:194.

16. Chambers, *Samuel Taylor Coleridge,* 54; Griggs, *Collected Letters,* 1:208; Coleridge, *Biographia,* 1:120; Gillman, *Life of Coleridge,* 75; Campbell, *Coleridge: A Narrative,* 52.

17. Griggs, *Collected Letters,* 1:208.

18. Colmer, *Critic of Society,* 49.

19. Coleridge, *Biographia,* 1:121.

20. Campbell, *Coleridge: A Narrative,* 53–54.

21. Campbell, *Coleridge: A Narrative*, 53–54; Chambers, *Samuel Taylor Coleridge*, 41, 76, 147; Colmer, *Critic of Society*, 27.

22. Campbell, *Coleridge: A Narrative*, 54; Chambers, *Samuel Taylor Coleridge*, 59, 63.

23. Campbell, *Coleridge: A Narrative*, 53–54.

24. Richard Holmes, *Coleridge: Early Visions* (New York: Viking, 1990), 175–76; Griggs, *Collected Letters*, 359–60n.

25. Holmes, *Early Visions*, 175, 197.

26. Stuart, *Letters*, 19–23, 329–33, 384–86.

27. Coleridge, *Biographia*, 1:261; Cornwell, *Coleridge, Poet and Revolutionary*, 247, 254, 257, 263–64, 266.

28. Holmes, *Early Visions*, 238.

29. Holmes, *Early Visions*, 249; Cornwell, *Coleridge, Poet and Revolutionary*, 268–71.

30. Coleridge, *Biographia*, 1:141–42.

31. Holmes, *Early Visions*, 249.

32. Coleridge, *Biographia*, notebook entry for Nov. 24, 1799; Purton, *Coleridge Chronology*, 43; Stuart, *Letters*, 23.

33. Holmes, *Early Visions*, 254.

34. Holmes, *Early Visions*, 255.

35. Stuart, *Letters*, 11n. 1.

36. Coleridge, *Biographia*, 1:146, 148; Holmes, *Early Visions*, 256.

37. Traill, *Coleridge*, 77; Coleridge, *Biographia*, 145; Coleridge, *Essays*, 1:xci.

38. Holmes, *Early Visions*, 255–56; E. V. Lucas, *The Life of Charles Lamb* (New York: G. P. Putnam's Sons, 1905), 338.

39. Coleridge, *Biographia*, 144; Coleridge, *Essays*, xc–xci.

40. Coleridge, *Essays*, 1:lxvii; Traill, *Coleridge*, 79.

41. H. W. Boynton, "The Literary Aspect of Journalism," *Atlantic Monthly*, June 1904, 848.

42. Coleridge, *Biographia*, 2:397.

43. Coleridge, *Biographia*, 1:145–46.

44. Traill, *Coleridge*, 82; Griggs, *Collected Letters*, 1:569.

45. Coleridge, *Biographia*, 1:341.

46. Colmer, *Critic of Society*, 20, 71.

47. Campbell, *Coleridge: A Narrative*, 107; Stuart, *Letters*, 7, 11–15.

48. Stuart, *Letters*, x–xi.

49. Molly LeFebure, *Samuel Taylor Coleridge: A Bondage of Opium* (New York: Stein and Day, 1974), 496–99; Holmes, *Early Visions*, 338–39.

50. Purton, *Coleridge Chronology*, 76–77; Chambers, *Samuel Taylor Coleridge*, 3n; Campbell, *Coleridge: A Narrative*, 167; Stuart, *Letters*, 60–63.

51. Stuart, *Letters,* 351–53.

52. Edith J. Morley, ed., *Henry Crabb Robinson on Books and Their Writers* (London: J. M. Dent, 1938), 155; Stuart, *Letters,* 83–95.

53. Stuart, *Letters,* 119, 331, 351–53.

54. Stuart, *Letters,* 128–31.

55. Stuart, *Letters,* 141–42, 176, 181, 185–86.

56. Stuart, *Letters,* 173–77; Purton, *Coleridge Chronology,* 88.

57. Morley, *Henry Crabb Robinson,* 33; Aspinall, *Politics and the Press,* 89, 209; Stuart, *Letters,* 189–95.

58. Stuart, *Letters,* 185–201; Traill, 132; Chambers, 243.

59. Purton, *Coleridge Chronology,* 96.

60. Stuart, *Letters,* 219–36, 255–61.

61. Purton, *Coleridge Chronology,* 107–8, 127–29; Lucas, *Charles Lamb,* 427.

62. Purton, *Coleridge Chronology,* 110–11.

2. "A WONDERFUL AND PONDEROUS BOOK"

1. David S. Reynolds. *Walt Whitman's America: A Cultural Biography* (New York: Knopf, 1955), 99.

2. Reynolds, *Walt Whitman's America,* 99; Walt Whitman, "Defining our Position," *Brooklyn Eagle,* Mar. 30, 1842, reprinted in *Walt Whitman of the New York Aurora, Editor at Twenty-Two,* ed. Joseph Jay Rubin and Charles H. Brown (State College, Pa.: Bald Eagle Press, 1950), 63–64.

3. Herbert Bergman, "Walt Whitman as a Journalist, 1831–January, 1848," *Journalism Quarterly,* Summer 1971, 195, 198.

4. Rubin, 7, 110–11; Gay Wilson Allen, *The Solitary Singer: A Critical Biography of Walt Whitman* (New York: Macmillan, 1955), 55.

5. Walt Whitman, editorial, *Brooklyn Eagle,* Mar. 22, 1857, quoted in Reynolds, *Walt Whitman's America,* 32.

6. Whitman, article in the *Brooklyn Daily Times,* 1857, quoted in Reynolds, *Walt Whitman's America,* 106.

7. Reynolds, *Walt Whitman's America,* 32; Henry M. Christman, ed., *Walt Whitman's New York: From Manhattan to Montauk* (New York: Macmillan, 1963),103–7.

8. Whitman, "Our City," *New York Aurora,* Mar. 8, 1842, reprinted in Rubin and Brown, *Walt Whitman of the New York Aurora,* 17–19.

9. Whitman, *Aurora,* Apr. 9, 1842, quoted in Bergman, "Walt Whitman as a Journalist," 197.

10. *Camden Courier,* June 1, 1882, reprinted in *Walt Whitman: Prose Works 1892,* vol. 1, *Specimen Days,* ed. Floyd Stovall (New York: New York Univ. Press, 1963), 288;

Malcolm Cowley, ed., *The Complete Poetry and Prose of Walt Whitman* (Garden City, N.Y.: Garden City Books, 1954), 435.

11. Allen, *The Solitary Singer,* 18; Stovall, *Specimen Days,* 286–87.

12. Bergman, "Walt Whitman as a Journalist," 195–96; Stovall, *Specimen Days,* 287.

13. Allen, *The Solitary Singer,* 18–19; Reynolds, *Walt Whitman's America,* 46.

14. Allen,*The Solitary Singer,* 17–18; Bergman, "Walt Whitman as a Journalist," 196.

15. Allen, *The Solitary Singer,* 32; Bergman, "Walt Whitman as a Journalist," 196; Reynolds, *Walt Whitman's America,* 183; Stovall, *Specimen Days,* 287.

16. Allen, *The Solitary Singer,* 34–35; Bergman, "Walt Whitman as a Journalist," 196–97; Emory Holloway, ed., *The Uncollected Poetry and Prose of Walt Whitman* (Garden City, N.Y.: Doubleday, Page, 1921) 1:xxxiii–xxxiv, n; Herbert Bergman and William White, "Walt Whitman's Lost 'Sun-Down Papers', Nos. 1–3," *American Book Collector,* Jan. 1970, 17–20.

17. Holloway, *Uncollected Poetry and Prose,* 1:4, 5–7, 19, 72–78, 83–86; Bliss Perry, *Walt Whitman* (Boston: Houghton Mifflin, 1906), 24; Larzer Ziff, *The American 1890s: Life and Times of a Lost Generation* (New York: Viking, 1966), 150–51; Whitman, "Song of Myself," stanza 8.

18. Allen, *The Solitary Singer,* 45–47; Reynolds, *Walt Whitman's America,* 98; Bergman, "Walt Whitman as a Journalist," 197; Rubin and Brown, *Walt Whitman of the New York Aurora,* 2–3.

19. Frederic Hudson, *Journalism in the United States from 1690 to 1872* (New York: Harper and Brothers, 1873), 489; W. Dale Nelson, *Who Speaks for the President: The White House Press Secretary from Cleveland to Clinton* (Syracuse: Syracuse Univ. Press, 1998), 3, 7; Rubin and Brown, *Walt Whitman of the New York Aurora,* 112–14.

20. Allen, *The Solitary Singer,* 42, 49; Bergman, "Walt Whitman as a Journalist," 198; Rubin and Brown, *Walt Whitman of the New York Aurora,* 2, 5–6.

21. Bergman, "Walt Whitman as a Journalist," 199; William Cauldwell, "Walt Whitman as a Young Man," *New York Times,* Jan. 26, 1901; Holloway, *Uncollected Poetry and Prose,* 1:xxxiii–xxxiv, n; J. Johnston, M.D., and J. W. Wallace, *Visits to Walt Whitman in 1890–91 by Two Lancashire Friends* (London: George Allen and Unwin Ltd., 1917), 70–71; Horace L. Traubel, "Walt Whitman, Schoolmaster: Notes of a Conversation with Charles A. Roe, 1894," *Walt Whitman Fellowship Papers,* Apr. 1894.

22. Allen, *The Solitary Singer,* 49, 53; Reynolds, *Walt Whitman's America,* 83, 86.

23. Bergman, "Walt Whitman as a Journalist," 200; Reynolds, *Walt Whitman's America,* 83; Allen, *The Solitary Singer,* 61; Justin Kaplan, *Walt Whitman: A Life* (New York: Simon and Schuster, 1980), 105, 114; Charles Eliot Norton, *Letters of James Russell Lowell,* vol. 1 (New York: Harper and Brothers, 1984), 242–43; Whitman, "One's Self I Sing," *Leaves of Grass* (New York: Random House, 1921), 1.

24. Bergman, "Walt Whitman as a Journalist," 201–4; Allen, *The Solitary Singer,* 74.

25. Allen, *The Solitary Singer,* 75; William H. Sutton, proof sheet in the Brooklyn Public Library, cited in Bergman, "Walt Whitman as a Journalist," 202; Stovall, *Specimen Days,* 288; Holloway, *Uncollected Poetry and Prose,* 1:106–10, 113–17; Thomas L. Brasher, *Whitman as Editor of the Brooklyn Daily Eagle* (Detroit: Wayne State Univ. Press, 1970), 17; Whitman, *Ourselves and the Eagle,* in Holloway, *Uncollected Poetry and Prose,* 1:114–17; Edward Hungerford, "Walt Whitman and His Chart of Bumps," *American Literature,* Jan. 1931, 350–81.

26. Reynolds, *Walt Whitman's America,* 11–15; Cowley, *Complete Poetry and Prose,* 276.

27. Brasher, *Whitman as Editor,* 194–200; Holloway, *Uncollected Poetry and Prose,* 1:21–23.

28. Clara Barrus, *Whitman and Burroughs, Comrades* (Boston: Houghton Mifflin, 1931), 362; Brasher, *Whitman as Editor,* 13–14; Horace Traubel, *With Walt Whitman in Camden* (New York: Rowman and Littlefield, 1961), 1:249.

29. Bergman, "Walt Whitman as a Journalist," 203; Holloway, *Uncollected Poetry and Prose,* 1:114; Reynolds, *Walt Whitman's America,* 31; Theodore A. Zunder, "Whitman Interviews Barnum," *Modern Language Notes,* Jan. 1933, 40; A. H. Saxon, *P. T. Barnum: The Legend and the Man* (New York: Columbia Univ. Press, 1989), 255.

30. Holloway, *Uncollected Poetry and Prose,* 1:114–17.

31. Stovall, *Specimen Days,* 287–88; Brasher, *Whitman as Editor,* 104–7; Reynolds, *Walt Whitman's America,* 134–35.

32. Reynolds, *Walt Whitman's America,* 135–36; Stovall, *Specimen Days,* 288.

33. Kaplan, *A Life,* 136; Holloway, *Uncollected Poetry and Prose,* 1:183, 185.

34. Reynolds, *Walt Whitman's America,* 120–21; Kaplan, *A Life,* 138–39; Holloway, *Uncollected Poetry and Prose,* 1:191; Whitman, *Leaves of Grass,* 25.

35. Kaplan, *A Life,* 144–45; Reynolds, *Walt Whitman's America,* 121–22; Allen, *The Solitary Singer,* 99.

36. Allen, *The Solitary Singer,* 102–3; Holloway, *Uncollected Poetry and Prose,* 1:234–35.

37. Holloway, *Uncollected Poetry and Prose,* 1:25–27.

38. Edward F. Grier, "Walt Whitman's Earliest Known Notebook," *PMLA: Publications of the Modern Language Association of America,* Oct. 1968, 1453–56; Whitman, *Leaves of Grass,* 66, 189.

39. Kaplan, *A Life,* 224–26; Allen, *The Solitary Singer,* 208–16.

40. Allen, *The Solitary Singer,* 274, 288–90; Whitman, *Specimen Days in America* (London: Walter Scott, 1887), 303; Walter Teller, ed., *Walt Whitman's Camden Conversations* (New Brunswick, N.J.: Rutgers Univ. Press, 1973), 119.

41. Allen, *The Solitary Singer,* 264; Reynolds, *Walt Whitman's America,* 344–45; Kaplan, *A Life,* 355; Milton Hindus, ed., *Walt Whitman: The Critical Heritage* (New York: Barnes and Noble, 1971), 45, 70.

42. Reynolds, *Walt Whitman's America,* 532–33; Allen, *The Solitary Singer,* 487; Teller, *Camden Conversations,* 146–47; Whitman, *Specimen Days,* 303.

43. Cleveland Rodgers and John Black, eds., *Gathering of the Forces* (New York: G. P. Putnam's Sons, 1920), 274–75.

3. "SOMETHING MORE THAN ORDINARY JOURNALISTIC PROSE"

1. Rudyard Kipling, *Something of Myself: For My Friends Known and Unknown* (Garden City, N.Y.: Doubleday, 1899), 331.

2. Kipling, *Something,* 363; Lord Birkenhead, *Rudyard Kipling* (New York: Random House, 1978), 130–31.

3. Birkenhead, *Rudyard Kipling,* 7–8.

4. Birkenhead, *Rudyard Kipling,* 148, 207.

5. Birkenhead, *Rudyard Kipling,* 15–21; Martin Seymour-Smith, *Rudyard Kipling* (London: Queen Anne Press, 1989), 17–20; Kipling, *Something,* 7–13; C. E. Carrington, *The Life of Rudyard Kipling* (Garden City, N.Y: Doubleday, 1955), 10; Boynton, "Literary Aspect," 848.

6. Birkenhead, *Rudyard Kipling,* 35; Seymour-Smith, *Rudyard Kipling,* 33.

7. Kipling, *Something,* 331; Seymour-Smith, *Rudyard Kipling,* 33–34; Birkinhead, *Rudyard Kipling,* 34; Carrington, *Life,* 10.

8. Birkenhead, *Rudyard Kipling,* 40; Kipling, *Something,* 36, 39–40.

9. Seymour-Smith, *Rudyard Kipling,* 39, 52; Birkenhead, *Rudyard Kipling,* 49.

10. Rudyard Kipling, *The Writings in Prose and Verse of Rudyard Kipling* (New York: Charles Scribner's Sons, 1911), 18:265–66.

11. Birkenhead, *Rudyard Kipling,* 55, 58; Seymour-Smith, *Rudyard Kipling,* 52.

12. Kipling, *Something,* 41, 45; Birkenhead, *Rudyard Kipling,* 55.

13. Birkenhead, *Rudyard Kipling,* 57–58.

14. Birkenhead, *Rudyard Kipling,* 58–59; Kipling, *Something,* 41, 46–47, 57; Carrington, *Life,* 39.

15. Kipling, *Something,* 46–47; John Beecroft, ed., *Kipling: A Selection of His Stories and Poems* (Garden City, N.Y., Doubleday, 1956), 1:405–6; Thomas Pinney, ed., *Kipling's India: Uncollected Sketches 1884–1888* (London: Macmillan, 1986), 3–4.

16. E. Kay Robinson, "Kipling in India: Reminiscences by the Editor of the Newspaper on Which Kipling Served at Lahore," *McClure's Magazine,* July 1896, 101, 103; Pinney, *Kipling's India,* 5–6.

17. Kipling, *Something,* 333; Rudyard Kipling, *Complete Verse: Definitive Edition* (New York: Doubleday, 1989), 73–75; Pinney, *Kipling's India,* 3–4, 7, 9–10, 64–65.

18. Carrington, *Life,* 39.

19. Birkenhead, *Rudyard Kipling,* 84.

20. Kipling, *Something,* 49–51; Pinney, *Kipling's India,* 250; Rudyard Kipling, *Departmental Ditties* (New York: M. F. Mansfield, n.d.), 3.

21. Pinney, *Kipling's India,* 249–51.

22. Kipling, *Complete Verse,* 496–97.

23. Birkenhead, *Rudyard Kipling,* 63; Sandra Kemp and Lisa Lewis, eds., *Writings on Writing by Rudyard Kipling* (Cambridge: Cambridge Univ. Press, 1996), 3.

24. Kipling, *Something,* 335.

25. K. Bhaskara Rao, *Rudyard Kipling's India* (Norman: Univ. of Oklahoma Press, 1967), 5, 23.

26. Robinson, "Kipling in India," 99, 109; Carrington, *Life,* 57.

27. Kipling, *Something,* 54–55.

28. Kipling, *Something,* 48–49, 56–57.

29. Kipling, *Something,* 73.

30. Kipling, *Departmental Ditties,* 40–43.

31. Kipling, *Something,* 222.

32. Kipling, *Something,* 75.

33. Kipling, *Something,* 73; Birkenhead, *Rudyard Kipling,* 51–52, 75; Seymour-Smith, *Rudyard Kipling,* 66; Carrington, *Life,* 62.

34. Kipling, *Departmental Ditties,* 82.

35. Kipling, *Something,* 75–78.

36. Kipling, *Something,* 75; Kemp and Lewis, *Writings on Writing,* xvi; Seymour-Smith, *Rudyard Kipling,* 88; Thomas Pinney, ed., *The Letters of Rudyard Kipling* (Iowa City: Univ. of Iowa Press, 1990), 1:140.

37. Birkenhead, *Rudyard Kipling,* 94; Kemp and Lewis, *Writings on Writing,* 34–35.

38. Pinney, *Letters,* 1:182.

39. Pinney, *Letters,* 1:323; Rudyard Kipling, *From Sea to Sea: Letters of Travel, Part II,* in *The Writings in Prose and Verse of Rudyard Kipling* (New York: Charles Scribner's Sons, 1910), 16:114–17; Birkenhead, *Rudyard Kipling,* 107.

40. Beecroft, *Kipling,* 400; Kipling, *Complete Verse,* 233.

41. W. H. Auden, *The Collected Poetry of W. H. Auden* (New York: Random House, 1945), 50.

42. Rudyard Kipling, *The Light That Failed* (Garden City, N.Y.: Doubleday, 1899), 18–19, 22–23, 110.

43. Kipling, *Something,* 105.

44. Kipling, *Something,* 186; Carrington, *Life,* 136, 181–82; Birkenhead, *Rudyard Kipling,* 160–61.

45. Birkenhead, *Rudyard Kipling,* 148.

46. Carrington, *Life,* 182–84; Birkenhead, *Rudyard Kipling,* 166.

47. Carrington, *Life,* 177–78; Pinney, *Letters,* 2:225.

48. Carrington, *Life,* 187–89.

49. Birkenhead, *Rudyard Kipling,* 194–95.

50. Birkenhead, *Rudyard Kipling,* 206–9; Kipling, *Something,* 165.

51. Carrington, *Life,* 239; Birkenhead, *Rudyard Kipling,* 208–9.

52. Kipling, *Something,* 169–71; Birkenhead, *Rudyard Kipling,* 210–11.

53. Birkenhead, *Rudyard Kipling,* 251.

54. Jerome K. Jerome, *My Life and Times* (London: John Murray, 1893).

55. Birkenhead, *Rudyard Kipling,* 259, 266, 270.

56. Carrington, *Life,* 312.

57. Seymour-Smith, *Rudyard Kipling,* 350–51.

58. Kipling, *Something,* 247.

59. Beecroft, *Kipling,* 410.

4. "ANYTHING BUT MATTER-OF-FACT LIFE"

1. James A. Harrison, ed., *Life and Letters of Edgar Allan Poe* (New York, Thomas Y. Crowell, 1903), 2:20–21.

2. Bettina L. Knapp, *Edgar Allan Poe* (New York: Frederick Ungar, 1984), 10–17; Harrison, *Life and Letters,* 1:10.

3. David K. Jackson, *Poe and the Southern Literary Messenger* (New York: Haskell House, 1970), 1–2; Harrison, *Life and Letters,* 1:96.

4. Jackson, *Poe and the Southern Literary Messenger,* 1; Harrison, *Life and Letters,* 1:102–4, 106; Edgar Allan Poe, *Poetry and Tales* (New York, Viking, 1984), 89–91; Dwight Thomas and David K. Jackson, *The Poe Log: A Documentary Life of Edgar Allan Poe, 1809–1849* (Boston, G. K. Hall, 1987), 134.

5. Harrison, *Life and Letters,* 1:107–8; Henry Tuckerman, *The Life of John Pendleton Kennedy* (New York: G. P. Putnam and Sons, 1871), 376; Hervey Allen, *Israfel: The Life and Times of Edgar Allan Poe* (New York: George H. Doran, 1927), 1:365–66.

6. Harrison, *Life and Letters,* 1:116–18, 2:16–17, 25–26, 26–27; Knapp, *Edgar Allan Poe,* 24; Jackson, *Poe and the Southern Literary Messenger,* 97–98, 98–99.

7. Jackson, *Poe and the Southern Literary Messenger,* 101–4, 109–10; Thomas and Jackson, *Poe Log,* 148; James Southall Wilson, "Unpublished Letters of Edgar Allan Poe," *Century Magazine,* Mar. 1924, 655; James A. Harrison, ed., *The Complete Works of Edgar Allan Poe* (New York: George D. Sproul, 1902), 17:29–31.

8. Jackson, *Poe and the Southern Literary Messenger,* 101–2; Thomas and Jackson, *Poe Log,* 147, 214–16, 236; James Russell Lowell, "Our Contributors—No. XVII: Edgar Allan Poe," *Graham's Magazine,* Feb. 1845, 49–53.

9. Anonymous, editor's note, *Southern Literary Messenger,* Jan. 1837, 72; Mary E. Phillips, *Edgar Allan Poe the Man* (Chicago: John C. Winston, 1926), 1:544–45.

10. Harrison, *Life and Letters*, 2:172–80; Jackson, *Poe and the Southern Literary Messenger*, 111–12; Gordon S. Haight, *Mrs. Sigourney, the Sweet Singer of Hartford* (New Haven: Yale Univ. Press, 1930), 77.

11. Thomas and Jackson, *Poe Log*, 166, 287, 316–18; Harrison, *Life and Letters*, 2:53.

12. Thomas and Jackson, *Poe Log*, 318; Harrison, *Life and Letters*, 2:139–40, 148, 165–66, 2:53; Harrison, *Complete Works*, 17:45–46; J. C. G. Kennedy, *Catalogue of the Newspapers and Periodicals Published in the United States, Compiled from the United States Census Statistics of 1850* (J. Livingston, 1852), 45.

13. Harrison, *Life and Letters*, 1:172, 176–77, 2:112–13, 114–15.

14. Harrison, *Life and Letters*, 2:115, 203; Frank Luther Mott, *A History of American Magazines, 1741–1850* (New York: D. Appleton, 1930), 757–58; Heyward Ehrlich, "The *Broadway Journal* (I): Briggs's Dilemma and Poe's Strategy," *Bulletin of the New York Public Library*, Feb. 1969, 77, 81, 83; Burton R. Pollin, ed., *Collected Writings of Edgar Allan Poe* (New York: Gordian Press, 1986), ix–x.

15. Mott, *American Magazines*, 757, 760–61; John Bisco, "Our New Volume," *Broadway Journal*, July 12, 1845; Horace Greeley, *Recollections of a Busy Life* (New York: J. B. Ford, 1868), 196–97; Harrison, *Collected Works*, 17:217; Pollin, "Edgar Allan Poe and His Illustrators," *American Book Collector*, Mar.–Apr. 1981, 6.

16. Horace Elisha Scudder, *James Russell Lowell: A Biography* (Boston: Houghton Mifflin, 1901), 1:165; Perry, *Walt Whitman*, 29; Jeffrey Meyers, *Edgar Allan Poe: His Life and Legacy* (New York: Charles Scribner's Sons, 1992), 169, 186, 188.

17. Mott, *American Magazines*, 586; Anonymous, "The Authors and Mr. Poe," *Godey's Lady's Book*, May 1846, 288; Thomas and Jackson, *Poe Log*, 636–37.

18. Poe, "The Literati of New York City," *Godey's Lady's Book*, May 1846, 194–200.

19. Poe, "To Helen," *Southern Literary Messenger*, Mar. 1836, 238; *Graham's Magazine*, Sept. 1841, 123; Poe, "The Raven," *American Review*, Feb. 1845, 144–45; *Broadway Journal*, Feb. 8, 1845; *Southern Literary Messenger*, Mar. 1845, 186–88.

20. Anonymous, "Authors," 288.

21. Vernon Louis Parrington, *Main Currents in American Thought* (New York: Harcourt, Brace and World, 1927) 2:56.

5. "UNHAPPILY SMITTEN WITH THE LOVE OF RHYME"

1. Edmund Blunden, *Leigh Hunt and His Circle* (New York: Harper and Brothers, 1930), 2–6; Leigh Hunt, *The Autobiography of Leigh Hunt, with Reminiscences of Friends and Contemporaries* (New York: AMS Press, 1965), 1:18.

2. Blunden, *Leigh Hunt*, 5–7; Hunt, *Autobiography*, 1:19–26, 63; James R. Thompson, *Leigh Hunt* (Boston: G. K. Hall, 1977), 19.

3. Thompson, *Leigh Hunt*, 20; Hunt, *Autobiography*, 1:69, 72, 73–74, 92, 121.

4. Hunt, *Autobiography*, 1:123, 128, 166; Blunden, *Leigh Hunt*, 40.

5. Hunt, *Autobiography*, 1:24, 181–82.

6. Blunden, *Leigh Hunt*, 42–43; Lawrence Huston Houtchens and Carolyn Washburn Houtchens, eds., *Leigh Hunt's Dramatic Criticism, 1808–1831* (New York: Columbia Univ. Press, 1949), 7–8; Hunt, *Autobiography*, 1:182.

7. Blunden, *Leigh Hunt*, 46–47; Hunt, *Autobiography*, 1:202–4; Hunt, *Correspondence*, 1:41; R. Brimley Johnson, ed., *Prefaces by Leigh Hunt* (Chicago: Walter H. Hill, 1927), 28–29; Robert Stewart, *Henry Brougham, 1778–1868: His Public Career* (London: Bodley Head, 1986), 74–75, 82, 100.

8. Gregory Dart, "Cockneyism," *London Review of Books*, Dec. 18, 2003, 19; H. S. Milford, ed., *The Poetical Works of Leigh Hunt* (London: Oxford Univ. Press, 1923), 141–44; Charles Kent, ed. *Leigh Hunt as Poet and Essayist* (London: Frederick Warne, 1891), x.

9. Blunden, *Leigh Hunt*, 49; Hunt, *Autobiography*, 1:236–37.

10. Blunden, *Leigh Hunt*, 49; Hunt, *Autobiography*, 1:240; George Dumas Stout, *The Political History of Leigh Hunt's Examiner* (St. Louis: Washington Univ., 1949), 10–11.

11. Hunt, *Autobiography*, 1:241–42; Blunden, *Leigh Hunt*, 52; Blunden, *Leigh Hunt's "Examiner" Examined* ([Hamden, Conn.]: Archon Books, 1967), 12; Stout, *Political History*, 13.

12. Lucy Maynard Sampson, *The Newspaper and Authority* (New York: Oxford Univ. Press, 1923), 286n; Stout, *Political History*, 6; Blunden, *Leigh Hunt*, 55; Tom Paulin, "Gentlemen and ladies came to see the poet's cottage," *London Review of Books*, Feb. 19, 2004, 17; Stewart, *Henry Brougham*, 75–78; Chester W. New, *The Life of Henry Brougham to 1830* (Oxford: Clarendon Press, 1961), 52.

13. Hunt, *Autobiography*, 1:250; Stout, *Political History*, 6–7, 16; New, *Life of Henry Brougham*, 56.

14. Stout, *Political History*, 19–20; Hunt, *Autobiography*, 1:272–80; Anonymous, "Law Report," *Times*, Dec. 10, 1812; Kent, *Leigh Hunt as Poet*, 25.

15. Thomas Sadler, ed., *Diary, Reminiscences, and Correspondence of Henry Crabb Robinson* (London: Macmillan, 1869), 1:376; Stout, *Political History*, 22.

16. Stout, *Political History*, 5, 21–23; Anonymous, "Law Report."

17. Stout, *Political History*, 24; Hunt, *Autobiography*, 283; Blunden, *Leigh Hunt*, 73.

18. Timothy J. Lulofs and Hans Ostrom, *Leigh Hunt: A Reference Guide* (Boston: G. K. Hall, 1985), 12–13; Blunden, *Leigh Hunt*, 73–74; Aspinall, *Politics and the Press*, 57n.

19. Stout, *Political History*, 24–25; Hunt, *Autobiography*, 1:283, 296; Blunden, *Leigh Hunt*, 57.

20. Hunt, *Autobiography,* 1:290–93; Thompson, *Leigh Hunt,* 21; Hunt, *Correspondence,* 78; H. R. Fox Bourne, *English Newspapers: Chapters in the History of Journalism,* 2 vols. (London: Chatto and Windus, 1887), 1:348; Kent, xxii.

21. Hunt, *Correspondence,* 79; Thompson, *Leigh Hunt,* 22; Blunden, *Leigh Hunt,* 75; Bourne, *English Newspapers,* 1:348.

22. Hunt, *Correspondence,* 99; Blunden, *Leigh Hunt's "Examiner,"* 48; Thompson, *Leigh Hunt,* 29–36; Stout, *Political History,* 37–38; Hunt, *Autobiography,* 2:36–37, 51–52.

23. Fred Kaplan, *Dickens: A Biography* (New York: William Morrow, 1988), 311; Deshler Welch, "Dickens in Switzerland: Some Unpublished Letters and Reflections," *Harper's Magazine,* Apr. 1906, 714–19; Charles Dickens, *Bleak House* (New York: Modern Library, 1985), 384–85; Edgar Johnson, *Charles Dickens: His Tragedy and Triumph* (New York: Simon and Schuster, 1952), 1:254; David Paroissien, ed., *Selected Letters of Charles Dickens* (Boston: Twayne, 1985), 331; Hunt, *Autobiography,* 2:266.

24. Hunt, *Autobiography,* 1:292; William Hazlitt, *Table Talk* (London: Dent, 1959), 202; Fred Kaplan, *Thomas Carlyle: A Biography* (Ithaca, N.Y.: Cornell Univ. Press, 1983), 194–95.

25. A. Aspinall, ed., *Three Early Nineteenth Century Diaries* (London: Williams and Norgate, 1952), 278; Hunt, *Correspondence,* 2:79–80; New, *Life of Henry Brougham,* 90.

6. "THE CRANK OF AN OPINION-MILL"

1. John B. Pickard, ed., *The Letters of John Greenleaf Whittier* (Cambridge, Mass.: Belknap, 1975), 1:481, 499; John Greenleaf Whittier, *The Complete Poetical Works* (Boston: Houghton Mifflin, 1880), 215–16.

2. Whittier, *Complete Poetical Works,* 209–14.

3. Robert Penn Warren, *New and Selected Essays* (New York: Random House, 1989), 239.

4. Albert Mordell, *Quaker Militant: John Greenleaf Whittier* (Port Washington, N.Y.: Kennikat Press, 1969); Pickard, *Letters,* 1:4, 17n; Wendell Phillips Garrison and Francis Jackson Garrison *William Lloyd Garrison, 1805–1879: The Story of His Life as Told by His Children* (Boston: Houghton Mifflin, 1894), 1:115.

5. Pickard, *Letters,* 1:19–20; Anonymous, "Young American Writers: J. G. Whittier," *Philadelphia Album,* May 20, 1829, 406; Mordell, *Quaker Militant,* 24.

6. Pickard, *Letters,* 1:5–6, 32, 35, 36, 37n, 65, 66n, 3:438, 1:113–14; Whittier, *Complete Poetical Works,* 40–41.

7. Whittier, *Complete Poetical Works,* 42; John L. Thomas, *The Liberator: William Lloyd Garrison, a Biography* (Boston: Little, Brown, 1963), 172–75.

8. Pickard, *Letters,* 1:112, 142–43; Garrison and Garrison, *William Lloyd Garrison,* 517–18.

9. Pickard, *Letters*, 1:112–13, 185–90, 202–4, 236–37.

10. Mordell, *Quaker Militant*, 93–94, 107–8; Pickard, *Letters*, 1:69n; Edward D. Snyder, "Whittier Returns to Philadelphia after a Hundred Years," *Pennsylvania Magazine of History and Biography*, Apr. 1938, 141; Whittier, *Complete Poetical Works*, 48–49.

11. Snyder, "Whittier Returns," 141; Mordell, *Quaker Militant*, 94–95; Pickard, *Letters*, 1:278.

12. Mordell, *Quaker Militant*, 94–97; Snyder, "Whittier Returns," 141; Pickard, *Letters*, 1:218.

13. Mordell, *Quaker Militant*, 96–98; Maria Weston Chapman, *Right and Wrong in Massachusetts* (1839; repr., New York: Negro Universities Press, 1969) 12.

14. Garrison and Garrison, *William Lloyd Garrison*, 218; Mordell, *Quaker Militant*, 99; Pickard, *Letters*, 1:300–303, 303n.

15. Garrison and Garrison, *William Lloyd Garrison*, 276; Mordell, *Quaker Militant*, 104.

16. Mordell, *Quaker Militant*, 105–7.

17. Mordell, *Quaker Militant*, 107–8; Pickard, *Letters*, 1:375, 376n.

18. Pickard, *Letters*, 1:493, 555, 556.

19. Garrison and Garrison, *William Lloyd Garrison*, 35; Pickard, *Letters*, 1:481, 499.

20. Garrison and Garrison, *William Lloyd Garrison*, 35; Pickard, *Letters*, 1:621–22.

21. Pickard, *Letters*, 1:2, 2:ix.

22. I Samuel 4:21; Whittier, *Complete Poetical Works*, 112.

23. Pickard, *Letters*, 2:x, 317, 319, 393, 3:243, 368; Whittier, "Brown of Ossawotamie," in *Complete Poetical Works*, 188.

7. "THE REPUTATION OF A REFINED POET"

1. Parrington, *Main Currents*, 2:230; Justin McCarthy, *Reminiscences* (New York: Harper and Brothers, 1900), 1:170; Traubel, *With Walt Whitman in Camden*, 1:69–70.

2. Charles H. Brown, *William Cullen Bryant* (New York: Charles Scribner's Sons, 1971), 7, 10, 51; William Cullen Bryant, *The Poetical Works* (New York: D. Appleton and Company, 1903), 21.

3. Brown, *William Cullen Bryant*, 19, 73–74.

4. Brown, *William Cullen Bryant*, 78, 82–83, 96, 99; Parrington, *Main Currents*, 2:232.

5. Brown, *William Cullen Bryant*, 124, 126, 129.

6. Brown, *William Cullen Bryant*, 151–53, 157.

7. Brown, *William Cullen Bryant*, 158–60, 168.

8. Brown, *William Cullen Bryant*, 157, 173, 174–75.

9. Brown, *William Cullen Bryant*, 175, 185, 241–42; Frank Luther Mott, *American Journalism: A History: 1690–1960* (New York: Macmillan, 1962), 186–87; William Cullen Bryant, *The Poetical Works* (New York: D. Appleton and Company, 1903), 193–94.

10. Whitman, *Specimen Days*, 175–77.

11. Rubin and Brown, *Walt Whitman of the New York Aurora*, 112–13.

12. Rubin and Brown, 114; Reynolds, *Walt Whitman's America*, 99; Traubel, *With Walt Whitman in Camden*, 3:248.

13. Rodgers and Black, *Gathering of the Forces*, 261–62; Traubel, *With Walt Whitman in Camden*, 1:125–26, 3:514–15.

14. Traubel, *With Walt Whitman in Camden*, 3:424; McCarthy, *Reminiscences*, 1:171; Barrus, *Whitman and Burroughs, Comrades*, 175.

15. Parrington, *Main Currents*, 2:230, 234; Brown, *William Cullen Bryant*, 249.

16. Mott, *American Journalism*, 425–26; Brown, *William Cullen Bryant*, 518–22; Whitman, *Specimen Days*, 175–76.

8. "THE EXHUMING OF BURIED REPUTATIONS"

1. Kaplan, *A Life*, 98; Merle M. Hoover, *Park Benjamin: Poet and Editor* (New York: Columbia Univ. Press, 1948), 120–21, 180–81.

2. Hoover, *Park Benjamin*, 6, 44–45, 53; Mott, *American Magazines*, 358–59.

3. J. Henry Harper, *The House of Harper: A Century of Publishing in Franklin Square* (New York: Harper and Brothers, 1912), 23; Mott, *American Magazines*, 360.

4. Hoover, *Park Benjamin*, vii, 16, 198.

5. Hoover, *Park Benjamin*, 28; Rubin and Brown, *Walt Whitman of the New York Aurora*, 110–11; Edgar Allan Poe, "A Chapter on Autography," *Graham's Lady's and Gentleman's Magazine*, Nov. 1841, 224–34.

6. Hoover, *Park Benjamin*, 8, 72, 85; Poe, "Chapter on Autography," 226.

7. Hudson, *Journalism in the United States*, 456; Hoover, *Park Benjamin*, 100, 105, 107; Mott, *American Journalism*, 236.

8. Hoover, *Park Benjamin*, 164–65.

9. Laura Stedman and George M. Gould, *The Life and Letters of Edmund Clarence Stedman* (New York: Moffat, Yard, 1910), 1:230; Bruce Catton, *The Coming Fury* (New York: Pocket Books, 1967), 451.

10. Stedman and Gould, *Edmund Clarence Stedman*, 1:230–31.

11. Edmund Clarence Stedman, "The Battle of Manassas," *The World*, July 24, 1861.

12. Stedman and Gould, *Edmund Clarence Stedman*, 1:227, 234, 236; Stedman, "Battle."

13. Robert J. Scholnick, *Edmund Clarence Stedman* (Boston: G. K. Hall, 1977), 13, 18–19.

14. Stedman and Gould, *Edmund Clarence Stedman*, 1:109.

15. Scholnick, *Edmund Clarence Stedman*, 21–24.

16. Scholnick, *Edmund Clarence Stedman*, 24–25; Stedman and Gould, *Edmund Clarence Stedman*, 1:215, 217.

17. Stedman and Gould, *Edmund Clarence Stedman*, 1:207–8; Allen, *Israfel*, 229; Scholnick, *Edmund Clarence Stedman*, 25.

18. Stedman and Gould, *Edmund Clarence Stedman*, 1:224; Catton, *Coming Fury*, 393–94.

19. Scholnick, *Edmund Clarence Stedman*, 28–29; Stedman and Gould, *Edmund Clarence Stedman*, 1:254.

20. Edd Winfield Parks, *Henry Timrod* (New York: Twayne, 1964), 38, 98.

21. Stedman and Gould, *Edmund Clarence Stedman*, 1:322–23, 325; Edmund Clarence Stedman, *An American Anthology, 1787–1900: Selections Illustrating the Editor's Critical Review of American Poetry in the Nineteenth Century* (Boston: Houghton Mifflin, 1900), xxiv.

22. Parrington, *Main Currents*, 2:v.

9. "EVERY QUALITY THAT MADE REPORTING A MISERY"

1. Stephen Crane, *Prose and Poetry* (New York: Library of America, 1984), 1293, 1299–1351; Charles Michelson, introduction to *The Work of Stephen Crane*, ed. Wilson Follett (New York: Knopf, 1926), x, xi.

2. Richard Harding Davis, "Our War Correspondents in Cuba and Puerto Rico," *Harper's New Monthly Magazine*, May 1899, 941; Scott C. Osborn, "The 'Rivalry-Chivalry' of Richard Harding Davis and Stephen Crane," *American Literature*, Mar. 1956, 51; Ames W. Williams, "Stephen Crane, War Correspondent," *New Colophon*, Apr. 1948, 113–14; Stanley Wertheim and Paul Sorrentino, eds., *The Correspondence of Stephen Crane* (New York: Columbia Univ. Press, 1988), 1:232–33.

3. John Berryman, *Stephen Crane: A Critical Biography*, rev. ed. (New York: Cooper Square Press, 1962), 3, 16, 20–23, 28.

4. Victor A. Elconin, "Stephen Crane at Asbury Park," *American Literature*, Nov. 1948, 275–80.

5. Elconin, "Stephen Crane at Asbury Park," 281–86; Berryman, *Stephen Crane*, 37.

6. Elconin, "Stephen Crane at Asbury Park," 284–85.

7. Berryman, *Stephen Crane*, 44; Hamlin Garland, *Roadside Meetings* (Macmillan, 1931), 190.

8. Berryman, *Stephen Crane*, 75, 82; Wertheim and Sorrentino, *Correspondence*, 232; Berryman, *Stephen Crane*, 75; Garland, *Roadside Meetings*, 200.

9. Wertheim and Sorrentino, *Correspondence*, 1:104, 124–25, 187.

10. Crane, *Prose and Poetry*, 1299, 1325.

11. Wertheim and Sorrentino, *Correspondence,* 1:39; R. W. Stallman and E. R. Hagemann, eds., *The New York City Sketches of Stephen Crane and Related Pieces* (New York: New York Univ. Press, 1966), 289; Corwin K. Linson, *My Stephen Crane* (Syracuse: Syracuse Univ. Press, 1958), 65, 69–70; Joseph Katz, ed., *The Poems of Stephen Crane* (New York: Cooper Square, 1971); Ziff, *American 1890s,* 152.

12. Stallman and Hagemann, *New York City Sketches,* 97–102; Crane, *Prose and Poetry,* 1322.

13. Wertheim and Sorrentino, *Correspondence,* 1:45; Joseph Katz, ed., *Stephen Crane in the West and Mexico* (Kent, Ohio: Kent State Univ. Press, 1970), xi–xiii; Willa Cather, "When I Knew Stephen Crane," *Prairie Schooner,* Fall 1949, reprinted from *Library,* June 23, 1900, 231.

14. Katz, *Stephen Crane in the West,* 3–14.

15. Cather, "When I Knew Stephen Crane," 231–32, 234–35.

16. Stephen Crane, letter to Lucius L. Button, in Wertheim and Sorrentino, *Correspondence,* 1:100–101.

17. Irving Bacheller, *Coming Up the Road: Memories of a North Country Boyhood* (Indianapolis: Bobbs-Merrill, 1928), 280; Garland, *Roadside Meetings,* 203; Berryman, *Stephen Crane,* 118–19, 131, 136–37.

18. Wertheim and Sorrentino, *Correspondence,* 1:261–64; Crane, *Prose and Poetry,* 878–79.

19. Crane, *Prose and Poetry,* 880–84, 885, 909.

20. Berryman, *Stephen Crane,* 115; Thomas Beer, *Stephen Crane: A Study in American Letters* (New York: Knopf, 1923), 146; Wertheim and Sorrentino, *Correspondence,* 1:264; Ames W. Williams, "Stephen Crane, War Correspondent," *New Colophon,* Apr. 1948, 115; Follett, *Work of Stephen Crane,* x, xi.

21. Follett, *Work of Stephen Crane,* xii; Wertheim and Sorrentino, *Correspondence,* 1:264, 288n.

22. Arthur Lubow, *The Reporter Who Would Be King: A Biography of Richard Harding Davis* (New York: Scribner's, 1992), 146; Charles Belmont Davis, ed., *Adventures and Letters of Richard Harding Davis* (New York: Scribner's, 1917), 200.

23. R. W. Stallman and E. R. Hagemann, eds., *The War Dispatches of Stephen Crane* (New York: New York Univ. Press, 1964), 5–6, 8, 21–22, 25–26, 28; Beer, *Stephen Crane,* 154.

24. Stallman and Hagemann, *War Dispatches,* 29–30, 51–52.

25. Linson, *My Stephen Crane,* 109; Hamlin Garland, *My Friendly Contemporaries: A Literary Log* (New York: Macmillan, 1932), 499.

26. Wertheim and Sorrentino, *Correspondence,* 2:356–57; Williams, "Stephen Crane, War Correspondent," 116; Beer, *Stephen Crane,* 177–78; Cecil Carnes, *Jimmy Hare, News Photographer: Half a Century with a Camera* (New York: Macmillan, 1940), 60.

27. Wertheim and Sorrentino, *Correspondence,* 2:353; Crane, *Wounds in the Rain: War Stories* (Freeport, N.Y.: Books for Libraries Press, 1972), 253; Stallman and Hagemann, *War Dispatches,* 123.

28. Davis, "Our War Correspondents," 944.

29. Williams, "Stephen Crane, War Correspondent," 120; Follett, *Work of Stephen Crane,* 12:xiii; Stallman and Hagemann, *War Dispatches,* 111.

30. Follett, *Work of Stephen Crane,* 12:xxiii.

10. "IT IS ONLY IGNORANCE WHICH IS BOREDOM"

1. Hugh MacDiarmid [Christopher Murray Grieve], *Lucky Poet: A Self-Study in Literature and Political Ideas* (Berkeley: Univ. of California Press, 1972), 65, 228.

2. MacDiarmid, *Lucky Poet,* 189, 320; Robert Crawford, "Yesterday's Scotland and Tomorrow's World" (lecture, Univ. of Wyoming, Oct. 13, 2004); Nancy Gish, "An Interview with Hugh MacDiarmid," *Contemporary Literature,* Spring 1969, 138, 144.

3. MacDiarmid, *Lucky Poet,* 8; Hugh MacDiarmid, *The Company I've Kept* (Berkeley, Univ. of California Press, 1967), 154; Hugh MacDiarmid, *Selected Prose,* ed. Alan Riach (Manchester, U.K.: Carcanet, 1992), 206, 243.

4. MacDiarmid, *Selected Prose,* 205; MacDiarmid, *Lucky Poet,* 8, 225; Catherine Kerrigan, *Whaur Extremes Meet: The Poetry of Hugh MacDiarmid, 1920–1934* (Edinburgh: Mercat Press, 1983), 10–11.

5. MacDiarmid, *Lucky Poet,* 8, 228.

6. Kerrigan, *Whaur Extremes Meet,* 14–15; Alan Bold, ed., *The Letters of Hugh MacDiarmid* (London: Hamish Hamilton, 1984), 1, 4n; MacDiarmid, *Selected Prose,* 203; MacDiarmid, *Company,* 21.

7. MacDiarmid, *Lucky Poet,* 14, 228–29; Bold, 2, 63n, 64, 66–68.

8. Bold, *Letters,* 4n; Colin Holmes, "The Tredegar Riots of 1911: Anti-Jewish Disturbances in South Wales," *Welsh History Review,* Dec. 1982, 214–25.

9. Holmes, "Tredegar Riots," 216; Bold, *Letters,* 5.

10. Bold, *Letters,* 6, 11.

11. Bold, *Letters,* 12, 13, 367, 367n; MacDiarmid, *Lucky Poet,* 3; MacDiarmid, *Company,* 24; MacDiarmid, *Collected Poems of Hugh MacDiarmid* (New York: Macmillan, 1967), 184–85.

12. Bold, *Letters,* 7, 367; MacDiarmid, *Lucky Poet,* 105; Hugh MacDiarmid, *Annals of the Five Senses: The First Collected Work by Hugh MacDiarmid* (Edinburgh: Polygon Books, 1983), 11; Nancy Gish, *Hugh MacDiarmid: The Man and His Work* (London: Macmillan, 1984), 18.

13. Bold, *Letters,* 28–29, 366–67; MacDiarmid, *Company,* 184.

14. Bold, *Letters,* 26; MacDiarmid, *Annals,* 2, 5; MacDiarmid, *Lucky Poet,* 106.

15. Bold, *Letters*, 40n, 41, 62, 64, 73–74; MacDiarmid, *Annals*, 8.

16. Bold, *Letters*, 41, 65n, 71, 297; Gish, *Hugh MacDiarmid*, 23; MacDiarmid, *Annals*, 4.

17. MacDiarmid, *Annals*, 4; Kerrigan, *Whaur Extremes Meet*, 55; Edwin Muir, "The Scottish Renaissance," *Saturday Review of Literature*, Oct. 31, 1925, 259.

18. Bold, *Letters*, xxx, 64, 82, 84, 86.

19. Muir, "Renaissance," 259, in *Uncollected Scottish Criticism* (London: Vision Press, 1982), 85, 87.

20. Bold, *Letters*, xxii–iii, 227, 387, 399, 401.

21. Bold, *Letters*, 234, 379, 384, 399, 402, 633.

22. Bold, *Letters*, 102–3, 228.

23. Bold, *Letters*, 354, 355n.

24. Bold, *Letters*, 232, 232n; T. S. Eliot, ed., *The Criterion, 1922–1939* (London: Faber and Faber, 1967), 8:596, 598.

25. Bold, *Letters*, xxxiii, 114–15, 148; MacDiarmid, *Lucky Poet*, 52, 133; Kerrigan, *Whaur Extremes Meet*, 173; MacDiarmid, *Collected Poems*, 192.

26. MacDiarmid, *Lucky Poet*, 41, 45, 187; MacDiarmid, *Selected Prose*, 209; Bold, *Letters*, xxxii–xxxiii.

27. MacDiarmid, *Company*, 152–53; Bold, *Letters*, 252, 383.

28. MacDiarmid, *Company*, 188–89; Gish, "Interview," 145–46.

29. Bold, *Letters*, xxxv.

11. "AS HE LEARNED TO KNOW IT DAY BY DAY"

1. Carl Sandburg, "Fixing the Pay of Railroad Men," *International Socialist Review*, June 1915, 709; Carl Sandburg, *The People, Yes* (Harcourt, Brace and World, 1936), 101.

2. Harry Golden, *Carl Sandburg* (Cleveland: World Publishing, 1961), 41, 48.

3. Carl Sandburg, *Always the Young Strangers* (New York: Harcourt, Brace, 1953), 211–12, 226.

4. Golden, *Carl Sandburg*, 49, 50–51; Penelope Niven, *Carl Sandburg: A Biography* (New York: Scribner's, 1991), 292.

5. Golden, *Carl Sandburg*, 55, 57.

6. Golden, *Carl Sandburg*, 57–58.

7. Golden, *Carl Sandburg*, 59–62.

8. Golden, *Carl Sandburg*, 67; Gay Wilson Allen, "Carl Sandburg: Fire and Smoke," *South Atlantic Quarterly*, Summer 1960, 321.

9. Golden, *Carl Sandburg*, 40–49, 57, 87, 89; Herbert Mitgang, ed., *The Letters of Carl Sandburg* (New York: Harcourt Brace, 1968), 76–77.

10. Golden, *Carl Sandburg*, 86–87.

11. Golden, *Carl Sandburg*, 117, 188–89.

12. Golden, *Carl Sandburg,* 89–90, 189.

13. Niven, *Carl Sandburg,* 229–31; Golden, *Carl Sandburg,* 191–93; Ben Hecht, *A Child of the Century* (New York: Simon and Schuster, 1954), 245; Negley D. Cochran, *E. W. Scripps* (New York: Harcourt, Brace, 1930), 130–33, 139–41.

14. Niven, *Carl Sandburg,* 223–33; Mitgang, *Letters,* 98, 127–28; Golden, *Carl Sandburg,* 200–1.

15. Niven, *Carl Sandburg,* 234, 248.

16. Niven, *Carl Sandburg,* 236–38; Sandburg, "Chicago Poems," *Poetry: A Magazine of Verse,* Mar. 1914, 191–98; Carl Sandburg, *Chicago Poems* (New York: Henry Holt, 1916), 3; Carl Sandburg, *Complete Poems* (New York: Harcourt, Brace, 1950), 271–82.

17. Ellen Williams, *Harriet Monroe and the Poetry Renaissance: The First Ten Years of Poetry, 1912–22* (Urbana: Univ. of Illinois Press, 1977), 99, 101.

18. Niven, *Carl Sandburg,* 270, 276; Mitgang, *Letters,* 544–45; Sandburg, *Chicago Poems,* 71.

19. Niven, *Carl Sandburg,* 291–92; Golden, *Carl Sandburg,* 196–97.

20. Niven, *Carl Sandburg,* 299; Hecht, *Child of the Century,* 249, 252; Mitgang, *Letters,* 127n; Mary Welsh Hemingway, *How It Was* (New York: Knopf, 1976), 30; Albert Parry, *Garrets and Pretenders: A History of Bohemianism in America* (New York: Dover Publications, 1960), 295–96.

21. Golden, *Carl Sandburg,* 193.

22. Mitgang, *Letters,* 130, 131–32, 143–45, 443.

23. Niven, *Carl Sandburg,* 318, 320–21; Golden, *Carl Sandburg,* 137; Theodore Draper, *The Roots of American Communism* (New York: Viking, 1957), 236–37.

24. Draper, *Roots of American Communism,* 237; Niven, *Carl Sandburg,* 322.

25. Niven, *Carl Sandburg,* 323; Mitgang, *Letters,* 145, 148.

26. Mitgang, *Letters,* 145, 149.

27. Niven, *Carl Sandburg,* 326–27, 331–32; Mitgang, *Letters,* 137.

28. Niven, *Carl Sandburg,* 336, 340–41; Mitgang, *Letters,* 163.

29. Niven, *Carl Sandburg,* 341; Carl Sandburg, *The Chicago Race Riots: July, 1919* (New York: Harcourt, Brace and World, 1919), 3.

30. Sandburg, *Complete Poems,* 201.

31. Golden, *Carl Sandburg,* 173; Lincoln Steffens, *Autobiography* (New York: Harcourt, Brace and World, 1931), 314.

32. Mitgang, *Letters,* 394; Niven, *Carl Sandburg,* 374–76; Sandburg, *Complete Poems,* 302–4; Philip R. Yannella, *The Other Carl Sandburg* (Jackson: Univ. Press of Mississippi, 1996), 46.

33. Niven, *Carl Sandburg,* 413; Lilla S. Perry, *My Friend Carl Sandburg: The Biography of a Friendship* (Metuchen, N.J.: Scarecrow Press, 1981), 31.

34. Golden, *Carl Sandburg,* 158, 216; Sandburg, *Complete Poems,* xxix.

35. Allen, "Fire and Smoke," 316.

1 2 . "FOR TIME TO KEEP"

1. Niven, *Carl Sandburg,* 599; Scott Donaldson, *Archibald MacLeish: An American Life* (Boston: Houghton Mifflin, 1992), 1–2.

2. W. A. Swanberg, *Luce and His Empire* (New York: Scribner's, 1972), 40–41.

3. R. H. Winnick, ed., *Letters of Archibald MacLeish, 1907 to 1982* (Boston: Houghton Mifflin, 1983), 65.

4. "Education," *Time,* Mar. 3, 1923, 17.

5. Swanberg, *Luce and His Empire,* 58.

6. Archibald MacLeish, interview, *New York Times,* 1942.

7. Peter Griffin, *Less than a Treason: Hemingway in Paris* (New York: Oxford Univ. Press, 1990), 36; A. Scott Berg, *Max Perkins: Editor of Genius* (New York: E. P. Dutton, 1978), 178–79; Jacqueline Tavernier-Courbin, *Ernest Hemingway's "A Moveable Feast": The Making of Myth* (Boston: Northeastern Univ. Press, 1991), 96; Archibald MacLeish, "Years of the Dog," in *Collected Poems, 1917–1982* (Boston: Houghton Mifflin, 1985), 376–77.

8. Swanberg, *Luce and His Empire,* 75–82; Robert E. Hertzstein, *Henry R. Luce: A Political Portrait of the Man Who Created the American Century* (New York: Scribner's, 1994), 58.

9. Hertzstein, *Henry R. Luce,* 58–59; Swanberg, *Luce and His Empire,* 83; MacLeish, interview, 8–9; Carlos Baker, ed., *Ernest Hemingway: Selected Letters, 1917–1961* (New York: Scribner's, 1981), 317.

10. Matthew Josephson, *Infidel in the Temple: A Memoir of the Nineteen-Thirties* (New York: Knopf, 1967), 57; Galley Proof, Matthew Josephson Papers, Box 13, Folder 1, American Heritage Center, Univ. of Wyoming, Laramie.

11. MacLeish, interview, 7–8; Archibald MacLeish, Kreuger profile in *Fortune,* May 1933, 51; MacLeish, "La Trentiesme de Mon Eage," in *Collected Poems,* 81; *Fortune,* June 1932.

12. Beatrice Kaufman and Joseph Hennessey, eds., *The Letters of Alexander Woollcott* (New York: Viking, 1944), 145; Donaldson, *Archibald MacLeish,* 256; *Fortune,* Nov. 1935; MacLeish, interview, 8; Editors of *Fortune, Background of War* (Knopf, 1937), 54; MacLeish, *Collected Poems,* 380.

13. Swanberg, *Luce and His Empire,* 106; Max Freedman, ed., *Roosevelt and Frankfurter, Their Correspondence, 1928–1945* (Boston: Little, Brown, 1968), 158; *Fortune,* Dec. 1933; "The Case Against Roosevelt," *Fortune,* Dec. 1935.

14. Baker, *Selected Letters,* 317; MacLeish, letter to Sandburg, July 20, 1933, MacLeish Papers, Library of Congress; Golden, *Carl Sandburg,* 165; Sandburg, *Complete Poems,* 665.

15. Hart Crane, *The Bridge: A Poem* (New York: Liveright, 1970), 75; Thomas S. W. Lewis, ed., *Letters of Hart Crane and His Family* (New York: Columbia Univ. Press, 1974), 521.

16. John Unterecker, *Voyager: A Life of Hart Crane* (New York: Farrar, Straus and Giroux, 1969), 634–37.

17. MacLeish, "Lines for an Interment," in *Collected Poems,* 288.

18. MacLeish, Memos to Henry Luce, Nov. 12 and Nov. 14, 1935; letters to Felix Frankfurter, Nov. 30, 1935, and Jan. 10, 1936; MacLeish Papers, Library of Congress; anonymous, "Jews in America," *Fortune,* Feb. 1936, 85.

19. Hertzstein, *Henry R. Luce,* 86.

20. MacLeish, letter to Laird Goldsborough, Jan. 16, 1937, memo to Goldsborough, Feb. 22, 1937, MacLeish Papers, Library of Congress.

21. James Bryant Conant, *My Several Lives: Memoirs of a Social Inventor* (New York: Harper and Row, 1970), 399, 401; Louis M. Lyons, "Harvard Meets the Press: A Personal Account of the Early Nieman Years," 5, and Charles L. Whipple, "A Vignette— Louis M. Lyons on *The Boston Globe,*" 40, both in *Nieman Reports,* Spring 1989.

22. Conant, *My Several Lives,* 400, 402; Jerome Aumente, "Archibald MacLeish, First Nieman Curator, Talks about That Innovative Year," *Nieman Reports,* Spring 1989, 37–38.

23. Aumente, "MacLeish Talks," 34; Lyons, 14.

24. Aumente, "MacLeish Talks," 37; Lyons, 14; Anonymous, "Aunt Agnes' Fellows," *Time,* Jan. 9, 1939, 39.

25. Nancy L. Benco, "Archibald MacLeish: The Poet Librarian," *Quarterly Journal of the Library of Congress,* July 1976, 234–37.

26. Aumente, "MacLeish Talks," 38; anonymous, "Here's Where We Get OFF," *New York Herald-Tribune,* Oct. 9, 1941, MacLeish Papers, Library of Congress; Thomas L. Stokes, "Poet MacLeish Has a Double-Barreled Job on His Hands in the OFF," Raymond Clapper Collection, Censorship File, Library of Congress; Harold L. Ickes, *The Secret Diary,* vol. 3, 506–7; MacLeish, letters to Elmer Davis, Oct. 17, 1942, and Jan. 26, 1943, MacLeish Papers, Library of Congress.

27. Donaldson, *Archibald MacLeish,* 372, 381–82, 384.

28. MacLeish, letter to Joseph Barnes, Dec. 30, 1944, memo to Joseph C. Grew, Feb. 3, 1945, memo, Feb. 7, 1945, MacLeish papers, Library of Congress.

29. MacLeish, memorandum of conversation with Bert Andrews, Mar. 30, 1945, MacLeish Papers, Library of Congress; H. R. Baukhage, column in Hollywood *Citizen News,* Apr. 4, 1945; Edward R. Stettinius, memo to MacLeish, MacLeish Papers, Library of Congress.

30. William S. White, *Majesty and Mischief: A Mixed Tribute to FDR* (New York: McGraw Hill, 1961), 32–34.

31. MacLeish, letters to President Truman on Apr. 13 and Aug. 15, 1945, MacLeish Papers, Library of Congress.

32. MacLeish, "The Poet and the Press," *Atlantic Monthly,* Mar., 1949, 40; MacLeish, *Collected Poems,* 150, 323, 335, 387; MacLeish, interview, 7; Bill Moyers, "A

Conversation with Archibald MacLeish," Mar. 27, 1976, transcript from WNET, New York, 9.

33. MacLeish, *Collected Poems,* 332, 335; Sandburg, "Open Letter to the Poet Archibald MacLeish Who Has Forsaken His Massachusetts Home to Make Propaganda for Freedom," *Complete Poems,* 622.

34. MacLeish, *Collected Poems,* 387.

13. "PERHAPS I HAVE BECOME A MERE REPORTER"

1. Stanley Kunitz, remarks in reading at the Library of Congress, Oct. 7, 1974.

2. Stanley Kunitz, *The Poems of Stanley Kunitz, 1928–1978* (Boston: Little, Brown, 1979), 48, 97.

3. Stanley Kunitz, *Next-to-Last Things* (Boston: Atlantic Monthly Press, 1985), 100–101.

4. Kunitz, *Next-to-Last Things,* 101.

5. "Notes on Contributors," *Poetry: A Magazine of Verse,* Apr., 1945, 59–60; "Contents," and "Contributors," *South Carolina Review,* Fall 2004, 1–2, 214–16; Alan Swallow, ed., *New Signatures I: A Selection of College Writing* (Prairie City, Ill.: The Press of James A. Decker, 1947), x.

6. Joyce Kilmer, *Poems, Essays and Letters,* ed. with a memoir by Robert Cortes Holliday, 2 vols. (Garden City, N.Y.: Doubleday, 1946), 1:40, 63, 89.

7. Paul Ferris, ed., *The Collected Letters of Dylan Thomas* (London: J. M. Dent and Sons, 1985),10, 15n; Constantine Fitzgibbon, *The Life of Dylan Thomas* (Boston: Little, Brown, 1965), 62, 64–65; Jonathan Fryer, *Dylan: The Nine Lives of Dylan Thomas* (London: Kyle Cathie Ltd., 1993), 38–39, 42.

8. Roy Scheele, "Hayden Carruth: The Gift of Self," *Poets & Writers Magazine,* May/June 1996, 47.

9. A. Thomas Trusky, *Thomas Hornsby Ferril* (Boise, Idaho: Boise State College, 1973), 8–11; Thomas Hornsby Ferril, *New and Selected Poems* (New York: Harper and Brothers, 1952), 82–85.

10. Ted Olson, *Footnotes to Time, Selected Poems* (Laramie: Univ. of Wyoming, 1986), vii–x.

11. Charles Levendosky, remarks at Denver Press Club, May 6, 2003; "Fragments of Other Lives Cling to Ours," *Casper (Wyo.) Star-Tribune,* Sept. 21, 1986, A12.

12. Levendosky, Press Club remarks; "All the Blue Rooms," in *Circle of Light* (Glendo, Wyo.: High Plains Press, 1995), 24.

13. Ralph J. Mills Jr., ed. *Selected Letters of Theodore Roethke* (Seattle: Univ. of Washington Press, 1968), 26–28, 172; Theodore Roethke, *On the Poet and His Craft* (Seattle: Univ. of Washington Press, 1965), 4.

Bibliography

ARCHIVAL SOURCES

Archibald MacLeish Papers, Library of Congress, Washington, D.C.

Raymond Clapper Collection, Censorship File, Library of Congress, Washington, D.C.

Matthew Josephson Papers, Box 13, Folder 1, American Heritage Center, Univ. of Wyoming, Laramie.

BOOKS

Allen, Gay Wilson. *The Solitary Singer: A Critical Biography of Walt Whitman.* New York: Macmillan, 1955.

Allen, Hervey, *Israfel: The Life and Times of Edgar Allan Poe.* 2 vols. New York: George H. Doran, 1927.

Aspinall, A. *Politics and the Press, c. 1780–1850.* London: Home and Van Thal, 1949.

———, ed. *Three Early Nineteenth Century Diaries.* London: Williams and Norgate, 1952.

Auden, W. H., *The Collected Poetry of W. H. Auden.* New York: Random House, 1945.

Bacheller, Irving. *Coming Up the Road: Memories of a North Country Boyhood.* Indianapolis: Bobbs-Merrill, 1928.

Baker, Carlos. ed. *Ernest Hemingway: Selected Letters, 1917–1961.* New York: Scribner's, 1981.

Barrus, Clara. *Whitman and Burroughs, Comrades.* Boston: Houghton Mifflin, 1931.

Barth, R. L. *Selected Letters of Yvor Winters,* edited by R. L. Barth. Athens: Swallow Press/Ohio Univ. Press, 2000.

213

Beecroft, John, ed. *Kipling: A Selection of His Stories and Poems.* 2 vols. Garden City, N.Y.: Doubleday, 1956.

Beer, Thomas. *Stephen Crane: A Study in American Letters.* New York: Knopf, 1923.

Berg, A. Scott. *Max Perkins: Editor of Genius.* New York: E. P. Dutton, 1978.

Berryman, John. *Stephen Crane: A Critical Biography.* Rev. ed. New York: Cooper Square Press, 1977.

Birkenhead, Lord. *Rudyard Kipling.* New York: Random House, 1978.

Blunden, Edmund. *Leigh Hunt and His Circle.* New York: Harper and Brothers, 1930.

———. *Leigh Hunt's "Examiner" Examined.* [Hamden, Conn.]: Archon Books, 1967.

Bold, Alan, ed. *The Letters of Hugh MacDiarmid.* London: Hamish Hamilton, 1984.

Bourne, H. R. Fox. *English Newspapers: Chapters in the History of Journalism.* 2 vols. London: Chatto and Windus, 1887.

Brasher, Thomas L. *Whitman as Editor of the Brooklyn Daily Eagle.* Detroit: Wayne State Univ. Press, 1970.

Brooks, Van Wyck. *Sketches in Criticism.* New York: E. P. Dutton, 1932.

Brown, Charles H. *William Cullen Bryant.* New York: Charles Scribner's Sons, 1971.

Bryant, William Cullen. *The Poetical Works.* New York: D. Appleton and Company, 1903.

Campbell, James Dykes, *Samuel Taylor Coleridge: A Narrative of the Events of His Life.* London: Macmillan, 1896.

———, ed. *The Poetical Works of Samuel Taylor Coleridge.* London: Macmillan, 1893.

Carnes, Cecil. *Jimmy Hare, News Photographer: Half a Century with a Camera.* New York: Macmillan, 1940.

Carrington, C. E. *The Life of Rudyard Kipling.* Garden City, N.Y.: Doubleday, 1955.

Catton, Bruce. *The Coming Fury.* New York: Pocket Books, 1967.

Chambers, E. K. *Samuel Taylor Coleridge: A Biographical Study.* Oxford: Clarendon Press, 1938.

Chapman, Maria Weston. *Right and Wrong in Massachusetts.* Boston: Dow and Jackson Anti-Slavery Press, 1839. Reprint, New York: Negro Universities Press, 1969.

Chaudhuri, Nirad C. *Thy Hand, Great Anarch! India: 1921–1952*. Reading, Mass.: Addison-Wesley, 1988.

Chivers, Thomas Holley. *Chivers' Life of Poe*. Edited with an introduction by Richard Beale Davis. New York: Dutton, 1952.

Christman, Henry M. *Walt Whitman's New York: From Manhattan to Montauk*. New York: Macmillan, 1963.

Cochran, Negley D. *E. W. Scripps*. New York: Harcourt, Brace, 1930.

Coleman, Deirdre. *Coleridge and The Friend (1809–1810)*. Oxford: Clarendon Press, 1988.

Coleridge, E. H., ed. *Complete Poetical Works of Samuel Taylor Coleridge*. 2 vols. Oxford, 1912.

Coleridge, Samuel Taylor. *Biographia Literaria*. 2 vols. London: Oxford Univ. Press, 1907.

———. *Essays on His Own Times: Forming A Second Series of The Friend*. London: William Pickering, 1850.

Colmer, John. *Coleridge: Critic of Society*. Oxford: Clarendon Press, 1959.

Conant, James Bryant. *My Several Lives: Memoirs of a Social Inventor*. New York: Harper and Row, 1970.

Cornell, Louis L. *Kipling in India*. New York: St. Martin's, 1966.

Cornwell, John. *Coleridge, Poet and Revolutionary, 1772–1804: A Critical Biography*. London: Allen Lane, 1973.

Cowley, Malcolm, ed. *The Complete Poetry and Prose of Walt Whitman*. Garden City, N.Y.: Garden City Books, 1954.

Crane, Hart. *The Bridge: A Poem*. New York: Liveright, 1970.

Crane, Stephen. *Prose and Poetry*. New York: Library of America, 1984.

———. *Wounds in the Rain: War Stories*. Freeport, N.Y.: Books for Libraries Press, 1972.

Davison, Peter. *The Fading Smile: from Robert Frost to Robert Lowell to Sylvia Plath*. New York: Knopf, 1994.

Davis, Charles Belmont, ed. *Adventures and Letters of Richard Harding Davis*. New York: Scribner's, 1917.

Deutsch, Babette. *This Modern Poetry*. New York: Norton, 1935.

Dickens, Charles. *Bleak House*. New York: Modern Library, 1985.

Donaldson, Scott. *Archibald MacLeish: An American Life*. Boston: Houghton Mifflin, 1992.

Downey, Fairfax. *Richard Harding Davis: His Day*. New York: Scribner's, 1933.

Draper, Theodore. *The Roots of American Communism*. New York: Viking, 1957.

Editors of *Fortune*. *Background of War*. Knopf, 1937.

Eliot, T. S., ed. *The Criterion, 1922–1939*. 18 vols. London: Faber and Faber, 1967.

Ferril, Thomas Hornsby. *New and Selected Poems*. New York: Harper and Brothers, 1952.

Ferris, Paul, ed. *The Collected Letters of Dylan Thomas*. London: J. M. Dent and Sons, 1985.

Fitzgibbon, Constantine. *The Life of Dylan Thomas*. Boston: Little Brown, 1965.

Follet, Wilson, ed. *The Work of Stephen Crane*. 12 vols. New York: Knopf, 1926.

Freedman, Max, ed. *Roosevelt and Frankfurter, Their Correspondence, 1928–1945*. Boston: Little Brown, 1967.

Fryer, Jonathan. *Dylan: The Nine Lives of Dylan Thomas*. London: Kyle Cathie Limited, 1993.

Garland, Hamlin. *My Friendly Contemporaries: A Literary Log*. New York: Macmillan, 1932.

———. *Roadside Meetings*. New York: Macmillan, 1931.

Garrison, Wendell Phillips, and Andrew Jackson Garrison. *William Lloyd Garrison, 1805–1879: The Story of His Life as Told by His Children*. 4 vols. Boston: Houghton Mifflin, 1894.

Gillman, James. *The Life of Samuel Taylor Coleridge*. London: William Pickering, 1938.

Gish, Nancy K. *Hugh MacDiarmid: The Man and His Work*. London: Macmillan, 1984.

Glen, Duncan, ed. *Selected Essays of Hugh MacDiarmid*. Berkeley: Univ. of California Press, 1970.

Golden, Harry. *Carl Sandburg*. Cleveland: World Publishing, 1961.

Greeley, Horace. *Recollections of a Busy Life*. New York: J. B. Ford, 1868.

Griffin, Peter. *Less than a Treason: Hemingway in Paris*. New York: Oxford Univ. Press, 1990.

Griggs, Earl Leslie, ed. *Collected Letters of Samuel Taylor Coleridge*. 2 vols. Oxford: Clarendon Press, 1956.

Haight, Gordon S. *Mrs. Sigourney: The Sweet Singer of Hartford*. New Haven: Yale Univ. Press, 1930.

Harper, J. Henry. *The House of Harper: A Century of Publishing in Franklin Square.* New York: Harper and Brothers, 1912.

Harrison, James A., ed. *The Complete Works of Edgar Allan Poe.* 17 vols. New York: George D. Sproul, 1902.

———. *Life and Letters of Edgar Allan Poe.* 2 vols. New York: Thomas Y. Crowell, 1903.

Hazlitt, William. *Table Talk.* London: Dent, 1959.

Hecht, Ben. *A Child of the Century.* New York: Simon and Schuster, 1954.

Hemingway, Mary Welsh. *How It Was.* New York: Knopf, 1976.

Hertzstein, Robert E. *Henry R. Luce: A Political Portrait of the Man Who Created the American Century.* New York: Scribner's, 1994.

Hindus, Milton, ed. *Walt Whitman: The Critical Heritage.* New York: Barnes and Noble, 1971.

Holloway, Emory. *The Uncollected Poetry and Prose of Walt Whitman: Much of Which Has Been but Recently Discovered, with Various Early Manuscripts Now First Published.* 2 vols. Garden City, N.Y.: Doubleday, Page, 1921.

Holmes, Richard. *Coleridge: Early Visions.* New York: Viking, 1990.

Hoover, Merle M. *Park Benjamin: Poet and Editor.* New York, Columbia Univ. Press, 1948.

Houtchens, Lawrence Huston, and Carolyn Washburn Houtchens. *Leigh Hunt's Dramatic Criticism, 1808–1831.* New York: Columbia Univ. Press, 1949.

Hudson, Frederic. *Journalism in the United States from 1690 to 1872.* New York: Harper and Brothers, 1873.

Hunt, Leigh. *The Autobiography of Leigh Hunt, with Reminiscences of Friends and Contemporaries.* 2 vols. New York: AMS Press, 1965.

———. *The Correspondence of Leigh Hunt, Edited by His Eldest Son.* 2 vols. London: Smith, Elder and Co., 1862.

Jackson, David K. *Poe and the Southern Literary Messenger.* New York: Haskell House, 1970.

James, Henry. *A London Life and The Reverberator.* Oxford: Oxford Univ. Press, 1989.

———. *The Novels and Tales: New York Edition.* New York: Charles Scribner's Sons, 1908.

Jerome, Jerome K. *My Life and Times.* London: John Murray, 1893.

Johnson, Edgar. *Charles Dickens: His Tragedy and Triumph.* 2 vols. New York: Simon and Schuster, 1952.

Johnson, R. Brimley, ed. *Prefaces by Leigh Hunt*. Chicago: Walter H. Hill, 1927.

Johnston, J, and J. W. Wallace. *Visits to Walt Whitman in 1890–91 by Two Lancashire Friends*. London: George Allen and Unwin, 1917.

Josephson, Matthew. *Infidel in the Temple: A Memoir of the Nineteen-Thirties*. New York: Knopf, 1967.

Kaplan, Fred. *Dickens: A Biography*. New York: William Morrow, 1988.

———. *Thomas Carlyle: A Biography*. Ithaca, N.Y.: Cornell Univ. Press, 1983.

Kaplan, Justin. *Lincoln Steffens: A Biography*. New York: Simon and Schuster, 1947.

———. *Walt Whitman: A Life*. New York: Simon and Schuster, 1980.

Katz, Joseph, ed. *The Poems of Stephen Crane*. New York: Cooper Square, 1971.

———. *Stephen Crane in the West and Mexico*. Kent, Ohio: Kent State Univ. Press, 1970.

Kaufman, Beatrice, and Joseph Hennessey, eds. *The Letters of Alexander Woollcott*. New York: Viking, 1944.

Keating, Peter. *Kipling the Poet*. London: Secker and Warburg, 1994.

Kemp, Sandra, and Lisa Lewis, eds. *Writings on Writing by Rudyard Kipling*. Cambridge: Cambridge Univ. Press, 1996.

Kennedy, J. C. G. *Catalogue of the Newspapers and Periodicals Published in the United States, Compiled from the United States Census Statistics of 1850*. New York: J. Livingston, 1852.

Kent, Charles, ed. *Leigh Hunt as Poet and Essayist*. London: Frederick Warne, 1891.

Kerrigan, Catherine. *Whaur Extremes Meet: The Poetry of Hugh MacDiarmid, 1920–1934*. Edinburgh: Mercat Press, 1983.

Kilmer, Joyce. *Poems, Essays and Letters*. Edited with a memoir by Robert Cortes Holliday. 2 vols. Garden City, N.Y.: Doubleday, 1946.

Kipling, Rudyard. *American Notes*. Edited by Arrell Morgan Gibson with the subtitle *Rudyard Kipling's West*. Norman: Univ. of Oklahoma Press, 1981.

———. *The Collected Works of Rudyard Kipling*. 27 vols. New York: Ames Press, 1970.

———. *Complete Verse: Definitive Edition*. New York: Doubleday, 1989.

———. *Departmental Ditties*. New York: M. F. Mansfield, n.d.

———. *From Sea to Sea: Letters of Travel, Part II*. In *The Writings in Prose and Verse of Rudyard Kipling*, vol. 16. New York: Charles Scribner's Sons, 1910.

———. *The Light That Failed*. Garden City, N.Y.: Doubleday, 1899.

———. *Something of Myself: For My Friends Known and Unknown.* Garden City, N.Y.: Doubleday, 1899.

———. *Stalky & Co.* In *The New World Edition of the Works of Rudyard Kipling.* Garden City, N.Y.: Doubleday, Page, 1907.

Knapp, Benita L. *Edgar Allan Poe.* New York: Frederick Ungar, 1984.

Kobler, J. F. *Ernest Hemingway: Journalist and Artist.* Ann Arbor, Mich.: UMI Research Press, 1985.

Kunitz, Stanley. *Next-to-Last Things.* Boston: Atlantic Monthly Press, 1985.

———. *The Poems of Stanley Kunitz, 1928–1978.* Boston: Little, Brown, 1979.

Langford, Gerald. *The Richard Harding Davis Years: A Biography of a Mother and Son.* New York: Holt, Rinehart and Winston, 1961.

Lefebure, Molly. *Samuel Taylor Coleridge: A Bondage of Opium.* New York: Stein and Day, 1974.

Levendosky, Charles. *Circle of Light.* Glendo, Wyo.: High Plains Press, 1995.

Lewis, C. Day. *The Poetic Image: The Creative Power of the Visual Word.* Los Angeles: Jerry P. Tarcher, 1984.

Lewis, Thomas S. W., ed. *Letters of Hart Crane and His Family.* New York: Columbia Univ. Press, 1974.

Linson, Corwin K. *My Stephen Crane.* Syracuse: Syracuse Univ. Press, 1958.

Lubow, Arthur. *The Reporter Who Would Be King: A Biography of Richard Harding Davis.* New York: Scribner's, 1992.

Lucas, E. V. *The Life of Charles Lamb.* 2 vols. New York: G. P. Putnam's Sons, 1905.

Lulofs, Timothy J., and Hans Ostrom. *Leigh Hunt: A Reference Guide.* Boston: G. K. Hall, 1985.

Lycett, Andrew. *Dylan Thomas: A New Life,* Woodstock, N.Y.: The Overlook Press, 2003.

MacDiarmid, Hugh [Christopher Murray Grieve]. *Annals of the Five Senses.* Edinburgh: Polygon Books, 1983.

———. *Collected Poems of Hugh MacDiarmid.* New York: Macmillan, 1967.

———. *The Company I've Kept.* Berkeley: Univ. of California Press, 1967.

———. *Lucky Poet: A Self-Study in Literature and Political Ideas.* Berkeley: Univ. of California Press, 1972.

———. *The Raucle Tongue; Hitherto Uncollected Prose.* 2 vols. Edited by Angus Calder, Glen Murray and Alan Riach. Manchester, U.K.: Carcenet, 1997.

———. *Selected Poems.* Selected and Edited by David Craig and John Manson. Harmondsworth, U.K.: Penguin Books, 1970.

———. *Selected Prose.* Edited by Alan Riach. Manchester: Carcanet, U.K., 1992.

MacLeish, Archibald. *Collected Poems, 1917–1982.* Boston: Houghton Mifflin, 1985.

Martin, John Barlow. *Adlai Stevenson of Illinois: The Life of Adlai E. Stevenson.* Garden City, N.Y.: Doubleday, 1976.

McCarthy, Justin. *Reminiscences.* 2 vols. New York: Harper and Brothers, 1900.

Meyers, Jeffrey. *Edgar Allan Poe: His Life and Legacy.* New York: Charles Scribner's Sons, 1992.

Milford, H. S., ed. *The Poetical Works of Leigh Hunt.* London: Oxford Univ. Press, 1923.

Mills, Ralph J., Jr., ed. *Selected Letters of Théodore Roethke.* Seattle: Univ. of Washington Press, 1968.

Mitgang, Herbert, ed. *The Letters of Carl Sandburg.* New York: Harcourt, Brace, 1968.

Mordell, Albert, *Quaker Militant: John Greenleaf Whittier.* Port Washington, N.Y.: Kennikat Press, 1969.

Morley, Edith J., ed. *Henry Crabb Robinson on Books and Their Authors.* 3 vols. London: J. M. Dent, 1938.

Mott, Frank Luther. *American Journalism: A History: 1690–1960.* New York: Macmillan, 1962.

———. *A History of American Magazines, 1741–1850.* New York: D. Appleton, 1930.

Muir, Edwin. *Uncollected Scottish Criticism.* London: Vision Press, 1982.

Nelson, W. Dale. *Who Speaks for the President? The White House Press Secretary from Cleveland to Clinton.* Syracuse: Syracuse Univ. Press, 1998.

New, Chester W. *The Life of Henry Brougham to 1830.* Oxford: Clarendon Press, 1961.

Newlin, Keith, and Joseph B. McCullough. *Selected Letters of Hamlin Garland.* Lincoln: Univ. of Nebraska Press, 1998.

Niven, Penelope. *Carl Sandburg: A Biography.* New York: Scribner's, 1991.

Norman, Charles. *Ezra Pound.* New York: Macmillan, 1960.

Norton, Charles Eliot. *Letters of James Russell Lowell.* Vol. 1. New York: Harper and Brothers, 1984.

O'Connor, Garry. *Sean O'Casey: A Life.* New York: Atheneum, 1988.

Olson, Ted. *Footnotes to Time, Selected Poems.* Laramie: Univ. of Wyoming, 1986.

Orel, Harold. *A Kipling Chronology.* Boston: G. K. Hall, 1990.

Ostrom, John Ward, ed., *The Letters of Edgar Allan Poe*. Cambridge, Mass.: Harvard Univ. Press, 1948.

Parks, Edd Winfield. *Henry Timrod*. New York: Twayne, 1964.

Paroissien, David, ed. *Selected Letters of Charles Dickens*. Boston: Twayne, 1985.

Parrington, Vernon Louis. *Main Currents in American Thought*. 3 vols. New York: Harcourt, Brace and World, 1927.

Parry, Albert. *Garrets and Pretenders: A History of Bohemianism in America*. New York: Dover Publications, 1960.

Perry, Bliss. *Walt Whitman*. Boston: Houghton Mifflin, 1906.

Perry, Lilla S. *My Friend Carl Sandburg: The Biography of a Friendship*. Metuchen, N.J.: Scarecrow Press, 1981.

Phillips, Mary E. *Edgar Allan Poe the Man*. 2 vols. Chicago. John C. Winston, 1926.

Pickard, John B. ed., *The Letters of John Greenleaf Whittier*. 3 vols. Cambridge, Mass.: Belknap, 1975.

Pinney, Thomas, ed., *Kipling's India: Uncollected Sketches 1884–88*. London: Macmillan, 1986.

———. *The Letters of Rudyard Kipling*. 3 vols. Iowa City: Univ. of Iowa Press, 1990.

Pizer, Donald, ed. *Hamlin Garland's Diaries*. San Marino, Calif.: Huntington Library, 1968.

Poe, Edgar Allan. *Poetry and Tales*. New York, Viking, 1984.

Pollin, Burton R. ed. *Collected Writings of Edgar Allan Poe*. 4 vols. New York: Gordian Press, 1986.

Potter, Stephen, ed. *Coleridge: Select Poetry and Prose*. London: Nonesuch, 1962.

Purton, Valerie. *A Coleridge Chronology*. London: Macmillan, 1993.

Rao, K. Bhaskara. *Rudyard Kipling's India*. Norman: Univ. of Oklahoma Press, 1967.

Reynolds, David S. *Walt Whitman's America: A Cultural Biography*. New York: Knopf, 1995.

Rodgers, Cleveland, and John Black, eds., *Gathering of the Forces*. New York: G. P. Putnam's Sons, 1920.

Roethke, Theodore. *On the Poet and His Craft*. Seattle: Univ. of Washington Press, 1965.

Ross, Charles G. *The Writing of News: A Handbook*. New York: Henry Holt, 1911.

Rubin, Joseph Jay, and Charles H. Brown, eds. *Walt Whitman of the New York Aurora, Editor at Twenty-Two: A Collection of Recently Discovered Writings*. State College, Pa.: Bald Eagle Press, 1950.

Sadler, Thomas, ed. *Diary, Reminiscences, and Correspondence of Henry Crabb Robinson*. 3 vols. London: Macmillan, 1869.

Sampson, Lucy Maynard. *The Newspaper and Authority*. New York: Oxford Univ. Press, 1923.

Sandburg, Carl. *Always the Young Strangers*. New York: Harcourt, Brace, 1953.

———. *Chicago Poems*. New York: Henry Holt, 1916.

———. *The Chicago Race Riots: July, 1919*. New York: Harcourt, Brace and World, 1919.

———. *Complete Poems*. New York: Harcourt, Brace and World, 1950.

———. *The People, Yes*. Harcourt, Brace and World, 1936.

Saxon, A. H. *P. T. Barnum: The Legend and the Man*. New York: Columbia Univ. Press, 1989.

Schmidgall, Gary, ed. *Intimate with Walt: Selections from Whitman's Conversations with Horace Traubel, 1888–1892*. Iowa City: Univ. of Iowa Press, 2001.

Scholnick, Robert J. *Edmund Clarence Stedman*. Boston: G. K. Hall, 1977.

Scudder, Horace Elisha. *James Russell Lowell: A Biography*. 2 vols. Boston: Houghton Mifflin, 1901.

Seymour-Smith, Martin. *Rudyard Kipling*. London: Queen Anne Press, 1989.

Southworth, James G. *Sowing the Spring: Studies in British Poets from Hopkins to MacNiece*. Freeport, N.Y.: Books for Libraries Press, 1968 (first printed 1940 by Basil Blackwell and Mott).

Stallman, R. W. *Stephen Crane: A Biography*. New York: George Braziller, 1968.

———, ed. *Stephen Crane: Sullivan County Tales and Sketches*. Ames: Iowa State Univ. Press, 1968.

Stallman, R. W., and E. R. Hagemann. *The New York City Sketches of Stephen Crane and Related Pieces*. New York: New York Univ. Press, 1966.

———. *The War Dispatches of Stephen Crane*. New York: New York Univ. Press, 1964.

Stedman, Edmund Clarence. *An American Anthology, 1787–1900: Selections Illustrating the Editor's Critical Review of American Poetry in the Nineteenth Century*. Boston: Houghton Mifflin, 1900.

Stedman, Laura, and George M. Gould. *The Life and Letters of Edmund Clarence Stedman*. 2 vols. New York: Moffat, Yard, 1910.

Steffens, Lincoln. *Autobiography.* New York: Harcourt, Brace and World, 1931.

Stewart, Robert. *Henry Brougham, 1778–1868: His Public Career.* London: Bodley Head, 1986.

Stout, George Dumas. *The Political History of Leigh Hunt's Examiner.* St. Louis: Washington Univ., 1949.

Stovall, Floyd, ed. *Walt Whitman: Prose Works.* 2 vols. New York: New York Univ. Press, 1963.

Stuart, Mary, ed. *Letters from the Lake Poets, Samuel Taylor Coleridge, William Wordsworth, Robert Southey, to Daniel Stuart, Editor of the* Morning Post *and the* Courier, *1800–1838.* London: Privately printed, 1889.

Swallow, Alan, ed. *New Signatures I: A Selection of College Writing.* Prairie City, Ill.: Press of James A. Decker, 1947.

Swanberg, W. A. *Luce and His Empire.* New York: Scribner's, 1972.

Tavernier-Courbin, Jacqueline. *Ernest Hemingway's "A Moveable Feast": The Making of Myth.* Boston: Northeastern Univ. Press, 1991.

Teller, Walter, ed. *Walt Whitman's Camden Conversations.* New Brunswick, N.J.: Rutgers Univ. Press, 1973.

Thomas, Dwight, and David K. Jackson. *The Poe Log: A Documentary Life of Edgar Allan Poe, 1809–1849.* Boston: G. K. Hall, 1987.

Thomas, John L. *The Liberator: William Lloyd Garrison, a Biography.* Boston: Little, Brown, 1963.

Thompson, James R. *Leigh Hunt.* Boston: G. K. Hall, 1977.

Thompson, Lawrance. *Robert Frost: The Years of Triumph, 1915–1938.* New York: Holt, Rinehard and Winston, 1970.

Traill, H. D. *Coleridge.* New York: Harper and Brothers, 1899.

Traubel, Horace. "Walt Whitman, Schoolmaster: Notes of a Conversation with Charles A. Roe, 1894." *Walt Whitman Fellowship Papers,* April, 1895.

———. *With Walt Whitman in Camden.* 5 vols. New York: Rowman and Littlefield, 1961.

Traubel, Horace, Richard Maurice Bucke, and Thomas Harned, eds. *In Re Walt Whitman.* Philadelphia: David McKay, 1893.

Trusky, A. Thomas. *Thomas Hornsby Ferril.* Boise, Idaho: Boise State College, 1973.

Tuckerman, Henry T. *The Life of John Pendleton Kennedy.* New York: G. P. Putnam and Sons, 1871.

Unterecker, John. *Voyager: A Life of Hart Crane.* New York: Farrar, Straus and Giroux, 1969.

Warren, Robert Penn. *New and Selected Essays*. New York: Random House, 1989.

Wertheim, Stanley, and Paul Sorrentino. *The Correspondence of Stephen Crane*. 2 vols. New York: Columbia Univ. Press, 1988.

White, William S. *Majesty and Mischief: A Mixed Tribute to FDR*. New York: McGraw Hill, 1961.

Whitman, Walt. *Leaves of Grass*. Introduction by Carl Sandburg. New York: Random House, 1921.

———. *Specimen Days in America: Newly Revised by the Author, with Fresh Preface and Additional Note*. London: Walter Scott, 1887.

Whittier, John Greenleaf. *The Complete Poetical Works*. Boston: Houghton Mifflin, 1880.

Williams, Ellen. *Harriet Monroe and the Poetry Renaissance: The First Ten Years of Poetry, 1912–22*. Urbana: Univ. of Illinois Press, 1977.

Winnick, R. H., ed., *Letters of Archibald MacLeish, 1907 to 1982*. Boston: Houghton Mifflin, 1983.

Woolf, Leonard. *Beginning Again: An Autobiography of the Years 1911 to 1918*. New York: Harcourt, Brace and World, 1964.

Yannella, Philip R. *The Other Carl Sandburg*. Jackson: Univ. Press of Mississippi, 1996.

Ziff, Larzer. *The American 1890s: Life and Times of a Lost Generation*. New York: Viking, 1966.

ARTICLES

Allen, Gay Wilson. "Carl Sandburg: Fire and Smoke." *South Atlantic Quarterly,* Summer 1960.

Anonymous. "Aunt Agnes' Fellows." *Time,* January 9, 1939.

———. "The Authors and Mr. Poe." *Godey's Lady's Book,* May 1846.

———. "Jews in America." *Fortune,* Feb. 1936.

———. "Law Report." *Times,* Dec. 10, 1812.

———. Editor's note. *Southern Literary Messenger,* Jan. 1837.

———. "Young American Writers: J. G. Whittier." *Philadelphia Album,* May 20, 1829.

Aumente, Jerome. "Archibald MacLeish, First Nieman Curator, Talks about That Innovative Year." *Nieman Reports,* Spring 1989.

Benco, Nancy L. "Archibald MacLeish: The Poet Librarian." *Quarterly Journal of the Library of Congress,* July 1976.

Bergman, Herbert. "Walt Whitman as a Journalist, 1831–January, 1848." *Journalism Quarterly,* Summer 1971.

Bergman, Herbert, and William White. "Walt Whitman's Lost 'Sun-Down Papers.'" Nos. 1–3. American Book Collector, Jan. 1970.

Bisco, John. "Our New Volume." *Broadway Journal,* July 12, 1945.

———. "Prospectus of the Broadway Journal." Jan. 25, 1845.

Boynton, H. W. "The Literary Aspect of Journalism." *Atlantic Monthly,* June 1904.

Campbell, Killis. "Gleanings in the Bibliography of Poe." *Modern Language Notes,* May 1917.

Cather, Willa. "When I Knew Stephen Crane." *Prairie Schooner,* Fall 1949, reprinted from *Library,* June 23, 1900.

Cauldwell, William. "Walt Whitman as a Young Man." *New York Times,* Jan. 26, 1901.

Dart, Gregory. "Cockneyism." *London Review of Books,* Dec. 18, 2003.

Davis, Richard Harding. "A Derelict." *Scribner's Magazine,* August, 1901.

———. "Our War Correspondents in Cuba and Puerto Rico." *Harper's New Monthly Magazine,* May 1899.

Ehrlich, Heyward. "The *Broadway Journal* (I): Briggs' Dilemma and Poe's Strategy." *Bulletin of the New York Public Library,* Feb. 1969.

Elconin, Victor A. "Stephen Crane at Asbury Park." *American Literature,* Nov. 1948.

Gish, Nancy. "An Interview with Hugh McDiarmid." *Contemporary Literature,* Spring 1969.

Glicksberg, Charles I. "Whitman and Bryant." *Fantasy,* 1935.

Grier, Edward F. "Walt Whitman's Earliest Known Notebook." *PMLA: Publications of the Modern Language Association of America,* Oct. 1968, 1453–56.

Holmes, Colin. "The Tredegar Riots of 1911: Anti-Jewish Disturbances in South Wales." *Welsh History Review,* Dec. 1982.

Hungerford, Edward. "Walt Whitman and His Chart of Bumps." *American Literature,* Jan. 1931.

Lowell, James Russell. "Our Contributors—No. XVII: Edgar Allan Poe." *Graham's Magazine,* Feb. 1845.

Lyons, Louis M. "Harvard Meets the Press: A Personal Account of the Early Nieman Years."*Nieman Reports,* Spring 1989.

MacLeish, Archibald. "The Poet and the Press." *Atlantic Monthly,* March 1949.

Nelson, W. Dale. "Reporting about the Earthquake." *Red Rock Review,* Winter 2002.

———. "Reporting about the Volcano." *Visions,* no. 19, 1985.

———. "With Jerry Falwell in Darkest Africa, or Forty Years as a Reporter for The Associated Press." *Connecticut Poetry Review,* 1996.

Osborn, Scott C. "The 'Rivalry-Chivalry' of Richard Harding Davis and Stephen Crane." *American Literature,* March 1956.

Paulin, Tom. "Gentlemen and ladies came to see the poet's cottage." *London Review of Books,* Feb. 19, 2004.

Poe, Edgar Allan. "Anthon's Cicero." *Southern Literary Messenger,* Jan. 1837.

———. "A Chapter on Autography." *Graham's Lady's and Gentleman's Magazine,* 1841.

———. "The Literati of New York City." *Godey's Lady's Book,* May 1946.

———. "The Magazines." *Broadway Journal,* Jan. 25, 1845; May 17, 1845.

———. "The Raven." *American Review,* Feb. 1845; *Broadway Journal,* Feb. 8, 1845; *Southern Literary Messenger,* March 1845.

———. "To Helen." *Southern Literary Messenger,* March 1836; *Graham's Magazine,* Sept. 1841.

Pollin, Burton R. "Edgar Allan Poe and His Illustrators." *American Book Collector,* March–April 1981.

Robinson, E. Kay. "Kipling in India: Reminiscences by the Editor of the Newspaper on Which Kipling Served at Lahore." *McClure's,* July, 1896.

Rosen, Roslyn. "Letter from Edinburgh." *The Nation,* Sept. 22, 1962.

Rubin, Joseph Jay. "Whitman in 1840: A Discovery." *Notes and Queries,* May 1937.

Sandburg, Carl. "Chicago Poems." *Poetry: A Magazine of Verse,* Mar. 1914

———. "Fixing the Pay of Railroad Men." *International Socialist Review,* April, May, and June 1915.

———. "Looking 'Em Over." *International Socialist Review,* Sept. 1915.

Scheele, Roy. "Hayden Carruth: The Gift of Self." *Poets & Writers Magazine,* May/June 1996.

Snyder, Edward D. "Whittier Returns to Philadelphia after a Hundred Years." *Pennsylvania Magazine of History and Biography,* April 1938.

Stedman, Edmund Clarence. "The Battle of Manassas." *The World*, July 24, 1861.

Welch, Deshler. "Dickens in Switzerland: Some Unpublished Letters and Reflections." *Harper's Magazine*, Apr. 1906.

Whipple, Charles L. "A Vignette-Louis M. Lyons on *Boston Globe*." *Nieman Reports*, Spring 1989.

Williams, Ames W. "Stephen Crane, War Correspondent." *New Colophon*, Apr. 1948.

Wilson, James Southall. "Unpublished Letters of Edgar Allan Poe." *Century Magazine*, Mar. 1924.

Zunder, Theodore A. "Whitman Interviews Barnum." *Modern Language Notes*, Jan. 1933.

OTHER SOURCES

Crawford, Robert. "Yesterday's Scotland and Tomorrow's World." Lecture, Univ. of Wyoming, Oct. 13, 2004.

Index

Italic page number denotes illustration.